3 | ALBA Patristic Library

The Paschal Mystery

ancient liturgies and patristic texts

Editor: A. Hamman, O.F.M.

English Editorial Supervisor: Thomas Halton

DIVISION OF THE SOCIETY OF ST. PAUL **alba house** STATEN ISLAND, N.Y. 10314

Original title: **Le Mystère de Paques,** published by Bernard
Grasset Editeur, Paris.

Translated by Thomas Halton

Nihil obstat: Donald A. Panella, M.A., S.S.L. — Censor Librorum

Imprimatur: Joseph P. O'Brien, S.T.D., V.G.
New York, New York, March 5, 1969

Library of Congress Catalog Number: 78-77646

Designed, printed and bound in the U.S.A. by the Pauline Fathers and
Brothers of the Society of St. Paul at Staten Island, New York as a part of
their communications apostolate.

Contents

Introduction 7
   I. Historical Survey 7
   II. Doctrine 15

I. The Greek Church

Melito of Sardis 25
   Paschal Homily 26
Origen 39
   The Sacrifice of Abraham 40
Derivatives from Hippolytus 49
   I. The Pasch History 50
   II. The Spiritual Pasch 68
Gregory of Nazianzus 74
   The Sacerdotal Sacrifice 75
Gregory of Nyssa 78
   I. The Resurrection of the Dead 79
   II. The Promise of God 96
John Chrysostom 98
   I. Victory over Death 98
   II. Those Invited 106
Asterius of Amasea 107
   Joseph and Jesus 108
Proclus of Constantinople 112
   I. The Coming of God 113
   II. The Model and the Statue 116
Basil of Seleucia 119
   The Christian Combat 119
Gregory Palamas 125
   Mary Magdalene 126

II. The Latin Church

Chromatius of Aquileia 135
   The Universal Vigil 136

Jerome 138
    As the Hind Longs for the Running Water 139
    The Gates of Heaven 142
Augustine of Hippo 144
    The World keep Vigil 147
    The Vigil of Vigils 148
    God the Creator 152
    The Death of Death 159
    Survival and Life 163
    Believe and Touch 167
    The Presence of Christ 169
    The One Shepherd 172
    The Love of Peter 175
    The Day the Lord Has Made 178
    The New Chant 180
    Alleluia 185
Maximus of Turin 189
    The Joy of Creation 191
    The Birth of Faith 193
    Today 195
Peter Chrysologus 197
    The Sin of the Church 198
    The Disquietude of Faith 202
    The Mournful Feast 205
Leo the Great 209
    Faith in the Risen One 209
Gregory the Great 214
    The Grace of God 214
Bibliography 225

Index 229

Introduction

I. HISTORICAL SURVEY

In 60 A.D., Festus, a Roman official, summed up the conflict in which Paul was opposed to the Jews as: *a dispute among the Jews about a certain Jesus who had died but who Paul affirmed was alive* (*Acts* 25, 19), and then resurrected from the dead. The conflict which set the convert of Damascus at loggerheads with his coreligionist underlines the essential truth of the Christian faith: Christ is not dead: he is risen and living. The Church is the assembly of those grouped around the risen One.

Oscar Cullmann supposes that the first place of assembly of the Christians was the upper room where the risen Lord appeared to his disciples while they were eating on Easter Sunday (cf. *Luke* 24, 33). Thus supper and resurrection, linked to the same place, represent the point of departure and the terminus of the new exodus, where Jesus accomplished his *passage from this world to his Father*.

As the Jews had celebrated the exodus of the Hebrews from Egypt, the Christians now celebrate the decisive event of their salvation in celebrating "the pasch of the Lord," the resurrection of Jesus. The continuity between the two celebrations is obvious. Jesus is the fulfillment of the messianic figures and prophecies.

The Jewish Pasch

The Jewish Pasch seems to have an even earlier origin than the historical event it commemorates. It actually originated from a feast of nomadic shepherds celebrated long before Moses. The shepherds offered, at the return of spring, the first fruits of the flocks to the divinity to ensure their fecundity. After the entry to Canaan, this rite was combined with another spring feast, the feast of the Azymes, or the Unleavened Bread, in which the

Canaanites, an agricultural people, offered the first-fruits of the harvest to their god.

Later this feast, enriched with new rites, was related to the most important event of the history of Israel: the exodus from Egypt. The historical commemoration lost its agricultural aspect to the Pasch which the rites still attested and gave it an entirely new aspect. The etymology of the name of Pasch (in Hebrew Pésakh, from Pasakh, passover) has undoubtedly contributed to this confusion. The meaning of "passage," perhaps was only an indication of astronomy but the word recalled the exodus of the Hebrews from the land of Egypt.

After the *Exodus*, the Pasch was instituted by Moses, under the command of God, the vigil of the departure from Egypt. The Jews pick for immolation on the fourteenth of Nisan,[1] in each family, a lamb, male and without blemish, to anoint with its blood the lintels and posts of the doors so as to keep at a distance the destroyer whom God would send that same night to destroy the firstborn of the Egyptians. They had also to roast the lamb, eat it at night with bitter herbs and unleavened bread, eating this meal in haste, with loins girt and feet shod, staff in hand, and no leftovers. They consumed the unleavened bread this same evening and until the evening of the twenty first of Nisan. The first and seventh day of this feast were more solemn than the others: all work was prohibited.

It was in memory, then, of their miraculous departure from the land of Egypt and their deliverance that the Israelites celebrated the Pasch. At the heart of their faith it perpetuated from generation to generation the memory of this wonderful event. Down to our own day the Samaritans, to celebrate the Pasch, slaughter sheep on Mt. Gerizim and eat them by night, according to the rites prescribed by Moses.

In each Jewish family today that is faithful to the traditional faith, the paschal *séder* commemorates "the marvel of all the marvels of its history. Without it, there would be no Torah, no prophecy" (Edmond Fleg).

Jewish children spend weeks in watchful expectation of this evening. They are prepared by a course of religious instruction, in which the details of the rites and texts are explained to them.

---

1. The Jewish year begins with the month of Nisan, between March and April.

When the evening arrives, the youngest child, the principal character, asks the father about the meaning of the feast. "You will tell your son on this day, saying, it was in view of this (this ceremonial of *séder*) that God has acted in my favor, so that I have come out of Egypt."

The father recounts the great event of history. The paschal meal is rhythmically interrupted by the traditional chants. Those participating raise their cup proclaiming: "This is why there is an obligation on us to give thanks, to praise, to rejoice, to celebrate, to elevate, to exalt, to magnify, to glorify, and to bless him who made these signs for our fathers and for us; who draws us from slavery to liberty, from distress to joy, from mourning to celebration, from darkness to shining light, and from oppression to freedom. Now let us chant before his face a new chant: Alleluia."

The first Pasch commemorated the immediate salvation of the Hebrews. The Paschs which followed, from generation to generation, perpetuated and re-enacted the event of salvation. With the re-enacted reminder of the historical deliverance was fused the expectation of future liberation. The Pasch is a feast of hope which deepens messianic expectation; in the course of a paschal night, the Messiah will come!

The Christian Pasch

For Christians the Messiah has come. The Gospels show us how he has deliberately situated himself in the extension of the historical experience of Israel: the journey begun by the people of God terminates in him. In him, the veiled presence of the desert became a presence incarnate; he is the manna who nourishes his people, the true Pasch where the lamb preserves from extermination and seals the new and definitive covenant in his blood. In his own exodus he brings about "passage" of the sinful world to his Father's kingdom.

Evangelists and apostles demonstrate that the first Exodus is fulfilled in Jesus. The whole of the Fourth Gospel is written in the framework of the paschal celebration. The Synoptics describe the Lord's last supper as a paschal meal. Its celebration is the last prophecy of immolation on the cross of the true paschal victim, which assembles the community of the new covenant in the Church.

The apostolic community is united around the risen Christ who is invisibly present to the entire assembly. To indicate clearly the paschal character of their unions as of their faith, the faithful chose "the day after the sabbath" as the day of union, or in other words the first day of the week, the day of the Resurrection of their Master. The annual feast of the Pasch, the fourteenth of Nisan, received a new meaning: it celebrated the coming of universal salvation, accomplished by the death and resurrection of Jesus.

The catechesis of the apostles describes the Christian event as a paschal mystery. Those baptized are the people of God, as we are told in I *Peter;* they march with loins girt, delivered from their trial like *a chosen race, a royal priesthood, a holy nation, a purchased people* (I *Pet.* 2, 9) toward the promised land and the kingdom of heaven.

As Paul explains to the Christians of Corinth, Christ henceforth is their true Pasch on which the true paschal lamb has been immolated. In the spirit of the Jewish *séder* which explains the meaning of the celebration, the Apostle shows that the Christian has personally lived the paschal mystery on the day of his baptism in dying to sin and rising to the life of God. Like the Jews they must get rid of the old leaven of iniquity to become, in St. Paul's words, *the unleavened bread of purity and truth.* The Eucharist perpetuates the paschal feast in the Christian communities.

This perfect interpretation of the Jewish Pasch, joined to the coincidence of dates (Jesus died during the Pasch), the Christian utilization of the texts and rites of Israel, explain why for two centuries the accent is on the immolation of the cross. The Resurrection is never excluded, but it will emerge more clearly when Roman usage will make the celebration coincide with the following Sunday. Between one usage and the other there is no question of an opposition between passion and resurrection, but of a different emphasis: both constitute the same mystery.

Origins of the Paschal Liturgy

The practices of the primitive Christian communities are not very well known to us. But from the apostolic age, Sunday, the Lord's day and the day of the Resurrection is solemnized: it is the day of the liturgical assembly. The vision of John on Patmos is placed on this day, to effect rapport between the liturgy of earth and that of heaven.

Melito of Sardis tells us that in the middle of the second century, the paschal celebration consisted in a vigil of fast, from nightfall to cockcrow. It was completed at dawn by a repast of the brethren and the celebration of the Eucharist. The Church recalled the memory of "the night when it was delivered."

The primitive liturgy is founded on the *séder* or the Jewish paschal ritual. The eating of the lamb was replaced by the vigil of fast, in contrast to the feast of Israel. During the vigil the community read, like Israel, the *Exodus* narrative, chapter 12, applied typologically to Christ who had brought figure and promise to realization.

Melito of Sardis provides us with the oldest example of the paschal homily, which gives an exposition to the faithful of the parallelism and progression from Jewish to Christian Exodus. Christ by his cross and death put an end to the era of preparation and definitively introduced the chosen people to the land of God. This venerable text restored in its integrity opens the series of commentaries published here.

From the second century we witness a two-fold change: a displacement of the day of the feast and an enlargement of the liturgy.

Syria, close to the usage of the Jewish-Christian community, continued to celebrate the Pasch, like the Jews, on the fourteenth Nisan, the anniversary of the night when Jesus was delivered on whatever day of the week it might occur; the fast lasted a day. The other churches, in Palestine, Egypt, Greece, Pontus and Rome, departed from Jewish usage and celebrated the paschal mystery the following Sunday, the anniversary day of the Resurrection, on whatever day of the month. The fast began on Saturday and lasted until Sunday morning. As there was little or no inter-relationship between the churches there was no sharp division noticed between them on this matter, except that at Rome in the reign of Pope Sixtus about 120 there was a confrontation between the Roman and Asian communities. But attention was awakened in 155 when Polycarp of Smyrna paid a visit to Pope Anicetus. This meeting ended in an agreement on mutual tolerance.

The debate resumed around 190. Melito had already written a work which justified the quartodeciman practice of the Jews.

In his *Paschal Homily* reference to this usage will be found. Synods were held.

Rome was in the main followed by the oriental churches and opposed by the bishops of Asia. Pope Victor reacted strongly, excommunicating the churches of Asia. Only under protestations raised by a number of bishops, including Irenaeus of Lyons, did he agree to accept the two-fold practice. The Council of Nicaea closed the debate in 325. The Roman usage was imposed in the entire Church. And in 341, at the Council of Antioch, the remaining adherents of the quartodeciman Pasch were declared excommunicated.

It was also during the second century that the paschal liturgy lost its original simplicity. At the beginning of the vigil, lamps were lighted in accordance with Jewish usage. Tertullian has the first explicit reference to the practice of baptizing at cockcrow. The sacraments of Christian initiation enabled the faithful to participate in the death and resurrection of Christ.

At this time the celebration of the paschal mystery lasted fifty days; after the Pasch which began on Saturday was devoted to fasting and which terminated on Sunday by the reception of the Eucharist. The feast of the Resurrection lasted until Pentecost.

In the third century here is how the *Didascalia of the Twelve Apostles* (21, 19) describes the celebration: "Unite yourselves and do not sleep; keep vigil all the night in prayer and read the Prophets, the Gospels and the psalms, until the third hour of the night of Saturday. Then cease fasting, offer sacrifice, eat and join in joyous jubilation because Christ, the first-fruits of your resurrection, is risen."

It is also in the third century that baptism is definitively incorporated on the paschal liturgy.

We must not conclude from difference of usage to a difference of meaning. For Christian antiquity the paschal mystery was conceived as a totality; it is the exodus of Christ, his passage from the world to his Father, through death which obtained his glorification and his overlordship of the universe. He involves humanity in his movement of salvation.

The term Pasch, Latin *pascha,* used by the Church, confirms this observation. The Fathers were not concerned about philology. They were nevertheless forced to explain the term chosen.

The Greek retained a preference for the idea of "passage," the Lord's passage through his own people, the passage of the

frontier by the people, the passage from fast to joy, from death
to life. It has to do with the movement itself in which the paschal
mystery involved redeemed humanity. The Latins, however, con-
necting *pascha* and *pati* (to suffer), attach to the word "passion"
not just simply the idea of suffering but the witness rendered to
Christ by the martyrs in the hour of persecution; as Christine
Morhmann puts it: "The passion associates the confessors of the
faith to the resurrection and to glory."

In the fourth century, the paschal liturgy is developed. The
readings from the Bible take account of the two sacraments ad-
ministered in the course of the vigil. To the traditional reading of
the account of the paschal lamb that of the sacrifice of Abraham
came to be added. The baptismal typology finds support in the
account of creation, a figure of the new creation, and in the
crossing the Red Sea in which St. Paul had already discovered
the figure of baptism and Eucharist. The catechesis of the Fathers
gave priority of place to the explanation of paschal baptism.

The paschal celebration was preceded by a fast which varied
in length at different times and in different churches. The Roman
Church fixed it at forty days, in commemoration of the forty
sacred days spent by Jesus in the desert. This period is called
Lent, a popular form of the word Quadragesima, which means
forty days. Lent ended with Holy Week. Liturgical offices were
held daily, morning and evening. The fast became more rigorous
and the faithful practiced a severe asceticism.

The three last days were the most solemn. On Holy Saturday
night the whole town was illuminated, torches lighted the streets,
while the faithful, candles in hand, came to the liturgical assembly. Solemnly the Christians listened to the reading of the great
pages of the Bible. The catechumens heard for the last time the
main stages of salvation, the history of the people of God, which
they made their own on this night. At the end of the vigil the
bishop, surrounded by his clergy, preached the homily. How
often Augustine stirred up emotion by one of those sermons
which we still enjoy reading. Like John Chrysostom, Augustine
could recall the paschal vigil when he himself (at Milan) had
received the sacrament of the new life.

The great vigil of reading and prayer was brought to an end
by baptism. The candidates went to the baptismal fonts and
descended naked into the baptistery. On returning they were
dressed in white garments in which they entered the church in

procession to participate for the first time in the Lord's supper. At dawn each returned home, his eyes aglow with the joy of Easter.

In the morning the Christians exchanged greetings and felicitations. The whole of Sunday was a day of joy. At Hippo, Augustine preached again in the morning and often in the afternoon. The paschal theme was inexhaustible. The feast extended through the entire week, during which the faithful heard at Mass the Gospel narratives of the apparitions of the risen Christ. We publish here a selection of the commentaries. This octave originating from the Jewish *azymes*, gave to the week the name *Septimana in albis*, or the Week in White. The octave, called *octava infantium, dominica in albis (deponendis)*, or *dies novorum*, when neophytes laid aside their white garments and returned to everyday life, generally completed the paschal celebrations.

Rome, which had gone away from the liturgical usage which was indubitably Judeo-Christian, came under the influence of Jerusalem where because of the holy places the pilgrims disrupted the unity of the paschal mystery to follow day by day the unfolding of the way of the cross. Etheria has left us a description of this in his *Journal of the Way*.

The liturgy of Jerusalem took account of the popular type of pilgrim and underlined in its presentation the dramatic character of events: the betrayal of Judas, the adoration of the cross, etc. This latter rite entered the Roman liturgy. But the most ancient rite was the blessing of the paschal candle carried by the deacon. This rite was borrowed from the Jewish vigil and was already in use since the third century in Spain and in Gaul perhaps in the time of Augustine. It was not introduced to Rome until the seventh or eighth century. It consisted in the blessing of a huge candle which symbolized the resurrected Christ, and the candle was pierced with five holes representing the five wounds.

Along with the baptism of the catechumens the reconciliation of penitents was a rite developed in the fourth and fifth centuries. It took place on Holy Saturday to enable them to participate in the paschal celebration. When baptisms became rarer in the sixth and seventh centuries, Rome developed the liturgy of the paschal *triduum*, which followed the historical unfolding of events from the processional entry into Jerusalem to the resurrection.

This reconstruction ended by concealing the essential. The

paschal night, the core of the original celebration, was anticipated on Holy Saturday morning from the seventh century. The Mass of the Day of Easter would take the place of the eucharistic celebration. This was the crowning act of the whole vigil, the sacrament of the paschal mystery.

Be that as it may in regard to later developments, the earliest core of the mystery lay in the great vigil, "the vigil of all vigils," passed in prayer until cockcrow. It terminated after the baptism of the catechumens in the Eucharist in which the Christian people united in the same celebration the mystery of the passion and of the resurrection.

The homilies of the Fathers give an exposition better than any abstract treatise of the essence of the Christian faith in commenting on the paschal mystery to their flocks. In them we will find a theology of salvation which it now remains to deal with.

II. DOCTRINE

The Pasch appears in Christian antiquity as "the feast of feasts," commemorating not merely the resurrection of Christ but the Christian mystery in its entirety, and the realization of the design of salvation in respect to man and the world. The Pasch is the feast of Christ and the Christian feast *par excellence,* the center of all the truths of the faith.

This essential unity gives the liturgical drama its action, its movement, and its meaning: the plan of *God* inscribed in creation in which history fulfills itself. Christ conducts it to its triumphal conclusion.

From promise to reality

Christ our Pasch has been immolated. Let us then celebrate, writes St. Paul. The Christian Pasch replaces the Jewish Pasch. In Christ the promises take figure and are fulfilled, the marvels which mark the history of the people of God find in him their fulfillment. On the road to Emmaus the risen Christ reveals to his companions how the Sacred Scripture announced the introduction by suffering to the glory of the resurrection. The paschal light illuminates the whole history of salvation.

The announcement of salvation which the ancient Pasch proclaimed — in figure — witnesses to the permanence of God and the dependability of his plan in regard to history. The similarities between the two Paschs, which are dwelt on by almost all our preachers, afford precise evidence of the unity of the divine plan.

This is brought about in two stages: The time of prophecy and the time of fulfillment, the time of the letter and the time of the spirit, the time of the law and the time of grace, the time of figure and the time of reality. The history of Israel is thus accomplished in the perspective of the future: its different events are an expression of the future and are charged with the whole mystery of the promise. That is why the Fathers are not content just to establish the most obvious relations between the two Paschs, between the lamb and the immolated Christ. The Scriptures as a whole hold and contain Christ: correspondences are discovered between the two histories of the world: traditional ones like those of the crossing of the Red Sea and the salvation of the newly baptized (Proclus), the sacrifice of Abraham and that of the Father (Origen), the new day chanted in the psalms and the new man (Augustine); but also new and unusual similarities, like that of Joseph and Jesus (Asterius), Noah's ark and the octave of Easter (Jerome), the mercy seat and the Lord, the pierced Leviathan and vanquished death (Gregory the Great), etc.

In the light of revelation, then, the true meaning of the Scriptures is uncovered in every sense of the term, for there is question of a direction given to history: "the Old Testament announces the future history of the Lord, the New recounts it, while it is accomplished" (Gregory the Great). Almost all our homilies, and particularly those inspired by Hippolytus of Rome, insist on this division of history, on yesterday and today. This is a fundamental preoccupation. The typological development which it inspires can sometimes be tiresome to us, or puerile, or too ingenious, but the principle itself is never at stake: they really pursue a Christian vision of the universe on which the whole Christian faith revolves: the accomplishment of salvation in regard to history.

From creation to fulfillment

The Israelite had discovered in the Exodus that God was his savior and the father of his people. In reflecting on these gifts, he enlarges their meaning. "He goes back in amazement to the beginnings: creation becomes then, apart from an experience proper to one people, the foundation of special relations with God, in a perspective enlarged and admitting the cosmos and the whole of humanity. Thereafter the hope of Israel itself rests on an understanding of the omnipotence of Yahweh the creator."[2]

History presents itself as the continued action of the creator, always at work, leading it to its fulfillment. Creation in the *Apocalypse* is the beginning of a work which embraces the whole duration of time, from beginning to end. Of this history, entering its last phase with Christ, the death and resurrection constitute a unique and decisive event. His action extends to the whole span of time, to the whole of creation. In the Byzantine mosaics the risen Christ delivers the whole of humanity from hell, including Adam and Eve to whom he extends a liberating hand. The *Book of Genesis* complements the *Book of Exodus* to express the entire riches of the paschal mystery. It is the reason for which the liturgy of the paschal vigil returns to the reading of the creation narrative.

The wood of the cross becomes the tree of knowledge which grew in the garden of Eden. Painters in the catacombs depict it covered with blossoms and flowers. Christ is compared with Adam. From his open side redeemed humanity is born. Syrian theology represents baptism as a return to earthly paradise. But the paschal victory is not merely the recapitulation of past history — as earlier times are a prophecy of later — but brings about the future times, called eschatological, and definitively establishes the economy of salvation and of grace.

There is question then of a definitive victory, an unfailing light, a life with immunity from death, a victory over time itself which enables the Christian to aspire not only to the height but to the eternity of God. The bodily resurrection of Christ equally expresses the integration of the universe in the salvation of reborn man. The work of Christ, the cosmic Adam, is extended to the whole of creation. The Pasch is the mystery of this universal reconstruction, virtually accomplished in Christ.

Human history, from its beginnings, is then on its way to kingship. The unfurling of the divine economy installs the two Paschs in a relationship of succession rather than of opposition. From there come this general comprehension in regard to the Jews and the moderation of grief which the Fathers devote to them, con-

---

2. R. Le Déaut, **Le Nuit Pascale** (Rome 1963), 90.

tent now to reproach them chiefly with their slowness to understand. Moreover, the resurrection reduces to naught the death of
Jesus of which the Fathers elsewhere accuse the Jews, and often
in violent terms. The mildness of their exhortation here is so
unusual as to merit underlining.

The Gospel narrative and Christian faith

The fullness of the paschal mystery is proportioned to the faith
which it calls for: in celebrating the Pasch, the Christian proclaims his faith in the resurrection of Christ and in his own
resurrection. "Our whole faith is founded on this resurrection,"
says Augustine, "pagans, infidels, and Jews have believed in the
passion of Christ, but only Christians in his resurrection." This
faith is rooted then in the Pasch. On what credentials? That of
the evangelists: the discovery of the empty tomb and the different
appearances of Christ. The time has not yet come to submit these
texts to the least criticism, external or internal. The contradic-
tions or even the silences ought not to arouse suspicion. "So
great is the authority of the Holy Gospel," says Augustine again,
(the same spirit spoke in the apostles) "that however strange its
testimony remains true." Let us then examine these witnesses.

The proofs of the resurrection given by the Gospel are of the
sensory order, and the witness of the senses is presented as irrefutable — *see the wounds of my body, notice the marks which
my enemies have made, touch me.* The apostles seek no further
proofs than those of the senses and among the senses in first
place are those which 'touch' the hand and eye: "My doubts will
persist until I see him. I will put my finger in the marks of the
nails and I will embrace this Lord whom I desire so much. So
Thomas expresses himself, refusing oral evidence and demanding
direct proof. Let him blame my lack of faith so long as he
satisfies my sight. Unbelieving until I shall see him, I shall
believe when I clasp him in my arms and contemplate him"
(Basil of Seleucia).

But these evidences of sight and touch are the sign of man's
weakness and of feeble faith. God is made known to man by the
Word, by the Good News. True faith is possessed by the people
who have heard and have believed. "Only announce me. They
will believe and will adore me. They will not demand any further
proofs. Tell them that they are called by grace and contemplate

their faith; truly blessed are they who have not seen and have believed" (Basil of Seleucia). It is this faith which permits entry into real contact with God. "Christ is better reached by faith than by touch," writes Augustine, "to touch him by faith is to touch him in every truth."

From the images to their theological meaning

To see the doctrinal significance of the paschal mystery, the Fathers have recourse to images inspired by religious symbolism sometimes used in the Bible. Down to the fourth century the faithful are still impregnated by pagan symbolism: light, the rebirth of spring. Instead of combatting them and trying to destroy them, they take them and give them a Christian signification, showing that Christ is come to fulfill them.

Rightly or wrongly the Greek Fathers translate the word "Pasch" as "passage." This passage, this transition from one plan to another, from one ceremony to another, can assume different meanings.

First, it expresses the transition from symbol to reality, from elementary signs to prophetic signs. The occurrence of Spring symbolizes the birth of a new creation, brought about by the resurrection of Christ. We will read in the homily of pseudo-Hippolytus the poetic meditation which the author is inspired to write by the return of the paschal Spring, and in the homily of Proclus the wonder caused by the renewal of everything. Under this heading it should be noted that the Christian preachers have restored to the Pasch some of its ancient pastoral meaning. To this theme, the equinox of the full moon, might be joined that of light, so dear to eastern sensibilities, and already encountered in the mystery of the Nativity as it is applied to Christ.

The lights of the paschal vigil, the passage from night to the light of dawn facilitate the application of the symbolism to the risen Christ.

At a deeper level the "passage" expresses the transition from a provisional to a definitive order, from the order of prophetic promise to that of realization. The biblical figures give way to fulfillment. Paschal time introduces us, not just to another order, or merely a new one, but to a completely different order, a definitive one which makes us pass from the order of the world to the time of God. It is not a question simply of the birth of the light of a new day, but of a light that is unfailing. Maximus of Turin describes this for us in a lyrical passage of great beauty.

The paschal victory initiates a new state of man which makes him participate in the condition of the resurrected Christ and gives him invulnerability, the appanage of life eternal.

The "passage" finally expresses, more than a succession of economies, an opposition, not, as we have seen, between the first and the second Pasch, between the order of the law and the order of the spirit, but between the order of God and everything which runs counter to it. The passion, the blood of Christ underline the dramatic character of the redemption. The victory of Christ is carried off by main force and presented as a singular and definitive combat which puts an end to the tryanny of the forces of evil.

Joy succeeds trials, liberty succeeds tyranny, and life, death. It is not just a question of succeeding, but of a drama, a confrontation where rival forces are at loggerheads and which is ended by the establishment of the sovereignty of God in the kingdom of his love.

The death of Christ tears the mask from imposture and imposter. Death, a consequence of sin, is vanquished by Christ. This defeat bursts forth in the paschal victory. The resurrection frees man from the twofold alienation of sin and of death. Regenerated man enters a new era, a new existence which enables him in faith and hope to partake in the condition of the risen Christ.

Christ's deed prolongs his saving action in the Church. The cult involved in the paschal celebration or the eucharistic celebration, far from being a denial is a proclamation of and an affirmation of the presence of the risen Christ and of his invisible action in the Church. The Eucharist is nothing but the sacrament of the passion and resurrection ever efficacious in the Church.

Humanity is saved provided that it participates in God's economy. Thus an ethic emerges from the paschal mystery, which the Fathers developed at length for their flocks. This moral teaching is no more than the application of faith to existence. It remains for us to sketch its outlines.

Outline of a paschal ethic

A renewal, a promise of eternity and plenitude, the Pasch is above all a hymn of joy. All our texts exalt in a body this happiness which is given not only to man on earth but also to the angels in the heavens and to the souls in hell. The vigil of the whole of creation is fulfilled, salvation is given on all sides. "All enter into the joy of the Master," says St. John Chrysostom, "those at the first hour and the second receive your reward, chant in choir, ye rich and poor; abstemious or careless, celebrate this day."

The whole life of the Christian ought to blossom forth here-after in the joy of the pasch which God in his goodness has sent to the heart of man, but this joy involves man: perfect harmony ought to reign in the breast of the Christian, between the lips which chant the "Alleluia" and the heart, between the words uttered and the inner conscience, to quote Augustine, while Leo speaks of the irruption of the paschal mystery in the life of be-lievers, and their obligation to bring their life into harmony with this feast.

What acts will retain this perfect accord? The Fathers never lose sight of the newly-baptized who after the feasts are going to return to their daily tasks, with the attendant difficulties and dangers. What of the white garment of their regeneration? John Chrysostom and Augustine never hide their joy and their emotion, but neither can they conceal their misgivings in thinking of the demands of the new life. So their counsels are pressing and diverse. There is a general exhortation to live the good life, to practice charity, to remain modest, to pardon one's enemies, to partake of the sacraments regularly and devoutly, to condemn earthly goods — riches and pleasures. But all these diverse coun-sels are synthesized in a single phrase, which is to live in imitation of Jesus Christ. "Become like Christ," says Gregory of Nazianzus, "since Christ has become like you. Become gods for him, since he has become man for you."

Jesus Christ here appears less as a model of perfection pro-posed to man than as the first example of the resurrection. He is the firstborn of a community of brothers. To imitate him is to enter into the risen community. The Pasch is then an exhortation to participate in the design of salvation begun in Jesus Christ. It is not simply the operation of individual salvation, but it arouses mankind to a realization of a massive transformation. All our texts insist at length on the cosmic nature of the resurrection in which the Christian participates, an artisan of collective renewal, which is no accepter of persons.

This fidelity demands a continuous warfare. Christ has not come to suppress the confrontation but to inure his soldiers to war. The baptismal catechesis puts the candidate on guard against the devil always lying in wait. The Christian should war against the devil's assualts, he should war against his own passions, which unceasingly threaten to overwhelm him. Suffering and death are not suppressed but vanquished. The paschal victory has taken away their sting. Henceforth, they can gain value from the redemption and serve the salvation of the world.

Joy and hope, gifts of the Pasch, are in no way causes for inertia. It is despair on the contrary, which the Pasch has come to abolish, which justified the inertia of men. Sure of being lost, man had no goal to attain and could freely abandon himself to sin. But today the Christian enjoys the certitude of the resurrection; better still, the gift of God, which comes first incites him to respond, to cooperate in the work of love. Sin would, in the word of a Greek homilist, be a veritable betrayal.

Such is the ambivalence of the Pasch; on the one hand it is pure grace of God, where man distracted with joy, to use Jerome's vivid expression, does not know how to chant his joy and his recognition. On the other hand it is a provocation, a challenge, made to man to participate in the salvation of the universe.

It is the expectation itself which is multiple, at once joy and toil. We have touched on the fundamental idea of this feast: the homily of Melito attests that waiting on the Lord characterizes the most ancient celebration. The vigil has no other meaning than to prepare the Church for his coming. This expectation of Christ in glory, of a universal resurrection, nourishes the Christian's joy but also reorientates his acts in the light of this coming, which they prepare for, and little by little get ready. Not only the celebrations, but the existence of the faithful prepare for it and they have no other meaning than to prepare for this return. The alleluia of the earth, the alleluia of hope, incites the traveller to chant the alleluia of his true country. "Here the chant must die, but there it will live for ever. Here the chant is in expectation, there it is in possession; here it is the alleluia *en route,* but there it is the alleluia of arriving home" (St. Augustine, sermon 256).

PART ONE

The Greek Church

MELITO OF SARDIS
(2nd Cent.)

Melito, Bishop of Sardis in the middle of the second century, was extremely popular in his lifetime and for long after his death, but later fell into disfavor. Only recently has he recovered his popularity. The historian Eusebius presents him as one of the great luminaries of his country and his age. He has become the delight of scholars since his works have become better known to us.

His homily on the Pasch, discovered in fragments and patiently reconstructed, is a document of capital importance. It is both one of the earliest of surviving sermons and the oldest homily giving a commentary on the paschal mystery.

This homily commemorates both the death and resurrection of Christ according to the quartodeciman practice followed by Melito.

The author compares at length the two Paschs, Jewish and Christian: the first saved Israel by the blood of the slaughtered lamb, the second brought about the salvation of all mankind by the sufferings and death of Christ. This parallel shows that the history of salvation began with that of Israel which received the signs in the lamb and in the patriarchs and prophets. Melito then treats of the passion of Christ and his account is rendered more dramatic by a series of apostrophies to Israel. Finally, he proclaims the glories of his resurrection and ends with a majestic evocation of Christ.

The homily unfolds the mystery of redemption in its signs, then in their realization. The thought of the *parousia* and the eschatological expectations dominate the narrative and reflexions, contributing a remarkable unity to the whole text.

In regard to style, it bears close affinities to primitive liturgical hymns: cadence, assonantal prose that is in J. Daniélou's words, "in part preaching and in part jubilation."

PASCHAL HOMILY

From Law to Logos

The text of the Hebrew Exodus has been read and the words of the mystery have been explained: how the sheep was sacrificed for the salvation of the people.

Now grasp this, dearly beloved: how it is new and old, eternal and transient, corruptible and incorruptible, mortal and immortal, the mystery of the Pasch.

It is old according to the Law, but new according to the Logos. It is transient in terms of figure, but eternal in terms of grace. It is corruptible because of the death of the sheep, but incorruptible because of the life of the Lord. It is mortal because of burial in the earth, but immortal because of resurrection from the dead.

The Law is old, the Logos new; the figure is transient, grace is eternal. The sheep is corruptible, the Lord is incorruptible, who was immolated as a lamb, but resurrected as God.

For as a sheep he was led to the slaughter but a sheep he was not; and *as a mute lamb,* but a lamb he was not. For the figure is past and the truth has been revealed: in place of a lamb it is God who has come, and in place of a sheep, man. And in man, Christ, who contains all.

Thus the immolation of the sheep, and the rite of the Pasch, and the letter of the Law are accomplished in Christ Jesus. For the Law has become Logos, and the old has become new, coming from Zion and Jerusalem. The commandment has become grace, and type has become reality, and the lamb the Son, and the sheep, man, and man, God.

For born Son-like, and led forth lamb-like, and slaughtered sheep-like, and buried man-like, he has risen God-like, being by nature God and man.

He is all things: in as much as he judges, Law; in as much as he teaches, Word; in as much as he saves, Grace; in as much as he begets, Father; in as much as he is begotten, Son; in as much as he suffers, sheep; in as much as he is buried, man; in as much as he has risen, God.

This is Jesus Christ to whom be glory for ever and ever. Amen.

The death of the firstborn

Such is the mystery of the Pasch as it is written in the Law according to the reading you have just heard. I am going to explain in detail the words of the Scripture: how God gave command to Moses in Egypt, when he wished to subject Pharaoh to the scourge and to deliver Israel from the scourge by the hand of Moses.

For behold, he says, *you will take a lamb without flaw or blemish, and toward evening you will slaughter it* in the midst of the sons of Israel, and by night you will eat it in haste, and not a bone of it will you break. These things, he said, you will do in a single night. You will eat it according to families and tribes, with loins girt and staff in hand. For this is the Passover of the Lord, an eternal memorial for the sons of Israel. Then with the blood of the sheep you will anoint the doors of your houses, so that the angel will be deterred before the blood. For behold I will smite Egypt and in a single night she will be left childless, both man and beast.

Then Moses slaughtered the sheep and accomplished the mystery at night in the presence of the sons of Israel. He sealed the doorposts of the houses to save the people and deter the angel.

When the sheep was slaughtered and the Pasch was eaten; when the mystery was completed and the people elated, and Israel was marked with the seal, then the angel came to smite Egypt, which was uninitiated in the mystery, without part in the Pasch, unsealed by the blood, unprotected by the Spirit, an enemy, an infidel.

In a single night he smote and left her childless. For the angel bypassed Israel, seeing it sealed by the blood of the sheep, and went forth against Egypt, and subdued the stiff-necked Pharaoh with grief, clothing him not in mourning garb, nor a mantle in shreds, but with all of Egypt in rent garments, mourning her firstborn.

For the whole of Egypt plunged in pain and plague, in tears and beatings of the breast, went to Pharaoh all in mourning not only in outward appearance but also in the heart, rending not just their outer garments but also their wanton breasts. It was a terrible sight: on one side, these beating their breasts, on the other, those bewailing, and in their midst Pharaoh grieving, seated in sackcloth and ashes, in a funeral robe of deep darkness, for Egypt draped him like a funeral garb. Such was the tunic woven for this tyrant's body; such was the garment which the angel of justice put on the hard-hearted Pharaoh: bitter mourning, and groping darkness, and the loss of children, and the angel's domination of the firstborn, for rapid and insatiable was the death that struck them.

There was a strange trophy to be seen over the fallen, cast down by a single blow. And the rout of those laid low became the nurture of death.

If you listen you will be astonished at this strange disaster. For this was the fate which struck the Egyptians; a long night, and impenetrable darkness, and death groping, and the angel exterminating, and hell devouring their firstborn.

But what was more astonishing and terrifying you have yet to hear: in the palpable darkness impalpable death was concealed, and in this darkness the unfortunate Egyptians were groping. And death was groping, seeking out the firstborn sons of the Egyptians at the angel's bidding. If anyone, then, groped in the darkness he was carried away by death. If any firstborn grasped a dark body by the hand, horror-stricken he cried out sharply in his terror:

"Whom does my right hand grasp? Whom does my soul dread? What darkness enfolds my body? If you are my father, help me. If you are my mother, console me. If you are my brother, speak to me. If you are my friend, be gentle to me. If you are my enemy, get away from me. For I am a firstborn."

Before the silencing of the firstborn, the great silence embraced him saying: "You are my firstborn. It is I who am destined for you, the silence of death." Another firstborn, perceiving the capture of the others, denied who he was to avoid a bitter death: "I am not a firstborn, but I am the third in the family." But death, incapable of being deceived, seized the firstborn, who fell, head foremost, in silence.

By one blow the firstborn of the Egyptians fell — the first sown, the first begotten, the long desired — on the ground, not only the men but also the brute beasts. And in the plains of the earth was heard the bellowing of beasts mourning their young, the cow her sucking calf, the mare her colt, and the other beasts who had brought forth, groaning and bitterly bewailing their firstborn.

And among men there was lamentation and beating of the breast at the disaster because of the death of the firstborn. The whole of Egypt stank of the odor of unburied corpses.

It was a dreadful sight: Egyptian mothers with dishevelled hair, fathers distracted in spirit, wailing woefully in Egyptian — "Unhappy are we. At one blow we have been deprived of our firstborn." And they were beating their breasts, and clapping their hands to the dance of the dead.

Such was the disaster that enveloped Egypt; in an instant she was deprived of her offspring. Israel, however, was protected by the sacrifice of the sheep and illuminated by the shedding of blood; and the death of the sheep was like a rampart for the people.

O strange, inexplicable mystery! The sacrifice of a sheep is the salvation of Israel, and the death of a sheep becomes the life of the people, and his blood deters the angel.

From design to work of art

Tell me, angel, what deterred you? The slaughter of the sheep or the life of the Lord? The death of the sheep or the figure of the Lord? The blood of the sheep or the spirit of the Lord? You were deterred because you witnessed the mystery of the Lord accomplished in the sheep, the life of the Lord in the sacrifice of the sheep, the figure of the Lord in the death of the sheep.

Therefore you did not strike Israel, but Egypt alone you deprived of her children. What is this mystery unprecedented: Egypt struck down to destruction and Israel protected and saved? Hear the meaning of this mystery.

Words and deeds, dearly beloved, are meaningless if they are separated from their symbol and prefigure. Everything said and everything done participates in this prefiguring — words in their parable, and deeds in their prefiguration; and so, just as deeds are indicated by their prototype, so words are illuminated by parable.

It is the same in a work of art. No work is undertaken without a model. Is not the future work already outlined in its design?

That is why a model is first constructed of wax, or clay, or wood, from which the future work can be seen emerging, loftier in height, more durable, gracious in line and rich in appointment, thanks to a miniature and perishable model.

And when the thing modeled has been realized, then the model itself is destroyed; it has outlived its use. Its image has passed over to reality. What was useful becomes useless, once the object of true value emerges.

Everything has its proper time: the model has its time, the object has its season. You construct a model of reality. You like it because you see in it the outline of the future work. You provide the materials for the model. You love the model, for from it will arise the work you have in mind. When you execute the work, it becomes the sole object of your desire, because in it alone you see model, materials, and reality.

Figure and Truth

As it is in the case of corruptible images so it is in incorruptible; as it is in the earth so it is in the heavenly. For the salvation and truth of the Lord have been prefigured in the people (of Israel), and the teachings of the Gospel have been proclaimed in the Law. The people were the outline of a plan and the Law a letter of a parable, but the Gospel is the explanation and fulfillment of the Law, and the Church is the receptacle of truth.

The model was precious before the reality, the parable splendid before its fulfillment. That is to say, the people was precious before the Church was established, the Law was marvelous before the Gospel shed its light.

But when the Church was established and the Gospel proclaimed, the figure was found wanting as its image had changed to reality. The Law was at an end as it had transmitted its strength to the Gospel. Just so, the figure becomes bankrupt when it transmits its image to reality, and the parable is bankrupt when it is clarified by interpretation.

So also the Law was terminated when the Gospel came to light, and the people lost its identity when the Church took its place. And the figure was abolished when the Lord became manifest and what was precious yesterday is today regarded as useless, because what is truly precious has appeared.

For the sacrifice of the sheep was once of value, but now it is valueless through the life of the Lord. The death of the sheep was once of value, but now it is valueless through the salvation of the Lord. The blood of the sheep was once of value, but now it is valueless through the Spirit of the Lord. The mute lamb was once of value, but now it is valueless through the sinlessness of the Son. The temple here below was once of value, but now it is valueless because of Christ above. The earthly Jerusalem was once of value, but now it is valueless because of the heavenly Jerusalem. The narrow inheritance was once of value, but now it is valueless because of the breadth of grace.

For it is not in one place or in a narrow piece of land that the glory of God resides, but his grace has been spread to the ends of the earth, and there the Almighty has pitched his tent, through Jesus Christ to whom is glory for ever and ever. Amen.

You have heard the explanation of the type and of its fulfillment. Hear now also the plan of the mystery.

Man's unhappiness

What is the Pasch? Its name is derived from what happened, from the verb "to suffer," to be suffering: learn then who it was who suffered, and who suffered along with the sufferer, and why the Lord is present on the earth. It is so that in the vesture of one who has suffered he may be taken up to the highest heavens.

In the beginning God made heaven and earth and everything in them. He formed man from the earth by his word and communicated the breath of life to this form. Then he placed him in paradise toward the East where he lived in happiness. Like a law he gave him this command: *From every tree of paradise you may eat for nourishment, but from the tree of knowledge of good and evil you shall not eat; for the day on which you shall eat of it you shall die* (*Gen.* 2, 16-17).

But man, by nature inclined to good and evil as a clod of earth admits of both kinds of seeds, received hostile and wanton advice. He ate of that tree, transgressing orders and disobeying God. Therefore he was cast into this world as into a prison for the condemned.

When he increased and multiplied he lived long and then returned to earth because of having tasted the tree. And he left an inheritance to his children.

This inheritance was not chastity but fornication, not incorruptibility but corruptibility, not honor but dishonor, not freedom but slavery, not kingship but tyranny, not life but death, not salvation but destruction.

Strange and dreadful was the destruction of men upon the earth. This is what happened to them: they were snatched by tyrannical sin and let into the turmoils of passion in which they were inundated by insatiable pleasures — adultery, fornication, impurity, bad thoughts, avarice, murder, bloodshed, the tyranny of lust, the tyranny of lawlessness.

For father took up sword against son, and son raised his hand against father, and impiously smote the breasts that nurtured him; brother killed brother, host was unjust to guest, friend assassinated friend, and man slaughtered man with tyrannical right hand. All on earth became homicides, fratricides, parricides, infanticides. But something more dreadful and strange remains to be told.

A mother touched the flesh she had brought into the world. Furthermore she touched those being fed at her breast and killed in her womb the fruit of her womb, making the ill-starred mother a fearful tomb, devouring the child carried in her womb.

I will say no more. Many other things were discovered among men — strange, dreadful, and disgraceful: a father in bed with his own child, son with his own mother, and brother with sister, and man with man, and *every man with every neighbor's wife* (*Jer.* 5, 8).

At such crimes sin rejoiced. As collaborator of death he first penetrated the souls of men, and prepared for death the souls as pasture. On every soul sin left his mark and those he marked were sealed for death. All flesh, then, succumbed to sin and every body to death, and every soul was driven from its house of flesh.

What had come from dust to dust returned, and the creation of God was imprisoned in Hades. There was a sundering of what had been fairly joined, for man was dissolved into his parts by death. A new disaster and terrible captivity enchained him. He was taken captive by the shadows of death. The image of the Father lay alone and abandoned.

The announcement of the Lord

That is why the Paschal mystery has been fulfilled in the body of the Lord. Already the Lord had preordained his own sufferings in the patriarchs, prophets, and the whole people, and on the Law and Prophets he placed his seal. For what is to be new and great is prepared for beforehand; a coming event derives credence from its distant prefiguration. Such, then, was the mystery of the Lord: for long prefigured but today revealed, finding credence in fulfillment although regarded as novel by man. For the mystery of the Lord is both old and new, old according to type but new according to grace.

If you look at this prefiguration you will see its truth through its fulfillment. If you wish to see the mystery of the Lord look to Abel likewise slaughtered, to Isaac likewise bound, to Joseph likewise sold, to Moses likewise exposed, to David likewise persecuted, to the prophets likewise maltreated because of Christ. Look also at the sheep sacrificed in the land of Egypt which smote Egypt and saved Israel by its blood.

By the voice of the prophets the mystery of the Lord has also been proclaimed. For Moses says to the people: *And you shall see your life hanging before your eyes night and day and you shall have no assurance of your life* (*Deut.* 28, 66).

And David says: *Why do the nations conspire and the people plot in vain? The kings of the earth and the rulers take counsel together against the Lord and against his anointed* (*Ps.* 2, 1).

And Jeremiah: *I was like a gentle lamb led to slaughter. They devised evil schemes against me, saying, "Come, let us cast wood on his bread and destroy him from the land of the living and his name shall not be remembered"* (*Jer.* 11, 19).

And Isaiah: *Like a lamb he was led to the slaughter and like a sheep dumb before his shearers this man did not open his mouth. Who shall tell his descent?* (*Isa.* 53, 7).

And many other things were proclaimed by many other prophets concerning the mystery of the Passover which is Christ; to him be glory for ever and ever. Amen.

The coming of Christ

He came on earth from heaven for suffering man, becoming incarnate in a virgin's womb from which he came forth as man; he took on himself the sufferings of suffering man through a body capable of suffering, and put an end to the sufferings of the flesh, and through his spirit incapable of death he became the death of death which is destructive of man.

For led like a lamb, and slaughtered like a sheep, he ransomed us from the slavery of the world of Egypt, and loosed us from the slavery of the devil as from the hand of Pharoah, and sealed our souls with his own spirit, and our bodily members with his own blood.

This is the one who covered death with a garment of reproach, who put the devil in mourning garb as Moses did Pharaoh. This is he who smote lawlessness and rendered injustice bereft of children as Moses did Egypt.

This is the one who rescued us from slavery to liberty, from darkness to light, from death to life, from tyranny to the kingdom of eternity (who made us a new priesthood, a people chosen, eternal).

This is he who is the Passover of our salvation; this is he who suffered many things in many men. This is he who in Abel was slaughtered, in Jacob was exiled, in Joseph was sold, in Moses was exposed, in the lamb was immolated, in David was persecuted, in the prophets was maltreated. This is he who in the virgin was made incarnate, on the cross was suspended, in the earth was buried, from the dead was resurrected, to the heights of heaven was lifted up.

This is the lamb without voice, this is the lamb slaughtered, this is the lamb born of the fair ewe, this is he who was taken from the flock, and dragged to immolation, and at evening slaughtered, and by night buried.

This is he who on the cross was not broken, and in the earth did not decay, but from the dead rose again, and raised up man from the depths of the tomb.

Israel's crime

He was put to death. Where? In the heart of Jerusalem. Why? Because he cured their lame, and cleansed their lepers, and restored sight to their blind, and raised to life their dead. That is why he suffered. For it is written in the Law and the Prophets: *They requite me evil for good, and my soul is forlorn, plotting evil against me, saying, "Let us bind the Just One, for he is burdensome to us"* (Gen. 44, 4; Ps. 38, 21; Jer. 11, 19).

Why Israel, have you committed this strange injustice? You have dishonored him who honored you. You have despised him who glorified you. You have denied him who confessed you. You have repudiated him who proclaimed you. You have killed him who gave life to you. What have you done, Israel?

For has he not written for you: *Do not shed innocent blood lest you die in misery?* But I, says Israel, have slaughtered the Lord. Why? "Because he had to suffer." You are wrong, Israel, in quibbling thus about the sacrifice of the Lord.

He had to suffer, but not by you. He had to be humiliated but not by you. He had to be judged, but not by you. He had to be crucified, but not by your right hand.

Israel, you ought to have raised this cry to the Lord: "Master, if your Son must suffer and such is your will, let him suffer, but not by me. Let him suffer by men of another race. Let him be judged by the uncircumcised. Let him be crucified by a tyrant's right hand. But not by me, no."

But you, Israel, have not raised this cry to God, nor have you expiated yourself before your Master. You have not been intimidated by his works: neither by the withered hand restored to the body, nor the eyes of the blind opened by his hand, nor the paralyzed bodies raised up by his voice, nor has the even more startling sign astonished you — the corpse raised from the tomb though dead for four days.

On the contrary, you have disdained all that. For the immolation of the Lord toward evening you have prepared sharp nails, and false witnesses, and cords and lashes, and vinegar and gall, and the sword and afflictions, as for a bloody brigand.

You have applied lashes to his body, and thorns to his head. You have bound his fair hands which fashioned you from the earth, and his beautiful mouth, which fed you with life, you fed with gall, and you have slain your Lord on the great festival.

And you have been cheerful while he was hungry; you have drunk wine and eaten bread while he took vinegar and gall; your face has been lit up with joy while his was sombre; you were rejoicing while he was oppressed; you were singing while he was condemned; you were dancing while he was being buried; you reclined on a soft cushion while he was in coffin and tomb.

Criminal Israel, why have you perpetrated this strange crime, casting new sufferings on the Lord, your Master, who has fashioned you, who has created you, who has honored you, who has named you "Israel"? (Cf. *Gen.* 35, 10).

But you have not proved to be "Israel" for you have not seen

God; you have not recognized the Lord; you have failed, Israel, to recognize that this is the firstborn of God who was begotten before the morning star, who made the light to rise, and the day resplendent; who separated the darkness, who set up the first limits, who fixed the earth in its place, and dried up the abyss, and spread out the firmament, and set in order the universe; who disposed the stars in the sky, who made the lights to shine, who created the heavenly angels, who placed there the thrones, who fashioned for himself man on earth.

This was he who chose you for himself, and was your guide, from Adam to Noah, from Noah to Abraham, from Abraham to Isaac and Jacob, and the twelve patriarchs.

This was he who led you to Egypt, and protected you, and nourished you there. This was he who led you by the pillar of fire, and hid you in the cloud, who divided the Red Sea and led you through it, and dispersed your enemy.

This is he who gave you manna from heaven, who gave you drink from the rock, who gave you his Law on Horeb, who gave you as inheritance the (Promised) land, who sent you the prophets, who raised up your kings.

This is he who came to you, who cared for your suffering ones, and resurrected your dead.

This is he whom you have blasphemed, this is he whom you have maltreated, this is he whom you have put to death, this is he whom you have sold for silver, having put the tribute shekel as price on his head.

Ungrateful Israel, come hither and be judged before me for your ingratitude. What value have you set on his direction? What value have you set on the election of your fathers? What value have you set on the descent to Egypt and your support there by goodly Joseph? What value have you set on the ten plagues? What value have you set on the column of fire by night, and the cloud by day, and the passage through the Red Sea? What value have you set on the manna from heaven, and the water from the rock, and the Law given on Horeb, the inheritance of the land, and the blessings given you there?

What value have you set on the sufferers whom he cured by his presence? Think of the withered hand, which he restored to the body. Think of those blind from birth whom he restored to sight by his word. Think of those dead and buried whom he recalled from the tomb three or four days after death.

Priceless are his gifts to you. But you, far from honoring him, have only given him ingratitude in exchange. You have returned evil for good, affliction for joy, and death for life to him for whom you ought to die.

If a pagan king is taken by enemies, for his sake wars are undertaken, for his sake ramparts are broken, for his sake towns are destroyed, for his sake ransom is sent, for his sake envoys are despatched, so that he may be returned alive, so that his life may be saved, or that, if dead, he may receive burial.

Now, however, you have cast your vote against your Lord. In fact he who is worshipped by the pagans, and admired by the circumcised, and glorified by strangers, of whom even Pilate washed his hands, has been put to death by you during the great festival.

That is why the Feast of Unleavened Bread is bitter, as your Scripture says: *You shall eat unleavened bread with bitter herbs.*

Bitter for you the nails which you sharpened. Bitter for you the tongue which you whetted. Bitter for you the false witnesses you presented. Bitter for you the scourges you prepared. Bitter for you the lashes you inflicted. Bitter for you Judas whom you hired. Bitter for you Herod whom you obeyed. Bitter for you Caiaphas whom you believed. Bitter for you the gall you prepared. Bitter for you the vinegar you cultivated. Bitter for you the thorns which you gathered. Bitter for you the hands which you bloodied.

The punishment of Christ

For you have slain your Lord in the midst of Jerusalem. Hear, all you families of mankind, and see: an unprecedented murder has taken place in the midst of Jerusalem, in the city of the Law, in the city of the Hebrews, in the city of the prophets, in the city considered just.

And who has been murdered? Who is the murderer? I am reluctant to tell, but I am constrained to say. For if the murder had taken place by night, or if the slaughter had occurred in a desert place, it would be easy to keep silent. But now, in the midst of the street and the town, in the midst of the city in full view of all, the Just One has been unjustly murdered.

And so he has been hoisted on a cross and a title added, indicating who was slaughtered. Who was he? To say it is hard, but not to say it more dreadful still. Only hear it trembling before him on whose account the earth trembled.

He who suspended the earth is himself suspended; he who fixed the heavens is himself transfixed; he who made all things fast is made fast upon the tree. The Master has been outraged. God has been slaughtered. The King of Israel has been slain by Israel's right hand.

O strange murder! O strange injustice! The Master has been insulted, his body stripped naked, and he has not been deemed worthy of a covering to keep him concealed. That is why the lights of heaven have been turned off, and the day darkened, to hide him who was naked on the cross, to drape, not the body of the Lord, but the eyes of mankind.

For in fact the people did not tremble, the tremor was in the earth; the people showed no fear, the fear was in the heavens; the people did not rend their garments, the rending of garments was done by the angel; the people did not lament, *the Lord thundered in the heavens and the Most High uttered his voice.*

Now why, Israel, before the Lord did you not tremble? Before the Lord did you not fear, before the Lord did you not lament, before your firstborn did you not grieve, before the crucified Lord did you not rend your garments?

You have abandoned the Lord, and have not found pity with him; you have destroyed the Lord, and you lie pulverized in turn. You lie prostrate, a corpse, while he has risen from the dead, and has ascended to the highest heavens.

The final triumph

(Being) Lord, having put on human nature, and having suffered for him who was suffering, and having been bound for him who was bound, and condemned for him who was condemned, and buried for him who was buried, he rose from the dead and exclaimed: Who is he that contends against me? Let him stand before me. I have freed the condemned. I have restored the dead to life. I have *raised* to life the buried. Who is he who speaks against me? I, he says, am the Christ. I am he who destroyed death, and triumphed over the enemy, and trampled Hades underfoot, and bound the strong one, and rescued man to the heights of the heavens; I, he says, am the Christ.

Come, then, to me all you families of mankind sullied with sin, and receive the remission of sins. For I am your forgiveness, I am the Pasch of salvation, I am the lamb immolated for you, I am your redemption, I am your life, I am your resurrection, I am your light, I am your salvation, I am your king. I lead you to the heights of heaven. I will show you the Father eternal. I will raise you by my right hand.

This is he who made heaven and earth, and who fashioned man when time began, who was announced by the Law and the prophets, who became incarnate in a virgin, who was hanged on a cross, buried in the earth, raised from the dead, and ascended to the heights of heaven, sits at the right hand of the Father, and who has power to judge and to save all.

By him the Father has created everything from the beginning and for ever and ever. He is *the alpha and the omega,* he is the beginning and the end, the inexplicable beginning, the incomprehensible end. This is the Christ. This is the King. This is Jesus. This is the commander. This is the Lord. This is he who rose from the dead. This is he who sits at the Father's right hand. This is he who carries the Father and is carried by the Father. To him be glory and power for ever and ever. Amen.

Peace to the writer, the reader, and to those who love the Lord in simplicity of heart.

ORIGEN
(†253/254)

Famous in his own lifetime and increasingly so after his death, Origen is one of the most imposing figures in Christian antiquity. Even his detractors have copiously pirated his works. East and West show literary dependence on him.

He was not merely a scholar and a popular exegete, but also a preacher, concerned about breaking the bread of the Word of God to the Christian people. Fortunately a number of his homilies have survived in which he comments on the books of the Bible.

His Genesis commentary affords him an opportunity to analyze the sacrifice of Abraham. Abraham is for him (and later for his disciple, Ambrose) a figure of the offering of God the Father sacrificing his only Son. The homily published here is a masterpiece of psychological finesse, religious feeling, and delicacy of touch, qualities which preserve in the text its original freshness. In the commentary we see Abraham vividly recreated, torn between love and faith.

In the commentary, the sacrifice of Christ, offered by his Father is also delicately interwoven.

ABRAHAM'S SACRIFICE[1]
(*On Genesis* 22, 1-14, Homily 8)

The Test of Abraham's Obedience

1. Lend an ear here, you who have come close to the Lord, you who believe yourselves to be the faithful; give your undivided attention to a consideration from the reading which you have just heard, of how the faithful are put to the test. *After these words,* Scripture says, *God tempted Abraham* and said to him, "*Abraham, Abraham.*" And he answered, "*Here I am.*" Consider each of the scriptural details. For he who knows how to dig deeply will discover a treasure in every detail and precious pearls of mysteries may be lurking where they are least expected.

The man of whom we are speaking is, first of all, called Abram. Yet we do not read any place that God has called him by that name or has said to him, "Abram, Abram." God cannot use a name which he is going to suppress. He calls him by the name which he has given him. Not content with calling him this name he twice repeats it. When he answers *"Here I am,"* God continues, *"Take your only begotten son Isaac whom you love and offer him to me." Go,* he adds, *to a high place and offer him for a holocaust upon one of the mountains which I will show you.*

God himself explains the name Abraham and why he has given it to him: *Because I have made you a father of many nations* (*Gen.* 17, 5). God made this promise to him, when he had a son Ismael, but he assured him that this promise would be fulfilled in the son to be born from Sara. He had inflamed his soul then with love for his son not only for the sake of posterity but also in the hope of the fulfillment of the promises.

---

1. PG 12, 203-210. Greek text is lost. Only Latin version of Rufinus remains.

The proving of Abraham

But this son in whom these great and marvelous promises were placed, this son whose name was called Abraham, he is ordered to offer as a holocaust to the Lord on one of the mountains. What have you to say to this, Abraham? What kind of thoughts arise in your heart? A word is brought forth from God to test and prove your faith. What do you say to this? What are your thoughts? What misgivings have you? Or do you think in your heart that if in Isaac was given to me a promise and I offer him as a holocaust, it must be that there is no promise to be hoped for. Or rather you say and think this, that it is impossible that the one who made the promise is a liar that whatever this is, the promise will remain? But I, because of my lowliness, am not able to examine the thoughts of such a great patriarch, and am not able to know what was the voice of God which had come to tempt him, what thoughts moved him, what was on his mind when he was ordered to slay his only son. But since *the spirits of prophets are under the control of prophets* (I *Cor.* 14, 32), the Apostle Paul, who had learned, I believe, through the spirit, indicated Abraham's mind and plan, saying: *by faith Abraham offered Isaac. And he who had received the promises ... was about to offer up his only begotten son reasoning that God has power to raise up even from the dead* (*Heb.* 11, 17). The Apostle then has produced for us the thought of this man of faith, because the faith in a resurrection already began in Isaac. Abraham then hoped that Isaac would rise, and believed that what had not hitherto happened would. How then are they sons of Abraham who do not believe that that was not done in Christ which he believed would be done in Isaac? Nay rather, to speak more plainly, Abraham knew that an image of the future truth was performed in himself, he knew that Christ would rise from his seed, and that he was to be offered as a truer victim for the whole world and was going to rise from the dead.

The most beloved son

2. But now, again, we are told, *God tempted Abraham by saying to him: Take your most beloved son whom you love.* It was not enough to say "son," but "most beloved" is added, and

even that wasn't enough; "whom you love" is also added. Now see the gravity of the test. By the frequent repetition of terms of endearment paternal affections are aroused, the father's right hand is delayed in sacrificing the son by the vivid recollection of his love. And so that the whole force of his flesh might rebel against his faith of soul there is added at the time of trial, *Take then Isaac, your most beloved son whom you love.* Granted, Lord, that you remind the father of his son, yet you add "most beloved" about him whose slaughter you order. Let these three details be enough to torment the parent. Why must you add a fourth, *Isaac.* Surely Abraham knew that his son was most dear, that he loved him, that he was called Isaac. Why is this added in its place? So that Abraham might recall that he was told *in Isaac your seed will be called,* and because in Isaac will be for you the promises. The name is also mentioned to increase despair about the promise given in connection with this name. But all this was because God was testing Abraham.

Go to an elevated place

3. What is the next line? *Go into the high land to one of the mountains which I will show thee. There you shall offer him for a holocaust.* You see how each detail increases the trial. Go to the high land. Couldn't Abraham have been first led with the boy to that high place and first be placed on whatever mountain the Lord chose and there be told to offer his son? But first he is told that he should offer his son, and then he is ordered to go to that high place and climb the mountain. What is the point of this? In order that while he walks, while he makes his journey, he may be distracted all the way, tormented with conflicting thoughts of the urgency of the command and yet of his affection for his only son. Therefore, he is enjoined to make the journey, and to climb the mountain so that in all these things human affection and divine faith, love of God and earthly love, the grace of the present and the glory of the future, may make their conflicting claims. He is sent then to elevated land, and this elevation is not sufficient for the patriarch about to perform such a work for the Lord, but he is ordered to climb a mountain so that, elevated by faith, he may leave earthly things behind and ascend to the higher things.

Abraham's journey

4. *At dawn Abraham harnessed his ass and cut wood for the holocaust. He took with him his son Isaac and two servants. Then he came to the place which God had fixed on the third day* (*Gen.* 22, 3). Abraham got up at dawn. In adding "at dawn" he wished perhaps to show that the first signs of light were shining in his heart. He prepared his ass, prepared the wood, and took his son. He did not deliberate, or draw back, or communicate his plan to anybody, but immediately undertook the journey. *And he came*, we are told, *to the place which the Lord had told him on the third day.* For the moment I leave aside the symbolism of *the third day* and direct attention to the wisdom and sagacity of the one testing him. So on the next day there was no certain mountain since it was all mountains but the journey continued for three days so that paternal concern might extend over the three-day period, so that his father's heart might be torn to pieces, looking at his son throughout this extended period, eating with him, his son sleeping in his arms at night, clinging to his breast, nestling in his arms.

See how the testing increases. The *third day*, however, is always suitable for signs. For when the (chosen) people came from Egypt, they offered sacrifice on the third day and were purified on the third day. The Lord's resurrection was on the third day and many other mysteries are concluded on this day.

The order to the servants

5. *Looking*, we are told, *Abraham saw the place at a distance and said to his servants: stay here with the ass; the boy and I will go yonder and when we adore we will return to you.*

He dismisses the servants. For they could not go up with Abraham to the place of holocaust which God had shown him. *You then*, he said, *stay here: the child and I will go and when we adore we will return to you.* Tell me, Abraham, was it true or a lie when you told the servants that you would adore with the child and return? If you are telling the truth, then you will not make him a holocaust. If you are lying, such a great patriarch as you should not lie. What then is the meaning of your words?

I am telling the truth, he says, and will offer my son in holocaust. That is why I am bringing wood with me and I will return to you with him. For I believe and this is my faith that *God has power to raise up even from the dead (Heb. 11, 19).*

Isaac, figure of Christ

6. *Abraham took the wood of holocaust and put it on his son Isaac; he himself took the fire in his hands and the sword and they went out together.*

Isaac who carries for himself the wood of holocaust in person is a figure of Christ who carried the cross in person. And yet to carry the wood of holocaust goes with the office of priest. So he becomes at the same time victim and priest. The word which follows *they both went out together* refers to this. For when Abraham carries the fire and the knife as if for the sacrifice, Isaac does not walk behind, but along with him to show that he shares his sacerdotal function.

What is next? *Isaac said to Abraham his father: Father.* And these words, at this juncture, uttered by the son, were the voice of temptation. For how do you think the father was smitten to the heart by these words of his son about to be sacrified? And, however rigid in faith Abraham was, he replies affectionately, *What is it, son?* But he said: *Behold fire and wood. Where is the sheep for holocaust?* To this Abraham answers: *The Lord will provide for himself a sheep for holocaust, son.*

This response of Abraham, at once affectionate and guarded, I find touching. I do not know what he saw in spirit, because he does not speak of the present but of the future when he says: *God himself will provide a sheep for himself.* His son asks about the present, in his reply he announces the future: because the Lord himself provided for himself a sheep in the person of Christ; in fact *wisdom has built itself a house (Prov. 9, 1)* and *humbled himself unto death (Phil 2, 8).*

Everything you read of Christ you will find that he did freely and not under constraints.

The place of sacrifice

7. *And they went together and arrived at the place of which*

God had told him (*Gen.* 22, 9). When Moses arrived at the place which God had indicated to him, he was not allowed to ascend but it was said to him first: *Remove the sandals from your feet* (*Exod.* 3, 5). Abraham and Isaac are not treated like this: they go up without taking off their sandals. The reason perhaps is that Moses, great as he was, nevertheless, came from Egypt: the shackles of mortality were knotted to his feet. Abraham and Isaac were not in the same situation.

They arrive then at the place. Abraham constructs the altar, sets up the wood on it, binds the child, and prepares to immolate him.

In this Church of God there is a large number of fathers listening to me. Do you think that any of you has acquired from the historical narrative such constancy, such strength of soul that if perchance your son were lost in death (which is universal and inescapable) even if he is your only son, beloved by you, would you think of the example of Abraham and place his magnanimity before your eyes?

And indeed not as much magnanimity is demanded from you as from him — to tie up your son, to prepare the sword, to slaughter your only son. All these mysterious deeds are not sought from you. Just be constant in intention and mind, rooted in faith and joyfully offer your son to God. Be the priest of your son's soul. A priest making sacrifice to God should not weep.

Do you want proof that this is demanded of you? In the Gospel the Lord says: *If you are the children of Abraham do the works of Abraham* (*John* 8, 39). Well, this is a work of Abraham. Do the works which Abraham did, but not tearfully. *God loves a cheerful giver* (*II Cor.* 9, 7). But if you too were prompt, God would say to you: *Go to an elevated place on a mountain that I will show you,* and there offer your son to me. Not in the depths of the earth, nor in the valley of tears, but on the heights, on the lofty mountains, offer your son.

Show that your faith in God is stronger than human affection. For Abraham, we are told, loved his son, Isaac, but he preferred love of God to earthly love, and he was found not in the bosom of the flesh, but in the bosom of Christ, that is, in the bosom of the word of God and of truth and wisdom.

The sacrifice of Abraham

8. *Abraham stretched out his hand, and took the knife to kill his son. But the angel of the Lord called to him from heaven, "Abraham, Abraham." He answered "Here I am." He said, "Do not lay a hand on the boy; do nothing to him. I know now that you fear God."* In regard to this text it is objected that God at this moment says that he knew that Abraham feared God, as if he did not know this previously.

God knew it, because nothing escapes him who *knows all things before they come to pass* (*Dan.* 13, 42).

It is for you that these words are written, because you too believed in God but if you have not done the works of faith, if you have not obeyed all the commandments, even the more difficult ones, if you have not offered sacrifice to show that you put God before even father and mother and sons, if you have given no proof of your fear of God no one will say to you: *I know now that you fear God.*

It must be noted also that Scripture places this word on the lips of an angel and the remainder of the incident shows conclusively that this angel is the Lord. I conclude that in the midst of men he is made like a man; likewise among angels he has taken the form of an angel. Following his example the angels in heaven rejoice over one sinner doing penance and take glory in man's progress. They are guardians of our souls; and we are committed to them for a definite time by the Father, when we are still in our childhood. They are our *guardians and stewards until the time set by his father* (*Gal.* 4, 2). And seeing the present progress of each of us they say: *Now I know that you fear God.*

For example, I am near martyrdom. The angel will not be able to say to me: *At present, I know that you fear God.* Because the intention of my heart is known to God alone. But if I enter into the arena, I confess my faith, and endure courageously all the blows. Then the angel can say, as it were confirming and corroborating me: *now I know that you fear God.*

These words were really said to Abraham to affirm that he feared God. Why? Because he did not spare his own son. Let us compare these words to those of the Apostle, when he spoke to God: *He did not spare his own son, but has delivered him up for us* (*Rom.* 8, 32). Behold God vies with men in munificence and liberality. Abraham offered a mortal son who was not going to die to God. God delivered an immortal Son to death for all. What will we say to this? *What return will we make to the Lord for all he has done for us?* God the Father has not spared his own Son for us. Which of you thinks he will one day hear the voice of an angel saying: Now I know that you fear God because you did not spare your son, or your daughter, or wife, or you did not spare money, or earthly honors, or worldly ambitions, but you made light of everything and *regarded everything as dung to gain Christ;* you sold everything and gave to the poor, and followed the word of God? Which of you, do you think, will hear a statement like that (from the angels). Again Abraham hears this voice and it is said to him: *you have not withheld your only son from me* (*Gen.* 22, 12).

The ram, figure of Christ

9. *Abraham looking back saw a ram among the briers sticking fast by the horns* (*Gen.* 22, 15). We have already said, I believe, that Isaac was a figure of Christ, but here too the ram seems to be no less a figure of Christ. But it is worth knowing how both can resemble Christ—Isaac who was not immolated and the ram who was.

Christ is the Word of God, but *the Word was made flesh* (*John* 1, 14). In Christ, then, there is one element from above, and one from human nature, got from the virginal womb. Christ then suffers, but in the flesh; he endured death but in the flesh of which here the ram is a figure, just as John said: *Behold the lamb of God who takes away the sin of the world.* The Word then remained incorruptible, which is Christ according to the spirit of which Isaac is a figure. So he is likewise a victim and priest according to the spirit. For he who offers the victim to the Father in the flesh, he is offered on the altar of the cross because as it is said of him: *Behold the lamb of God who takes away the sin of the world,* so it is also said of him, *you are a priest forever according to the order of Melchisedech* (*Ps.* 109, 4). Therefore, the ram is held by the horns among the briars.

The fruit of the sacrifice

10. *And the ram he took and offered for a holocaust instead of Isaac his son. And he called the name of that place the Lord sees* (*Gen.* 22, 13). To those who know how to understand this way of spiritual understanding is clearly open. All things which are done come to vision. The vision which the Lord has, however, is spiritual so that you who read what is written may see in spirit. Just as there is nothing corporeal in the Lord so you should understand these things in non-corporeal terms, but you will generate spiritually a son Isaac when you begin to have the fruit of the spirit, joy and peace. You will generate that kind of son if like Sara of whom it was written that she was past the age of childbearing when she gave birth to Isaac you should have nothing maternal or effeminate in your soul but should act like a man, girding your loins like a man; if your breast is fortified with the breastplate of justice, if the helmet of salvation and the sword of the spirit are girded on. When the things of woman were no longer in your soul you would generate a son fathered by virtue and wisdom—joy and happiness. You would generate joy however if you regard as joyful every fall into temptation, offering that joy as a sacrifice to the Lord. When you approach the Lord in joy he will give you back your offering and say to you: *A little while I will see you again and your heart will rejoice and your joy no one shall take from you* (*John* 16, 22). So your offerings to God will be returned to you multiplied.

Some such thing, though under another figure, is meant in the Scriptures, in the parable telling of a certain man getting a golden piece to trade with it and to seek money for the head of a family. But if you bring five multiplied to ten, they will be donated and granted to you. Hear what he says: *take this gold piece and give to him who has ten* (*Luke* 19, 24). So then we seem to do business for the Lord, but the gains in the transaction return to us, and we seem to offer sacrifices to the Lord but our offerings redound to ourselves. For God is in need of nothing but wishes us to be rich, wishes our perfection in all things. This figure is shown to us even in these things which were done concerning Job. For he when wealthy lost everything for God. But because he nobly endured the tests of patience and was magnanimous in all his sufferings and said: *The Lord has given, the Lord has taken away; blessed be the name of the Lord* (*Job* 1, 21). See what is written of him (at the end) *everything which he lost was doubled* (*Job* 42, 10).

You see that to lose something for God is to get it back multiplied for yourself. The Gospels promise other things besides: a hundred-fold is promised you and also eternal life in Christ Jesus our Lord, to whom is glory and power forever and ever. Amen.

DERIVATIVES FROM HIPPOLYTUS OF ROME

The two homilies presented here were inspired by a treatise on the Pasch (now lost) written by Hippolytus of Rome.

The first of these homilies was long regarded as a work of Hippolytus. P. Nautin has shown with supporting proofs that the bishop of Rome was not the author. It consists of two main parts dealing with the Jewish Passover, and secondly the passion of Christ. The author, faithful to the exegetical principles of Hippolytus, strives to discover a spiritual meaning in the Jewish rites; the mystery of Jesus Christ is also discovered, phrase by phrase, in the text of Exodus, chapter twelve. This part which is in the nature of a research project and which constitutes an attempt at an intellectual explanation is written in vigorous but often elliptical terms, sometimes reducing itself to the form of simple lecture notes.

The passion of Christ by contrast is a more artistic evocation. The sacrifice of Jesus, the gift of his grace move the preacher; prayers and poetical meditations — we are thinking especially of the admirable hymn of the Tree — confer extreme beauty and originality on this homily.

The second homily also derives from Hippolytus, but at the same time comes under another important influence on early Christian spirituality — that of Origen. These two traditions are not contradictory but complementary. The Jewish Passover is not only an historical figure of the redemption, but also assumes a more personal and more interior significance, which favors the etymology which Origen gave to the Pasch, the "passage"; the Pasch becomes the symbol of the renewal of the individual conscience. The co-existence of the two tendencies — historical and moral — give this homily a great spiritual value.

I
THE PASCH HISTORY[1]

INTRODUCTION

THE PASCH AND THE ECONOMY OF SALVATION

The Pasch: passage from figure to truth

Now is the time when the blessed light of Christ sheds its
rays; the pure rays of the pure Spirit rise and the heavenly
treasures of divine glory are opened up. Night's darkness and
obscurity have been swallowed up, and the dense blackness
dispersed in this light of day; crabbed death has been totally
eclipsed. Life has been extended to every creature and all things
are diffused in brightness. The dawn of dawn ascends over the
earth and *he who was before the morning star* (*Ps.* 109, 2) and
before the other stars, the mighty Christ, immortal and mighty,
sheds light brighter than the sun on the universe.

For us, his faithful, he has initiated a bright new day, long,
eternal and inextinguishable; it is the mystical Pasch, celebrated
in figures under the Law, but fulfilled in very truth by Christ,
the marvelous Pasch, the wonder of divine virtue, the work of
power, truly a feast, an everlasting memorial, impassibility born
of suffering, immortality born of death, life born in the tomb,
healing born from wounds, resurrection born from the fall, ascent
to heaven born from descent to hell.

God is the author of these wonders; from impossible beginnings he produces wonderful results, to show you that he alone
can accomplish everything he wills.

Let Egypt, then, announce beforehand the truth in figures,
let the Law interpret the figures of truth in advance, proclaiming
the glorious coming of a glorious King. Let the host of Egyptian
firstborn die and let Israel be saved by the mystical sign of the
blood: all this is a foreshadowing of what is to come. But for us
today the images have been realized; the figures are replaced by
the truth, and shadow gives way to what is substantial and complete. So the Law has come first to signify in type the true reality.
But type and figure are no more, now that truth has arrived. Then

---

1. PG 59, 735-746; SC 27, 117-191.

the lamb was taken from the flock; today the lamb has come down from heaven; then there was the sign of blood and the small phylactery of all; today there is the Word and the cup filled with blood and the Divine Spirit; then there was the sheep from the flock, today there is not just a sheep but the Shepherd in person.

Will not the reality announce the salvation of the whole world since even their types were already salutary? Exult, ye heavens of heavens, which as the Spirit exclaims, *proclaim the glory of God* (*Ps.* 18, 1) in that they are first to receive the paternal light of the Divine Spirit. Exult, angels and archangels of the heavens, and all you people, and the whole heavenly host as you look upon your heavenly King come down in bodily form to earth. Exult, you choir of stars pointing out him who rises *before the morning star.* Exult, air, which extends over the abysses and interminable spaces. Exult, briny water of the sea, honored by the sacred traces of his footsteps. Exult, earth washed by the divine blood. Exult, every soul of man, reanimated by the resurrection to a new birth.

O Pasch; common feast of the world; you proclaim to the earth the Father's will for the universe. You are the divine dawning of Christ on the earth, invisible feast for angels and archangels, immortal life of the entire world, fatal wound of death, indestructible nourishment of man, heavenly soul of the universe, sacred feast of heaven and earth, prophet of *mysteries old and new* (*Matt.* 13, 52), seen by the eyes here on earth and contemplated by the Spirit of the heavens.

After having consulted those who have been initiated into those *mysteries old and new* we will attempt to define briefly the universal feast of Pasch so that we may be nourished completely on the Word, feasting not on earthly but on heavenly food; let us eat the Pasch of the Word with the same spiritual desire with which the Lord wished to eat with us when he said, *with desire I have desired to eat the Pasch with you* (*Luke* 22, 15).

The figures of the paschal rite

Come now, let us first deal briefly with the nature of the Law, its necessity, and why it only came after Egypt. Secondly, what is the connection of the Pasch and Egypt, what is the inner meaning of the Pasch and the paschal mystery.

Let us first quote the Scripture itself, so that by comparison and reference we may see each of the points to be studied.

And the Lord spoke to Moses and Aaron in the land of Egypt, saying, this month shall be to you the beginning of months. It is the first to you among the months of the year. Speak to all the congregation of the children of Israel, saying, "On the tenth of this month let them take each man a lamb according to the houses of their families, every man a lamb for his household. And if they be few in a household, so that there are not enough for the lamb, he shall take with himself his neighbor that lives near to him,— as to the number of souls, every one according to that which suffices him shall make a reckoning for the lamb. It shall be to you a lamb unblemished, a male of a year old: you shall take it of the lambs or the kids. And it shall be kept by you till the fourteenth of this month, and all the multitude of the congregation of the children of Israel shall kill it toward evening. And they shall take of the blood, and shall put it on the two door-posts, and on the lintel, in the houses in which soever they shall eat them. And they shall eat the flesh in this night roast with fire, and they shall eat unleavened bread with bitter herbs. You shall not eat of it raw nor sodden in water, but only roast with fire, the head with feet and the entrails. Nothing shall be left of it till the morning and a bone of it you shall not break; but that which is left of it till the morning you shall burn with fire. And thus shall you eat it: your loins girded, and your sandals on your feet, and your staves in your hands, and you shall eat it in haste. It is a passover to the Lord. And I will go through the land of Egypt in that night, and will smite every firstborn in the land of Egypt both man and beast, and on all the gods of Egypt will I execute vengeance: I am the Lord. And the blood shall be for a sign to you on the houses in which you are, and I will see the blood and will protect you, and there shall not be on you the plague of destruction, when I smite in the land of Egypt.

And this day shall be to you a memorial, and you shall keep it a feast to the Lord through all your generations; you shall keep it a feast for a perpetual ordinance. Seven days you shall eat unleavened bread" (Exod. 12, 1-15).

And the Lord said to Moses and Aaron, "This is the law of the passover: no stranger shall eat of it. And every slave or servant bought with money — him you shall circumcise, and then shall he eat of it. A sojourner or hireling shall not eat of it. In one house shall it be eaten, and you shall not carry of the flesh out from the house: and a bone of it you shall not break. All the congregation of the children of Israel shall keep it. And if any proselyte shall come to you to keep the passover to the Lord, you shall circumcise every male of him, and then shall he approach to sacrifice it, and he shall be even as the original inhabitant of the land; no uncircumcised person shall eat of it. There shall be one law to the native, and to the proselyte coming among you" (*Exod.* 12, 43-49).

Scripture has announced this sacred feast in this figurative language. We will now examine the text in minute detail and interpret its hidden meaning in response to your prayers; we will not suppress the truth in what is written but study the reality of the mysteries underlying the figures.

For the Holy Spirit ordered Moses to erect the tabernacle *according to the plan which I will show you* (*Exod.* 26, 30). And so this dwelling-place made according to the original proposes a figure to the eyes and a mystery to the spirit.

Let us first say why this month is the *beginning of months* and why this month of the Passover is *the first of the months of the year*. Secondly, what is the lamb which is taken *on the tenth day of the month*, the *perfect* lamb *one year old;* who is *the neighbor* and *the one who lives near* who *is taken;* why is the lamb kept *until the fourteenth* day and then *killed toward evening – and all the multitude of the congregation of the children of Israel shall kill it toward evening*. What is *the blood on the two door-posts and on the lintel;* why is the meat eaten *at night, roasted on the fire*, and *not raw* or *boiled in water;* what is the meaning of the expression *the head with the feet and the entails* and why – *you shall not break a bone of the victim?* What is the meaning of *unleavened bread with bitter herbs;* why do you eat the Pasch *in haste?* What means *with your loins girt, sandals on your feet, and your staff in hand?* What is the meaning of *the Passover of the Lord* and *the blood will mark the houses where you are. Seeing the blood, I will pass over you; thus when I strike the land of Egypt, no destructive blow will come upon you*. And why does it say: *For seven days you must eat unleavened bread?* And why are transient aliens or slaves excluded, and what is the meaning of *it must be eaten in one and the same house; you may not take any of the flesh out of the house. You shall not break any of its bones. The whole community of Israel must celebrate this feast*. What is this "community"? And *if any aliens living among you wish to celebrate, all the males must first be circumcised. The law shall be the same for the resident alien as for the native.*

The Truth: Christ incarnate, dead and risen

Thus figures, symbols and signs in Israel were physically seen but among us they received their spiritual fulfillment. After these brief remarks, let us proceed to the mysteries of the Truth. Why was the coming of Jesus Christ after the Law; why did he become incarnate? What was the Pasch which he desired to eat with us? Why did he who raised the dead by his word not completely conquer death while still alive? Why did he endure death on the cross? What was the meaning of the crown of thorns, the vinegar and gall which he drank, his opened side from which blood and water flowed? Why did he pray that the cup might pass which he came on earth to drink? Who were the thieves who were crucified with him, one of whom joined him in paradise? Why was his Spirit placed in the hands of his Father and his body in the unused tomb? What means *shall be with me in paradise* and *today?* What were the *three days* he remained in the earth? Why were women the first to see him whom he summons to rejoice; as the Gospel says *women rejoice.*

This is for us the celebration of our sacred feast, this is our spiritual banquet, this is our immortal and delightful nourishment. Since we have been nourished on *the bread come down from heaven* and have drunk of the chalice of joy, that chalice which is full of fervor and warmth, containing blood signed from on high with the glow of the Spirit, let us speak first on what is the Law, what is the economy of the Law, for in this way we will learn in parable the meaning of the Word and the economy of the Word.

I. THE MYSTERY OF THE LAW

The Law of Moses

The Law of Moses is a collection of various important dogmas, a salutary guide to all that is beautiful in life, a mystical replica of life in heaven, a light, an illumination, a flame, a torch, a reflection of heavenly brightness. The Law of Moses is a prototype of piety and a rule for behavior and right order, an antidote to original sin, and a preview of the truth to come. The Law of Moses is the rejection of the error of Egypt written *with the finger of God*, because his *strong right arm* was in reserve for another purpose. The Law of Moses is a guide for piety and a directive for justice, a light for the blind, a rebuke for the foolish, a pedagogue for children, a restraint for the imprudent, a bridle for the stiff-necked and a restraining yoke for those who rebel. The Law of Moses is a messenger of Christ and a precursor of Jesus, a herald and prophet of the great King, a school for the wise, an essential academy, a university, a dogma formerly and a passing mystery. The Law of Moses was in the form of a symbol and a sign of future grace in epitome, announcing in images the plenitude of the truth to come, prefiguring the sacred victim in its sacrifices, the Blood in the blood, the Lamb in the lamb, the heavenly Dove in the dove, the High-priest in its altar, the abode of the divinity in its temple, and in the fire on the altar the fullness of the light of the world come down from above.

Egypt is God's first victory

The Law was thus first preordained for us in this figurative manner. But it came of necessity after the departure from Egypt because the soul had become materialistic and the heart Egyptianized. The Law had to eradicate the invisible roots of evil, and plough the rough, dense undergrowth of thorny thoughts and furrow the depths of the soul prior to making it the seedbed of the heavenly Divine Word. Therefore the Holy Spirit rightly exclaims: *Break fresh ground for yourselves and sow not among thorns* (*Jer.* 4, 3). That is why the Pasch began symbolically in Egypt, the first breach in the darkness of idolatry, the symbolical destruction of impious paganism, the avenging plague by night on the firstborn of a people in error.

Therefore Egypt first experienced the Pasch when the plague claimed its firstborn, and all its firstborn died, so that the stiff-necked Pharaoh might finally learn a lesson, having failed to get the message of the first plagues, and to let Israel be saved in this paradoxical fashion, while everything contributed to the glory of God. For Egypt there was a passion in the plague, for Israel a pasch in a feast, and so the feast was called the Pasch of the Lord.

There are many other figures of God's future mercy, and here is the reason: Egypt is a vast, dark image of darkness and profound error. It is the prime source of error. There they made false gods and false theologies around heifers, fish, birds, wild beasts and all such creatures. When the avenging anger descended from the heavens and the great wrath was unloosed on the earth then superstition and the error of idolatry were the first to be struck. For *on all the gods of Egypt will I execute vengeance* (*Exod.* 12, 12).

The plague was directed at all the firstborn, because they claimed for themselves the privileges of seniority and the slavery of idolatry got primacy of place.

The plague took place in darkness and in the night, because it is in the shadow of night far from the clear light of day that justice will be done to the devils and their black crimes: *I will give portents in the heavens and on the earth, blood and fire and columns of smoke. The sun shall be turned to darkness and the moon to blood before the great and terrible day of the Lord comes* (*Joel* 3, 3-4). And: *Woe to you who desire the day of the Lord. What is this day of the Lord to you? It is darkness and not light. As if a man should flee from the face of a lion and a bear should meet him and he should spring into his house and lean his hands on the wall and a serpent should bite him. Is not the day of the Lord darkness and not light? And is not this day gloom without brightness* (*Amos* 5, 18-20)?

The sign of blood

The *sign of blood* is a bloody type of the seal of Christ; and the sign is not so much the truth itself as a sign of the truth to come. For those who carry the sign of blood marked and anointed on their souls as on their houses, all those will be passed over by the avenging plague for it is said: *And the blood shall be for a sign to you on the houses in which you are, and I will see the blood, and will protect you, and there shall not be on you the plague of destruction when I smite in the land of Egypt* (*Exod.* 12, 13). The blood is a protective sign. *In the houses,* as in the souls where the Spirit of the Lord has his sacred dwelling by faith. *I will protect you*: the immense protection of the hands of Jesus extended over those who believe.

Such, then, is an overall view of the cosmic mystery of the

Pasch: but hear also a detailed account of the divine mystery from us to the best of our ability, for only God knows the whole truth in these matters, and the Word who has organized the Pasch in himself and for himself; if we fail in our efforts allowance should be made for our human frailty, beloved.

Why is the month of the Pasch the first month?

Let us return then to the first point. Why does this month come ahead of the others? Why is the month of the Pasch the first month of the year? A secret tradition among the Hebrews says that it was in this month that the Divine artist God, the creator of the universe, conceived his world. This was the first flower of creation, the beauty of the world, when the creator saw the statue of his artistic making move in harmonious accord with his intentions. They observe the order of the heavens, the blend of the seasons, the regular course of the sun, the rising of the full moon, the blossoming of fruits, the budding of plants, the flowering of trees, the birth of flocks; when the whole earth becomes green, and the shrubs burst forth, groaning, under their burden of fruits, and the farmer unyokes the plough and allows his lowing oxen to rest, and after casting the God-given seeds in the earth awaits the rains from heaven, when the shepherd milks the white sheep of his flocks and the beekeepers construct sweet honeycombs for the hives, when the sailor joyfully risks the hazards of the sea and in his search for gain defies the hoary waves. They see this harmony in the universe, this order in all things, this first-fruit, so to speak, of happiness and this sweet beginning of spring is for them the beginning of the year.

For my part, I do not disbelieve all this, but I feel, or rather I am certain, that it is rather because of the spiritual nature of the Pasch that it has been considered as the beginning, head, and leader of all times and all ages, this month of the Pasch in which this great mystery is accomplished and celebrated, so that, just as the Lord is the first-engendered and firstborn of all beings intelligible and invisible, likewise this month which celebrates the sacred solemnity becomes the first of the year and the beginning of all ages. And the year is that which is announced in the divine Scriptures: *Declare the acceptable year of the Lord* (*Isa.* 61, 2).

The immolated lamb

A sheep is the sacred victim: *As a sheep he was led to the slaughter, and like a lamb before the shearer* (*Isa.* 53, 7), and John says: *Behold the lamb of God who takes away the sins of the world* (*John* 1, 29).

The sheep is of perfect age of one year. It is perfect since it has come from the heavens, it is one year old since it lives on earth. Since a year is a measure of earth by time, its successions, its perpetual returns form a rhythmical eternity without measure. *He is taken on the tenth of the month,* a purely symbolical detail: the time prior to the Gospel was occupied by the Law and the Decalog is the Law's fundamental article; after the ten commandments of the Law the mystical sheep descends from the heavens. He is *kept* during the intervening days: The Scripture here indicates to us the interval before the passion and the captivity where he was held by the high priest.

The neighbor invited to eat the lamb is me. I am *the neighbor.* Because you, Israel, you have never received the lamb.

Then the lamb is immolated *toward evening.* And it was also toward sunset that the sacred lamb of God was immolated. *Then all the multitude of the congregations of the sons of Israel shall kill it.* For impious Israel has become responsible for this precious blood, those of old in shedding it, and those from then until now in refusing to believe. Therefore the Divine Spirit bears witness against them, exclaiming: *Your hands are full of blood* (*Isa.* 1, 15).

The blood is on the lintel as on the Church and on the two door-posts as on the two peoples. Because the Savior does not deny that he was sent first to you, Israel: *I have not been sent to you, but to the lost sheep of the house of Israel* (*Matt.* 15, 24). And I, like a house dog, have been beside the table of another, unable to eat the bread yet, but a parasite picking up the crumbs which fall from another man's table. But since you have failed to recognize the manna come down from heaven, the Bread has been given to me instead of you because of my faith and I am changed from a dog to a son.

This is *the night* on which the flesh is eaten, for the light of the world has set on the great body of Christ: *Take and eat; this is my body* (*Matt.* 26, 26).

The flesh is roasted with fire: for the spiritual body of Christ is on fire: *I have come to light a fire on the earth. How I wish the blaze were ignited* (*Luke* 12, 49). The flesh is not *raw*, so that the Word may be easily assimilated, easy to preach and easy to hear; it is not *boiled in water*, so that the Word may not be sodden, or watery, or running.

The head with the feet and the entrails . . . (God) as the invisible will, man as the feet. *The head with the feet and the entrails*, beginning, middle and end, containing all binding and uniting in itself with indissoluble bonds him who has truly become the *Mediator between God and man* (I *Tim.* 2, 5). *The head with the feet and the entrails*: God, Word, and man on earth. *The head with the feet and the entrails* in height, and depth, and breadth, (the skies, the earth) and the earth's foundations. *The head with the feet and the entrails*: the Law, the Word, and the apostles, the Law as beginning, the Word as will, and the apostles as feet. *How beautiful are the feet of those who announce good news* (*Rom.* 10, 15).

A bone of it you shall not break, so that the resurrection of the body may be recognized: *Put your fingers into the place of the nails that you may know that spirit has not flesh and bones* (*John* 20, 27). *You shall eat unleavened bread with bitter herbs;* a bitter mystery for you (Israel), a mystery of bitter things. *Your land is desolate, your cities burned with fire, your land, strangers devour it in your presence and it is made desolate, overthrown by strange nations* (*Isa.* 1, 7).

And you shall eat it in haste: for one must be keeping vigil and fasting when one approaches the great Body. *Your loins girded*: pollutions must cease, carnal intercourse, and shameful pleasures. *And your sandals on your feet;* a steady step, a solid support, rooted in truth. *Sandals on your feet*, those which Moses took off and Jesus put on. For Moses said, *Loose your sandals from your feet* (*Exod.* 3, 5) to show that the Law was transitory. And of Jesus it was said, *I am not worthy to loose his sandal strap* (*Luke* 3, 16) to show that the Word is well founded.

Your staffs in your hands: Signs of divine power, supports of the Word, the staff of Moses, the staff of Aaron, the nut-like staff, the staff which cleaves the depths of the (Red) sea, the staff which makes sweet the bitter waters, the staff on which repose the seven holy spirits of God: *the spirit of wisdom and under-*

*standing, the spirit of counsel and strength (the spirit of knowl-
edge and godliness), the spirit of the fear of God shall fill him
(Isa. 11, 2).*

The blood reconciled God and men

The Pasch is the *Pasch of the Lord.* The Spirit has proclaimed
this in the clearest terms, that the Pasch is no longer just a figure,
just a narrative, just a shadow but truly the Pasch of the Lord.
The blood is a sign, and a sign of the truth to come, a prototype
of the true spirit, an image of the great anointing.

And I will see the blood and will protect you. Truly, Jesus,
you have protected us from much danger and have extended your
paternal hands, clutching us under your wings; you have poured
out your divine blood on the earth to seal the alliance in blood in
your zeal for those whom you love. You have put far from us
the threats of anger, and have given us in its place the first
reconciliation from on high.

Seven days they (the Jews) shall eat unleavened bread, thus
spending a week as the world measures it and eating the food of
the earth as the Law ordains. But as for us, *Christ, our passover,
has been sacrificed* (I *Cor.* 5, 7). And we have received the new
leaven of his sacred mixing entirely fermented by a superior
power and kneaded by his Spirit. For my leaven has caused the
King of the heavens to rise like the three measures of meal (cf.
Matt. 13, 33).

That is why *no stranger shall eat of it* (cf. *Exod.* 12, 43-44).
For I do not *cast pearls before swine,* I do not *give what is holy
to dogs.* But he who was a slave to sin will be circumcised in his
heart and once freed from his odious servitude, he will approach
the mystery like one nobly born; in his newly-found state of freedom he will then eat the Pasch. For *Christ redeemed us* from
slavery *and from the curse, becoming a curse for us* (*Gal.* 3, 13).

*In one house shall it be eaten and you shall not carry any of
the flesh out from the house* (*Exod.* 12, 46) for the assembly is
one, the house is one, it is the one church where the sacred body
of Christ is eaten and therefore outside this one house — that is,
the Church — the meats shall not be carried; but he who eats
elsewhere will be punished as impious and a thief.

There shall be one law to the freeman and the proselyte

coming among you: for wherever Christ is there is liberty, there is equality for all, the same law, the same honor, for all have been redeemed with the precious blood, and so you are no longer a slave, no longer a Jew, but a free man; for we have all become free in Christ.

II. THE TRUTH: JESUS CHRIST

Now, having heard about the figures and economy of the Law, hear the reason why Christ descended to earth, and understand its full grandeur.

What is the meaning of the coming of Christ? It is deliverance from slavery, rejection of the old constraint, the beginning of freedom, the glory of adoption, the source of pardon and true immortality for all.

The coming of Jesus Christ

From heaven he saw us tyrannized by death, bound and loosed at the same time in the chains of death, traversing the fatal road which has no point of return. He came and assumed the first man's nature according to the design of his Father, and he did not entrust to his angels and archangels the charge of our souls, but he himself, the Word, undertook the entire challenge for us in obedience to his Father's orders.

As the Divine Spirit in his essence remained inaccessible to all things, so that nothing should be impermeable to the pure effusions of the Spirit, he willingly confined himself to himself and collecting and, compressing in himself all the greatness of the divinity, came in the dimensions of his own choice in no way diminished or lessened in himself, nor inferior in glory. By the extreme power of the Father he lost nothing of what he had, but taking on in addition something which he had not, he came in a way in which he could be comprehended. And since there had to be a receptacle for the Holy Spirit, so that the first might participate in human nature and existence, . . . he strained it and banished its excess and its impurities . . . and what he offered of pure, translucent and perfect, he illuminated. He filled it with radiance and fire, making it virginal and, so to speak, angelic. Such is the body that he models in the image of man, and keeping his spiritual beauty he has taken flesh. The Scripture calls this figurative names: *Behold the man whose name is the Branch* (*Zech.* 6, 12). In spirit he is a branch, but in body a man. *The Holy Spirit shall come upon thee and the power of the Most High shall overshadow you; and therefore the Holy One to be born shall be called the Son of the Most High* (*Luke* 1, 35). As this birth was unusual and divine, it is no wonder that the Spirit marveled, saying: *who shall declare his generation?* (*Isa.* 53, 8).

The four names of glory

The divinity has four principal names to characterize the Holy Spirit; lordship, divinity, sonship, and eternal kingship. Let us look and see if only Christ partakes of the honor of these virtues and these glories. Notice first that he is Lord: *The Lord said to my Lord: Sit at my right hand* (*Ps.* 109, 1). You see here that he is Lord, since he lives in the intimacy of the Lord.

See now that he is Son: *he shall say to me, You are my father and I will make him the firstborn* (*Ps.* 88, 27). And: *You are my son; this day I have begotten you. Ask of me and I will give you the nations for an inheritance* (*Ps.* 2, 7). You see here that he is Son, the only and firstborn; note also that he is God: *men of stature shall come over to you, and shall be yours: they shall walk after you, they shall go bound with miracles; and they shall worship you, and shall make supplication to you: only in you is God and there is no God besides you* (*Isa.* 45, 14). There you see he is God; notice too that he is eternal King: *Your throne, O God, stands forever and ever; a tempered rod is your royal scepter. You love justice and hate wickedness; therefore God your God, has anointed you with the oil of gladness above your fellow kings* (*Ps.* 44, 7-8). He is King, I say; but see, at the same time, he is all powerful Lord. *Lift up, O gates, your lintels; reach up, you ancient portals, that the king of glory may come in. Who is this King of glory? The Lord of hosts; he is the King of glory* (*Ps.* 23, 9).

You see that as well as being King he is Lord of Powers; see too that among his other titles he is also eternal High priest: *The Lord swore and will not repent, you are a priest forever according to the order of Melchisedech* (*Ps.* 109, 4). Now if he is Lord and God, Son and King, Lord of Powers and eternal High priest when he wishes *he is also man and who can know him* (*Jer.* 17, 9)? The words *also man* imply that he is God to begin with. And lest you think after the fashion of men that he came on earth by chance and without being born, a phantom or ghost, hear how he became a little child: *Hear now, O house of David; is it a little thing for you to contend with men? And how do you contend with the Lord? Therefore the Lord himself shall give you a sign: Behold, a virgin shall conceive in the womb and shall bring forth a son, and thou shalt call his name Emmanuel* (*Isa.* 7, 13-14). And: *they shall be willing, even if they were burned with fire. For a child is born to us whose government is upon his shoulders, and his name is called the Messenger of great counsel, admirable counsellor, God of power, prince of peace and Father of the world to come* (*Isa.* 9, 4-5).

As God and man Jesus in his goodness has dwelt among us — this let no one refuse to believe — and the sovereign Spirit has been contained in a human body. The first mystical breathing of the Father was received by Adam on the earth, clay though he was, for nothing could prevent the Divine Spirit from being united to a body when God willed it; if the primitive chaos received the Holy Spirit, a body endowed with a soul has contained the immortal life of Christ. If the Spirit alone had fallen into the slavery of sin and death this great coming of Christ in the body would have been superfluous and neither sin nor death would have been vanquished. But sin had to be suppressed and the body liberated. So *he himself practiced no iniquity nor was malice found in his mouth* (*Isa.* 53, 9).

So he first put on this miserable and mortal flesh: therefore the Holy Spirit has exclaimed: *And he shall grow up as a tender plant before him, and as a root out of a thirsty ground; there is no beauty in him, nor comeliness; and we have seen him, and there was no sightliness, that we should be desirous of him: Despised, and the most abject of men, a man of sorrows and acquainted with infirmity: and his look was as it were hidden and despised; whereupon we esteemed him not* (*Isa.* 53, 2-3).

He took care of all the maladies of our bodies and cured each of our diseases in virtue of his power so that the Word might be fulfilled: *I am the Lord God. I have called you in righteousness and will hold your right hand and will strengthen*

*you. And I have given you as the covenant of my race for a
light of the Gentiles to open the eyes of the blind, to bring those
bound and them that sit in darkness out of bonds and the prison
house. I am the Lord God, that is my name* (Isa. 42, 6-8). *The
deaf shall hear the words of a book; for those who sat in darkness a light is raised up* (Isa. 29, 18). *Then the lame man shall
leap as an hart and the tongue of the stammerers shall speak
plainly* (Isa. 35, 6). *And when every evil shall be suppressed the
last enemy to be destroyed will be death. O death, where is thy
sting?* (I Cor. 15, 26, 55).

The passion

This was the Pasch which Jesus desired to suffer for us. His
suffering has freed us from sufferings, his death has vanquished
death, the visible nourishment has procured his eternal life for us.
Such is the salutary desire of Jesus, such his love which is the
Spirit; to show the figures as figures and no more; to offer in their
place his holy body to his disciples. *Take and eat; this is my body
. . . drink of this for this is my blood of the new covenant which
is being shed for many unto the remission of sins.* Therefore he
desires not so much to eat as to suffer so that he might deliver us
from suffering in eating.

And so he plants a new tree in place of the old one; it is no
longer the old hand of wickedness which yesterday was extended
in an impious gesture; it is his pure hand in a gesture of piety he
shows his whole life truly stretched on the cross. But you, Israel,
were unable to eat, whereas we ate with a spiritual, indestructible
knowledge and eating, we shall not die.

This cross is the tree of my eternal salvation nourishing and
delighting me. I take root in its roots, I am extended in its
branches, I am delighted by its dew, I am fertilized by its spirit
as by a delightful breeze. In my tent I am shaded by its shade
and fleeing the excessive heat I find this refuge moist with dew.
Its flowers are my flowers; I am wholly delighted by its fruits
and I feast unrestrainedly on its fruits which are reserved for
me always. This is my nourishment when I am hungry, my fountain when I am thirsty, my covering when I am stripped, for my
leaves are no longer fig leaves but the breath of life. This is my
safeguard when I fear God, my support when I falter, my prize
when I enter combat, and my trophy when I triumph. This is

my narrow path, my steep way. This is the ladder of Jacob, the way of angels, at the summit of which the Lord is truly established. This is my tree, wide as the firmament, which extends from earth to the heavens, with its immortal trunk established between heaven and earth; it is the pillar of the universe, the support of the whole world, the joint of the world, holding together the variety of human nature, and riveted by the invisible bolts of the Spirit, so that it may remain fastened to the divinity and impossible to detach. Its top touches the highest heavens, its roots are planted in the earth, and in the midst its giant arms embrace the ever present breaths of air. It is wholly in all things and in all places.

And although he had permeated all things with himself, Christ stripped himself naked to war against the powers of the air. For an instant he calls for a drink so as to show that he was truly *also man*. Recalling the reason why he was sent and wishing to accomplish the economy which was the object of his mission he again exclaimed: *not my will but your will (Luke 22, 42). For the spirit is willing but the flesh is weak (Matt. 26, 41)*.

Since he ran to victory in the spiritual contest he received on his sacred brow the crown of thorns, effacing the entire ancient curse of the race, and eradicating the thorny undergrowth of sin from the world with his divine head. And when he drank the bitter gall of the serpent he opened up for us instead the sweet fountains which issued from himself.

For wishing to destroy the work of the woman, and to place an obstacle to him (Adam) from whose side she came, see how he opens his own sacred side from which issued the sacred blood and water, the plenary signs of the sacred nuptials, and of divine adoption and rebirth. For *he will baptize you in a holy spirit and fire*, the water being in the spirit and the blood in the fire.

Then there were crucified with him two thieves who were types of the two peoples: the one which confessed and repented of his sins, being filled with piety at the sight of the Master, the other offering resistance, for he was stiff-necked and denied his Lord, insulting him and persisting in crime. Or perhaps the two thieves signify the two dispositions of the soul: the first disavows its faults and returns clean in the sight of the Lord, and its repentance renders it worthy of mercy and compassion. The second is inexcusable because it refuses to change and so lives and dies a thief.

The death of death

When the cosmic struggle ended and Christ had struggled victoriously on all sides, neither elevated as God nor vanquished as man, but remaining solidly rooted in the confines of the universe, triumphantly producing on his own person a trophy of victory over the enemy. Then the world was in amazement at his long endurance. Then the heavens leaped with joy; the Powers were moved, the heavenly thrones and laws were moved at seeing the General of the great powers hanging on the cross; for a short time the stars of heaven were falling when they viewed stretched on the cross him who was *before the morning star.* For a time the sun's fire was extinguished, the great Light of the world suffered eclipse. Then the earth's rocks were rent, crying to ungrateful Israel: you have not recognized *the spiritual rock which you followed and from which you drank* (cf. I *Cor.* 10, 4). The veil of the temple was rent in sympathy, bearing witness to the true High priest of the heavens, and the world would have been dissolved in confusion and fear at the passion if the great Jesus had not expired saying: *Father, into your hands I commit my spirit (Luke* 23, 46). The whole universe trembled and quaked with fear, and everything was in a state of agitation, but when the Divine Spirit rose again the universe returned to life and regained its vitality and stability.

O divine presence in all things and everywhere! O crucifix which shelters the entire world. O thou who art unique among all things unique in the universe, may the heavens possess your spirit, and paradise your soul — for he said, *This day will I be with you in paradise* — and may the earth possess your body. For the indivisible is divided so that all may be saved, so that even the lowest place may be accessible to the divine coming. *For we have not seen his form, but we have heard his voice.*

The tomb

Already in his lifetime he had broken the bonds of death using his kingly power, as when he said: *Lazarus, come forth,* and *child, arise,* to show that he could also command with power. Accordingly he gave himself completely up to death so that the voracious beast and the insatiable prison might die completely themselves. In his sinless body he sought his own nourishment on all sides, not pleasure, nor anger, nor disobedience — in a word, not the old sin, the original nourishment of death: for *sin is the sting of death* (I *Cor.* 15, 56). As he found nothing in him that could nourish death, becoming completely isolated in himself and destroyed through lack of nourishment he brought about his own death.

And so, many of the just announced the good news and prophesied that he would be *the firstborn of the dead* by his resurrection. But he spent a period of three days in the earth to achieve the salvation of all three peoples — those before the Law, those under the Law, and those of his own time. Or perhaps the three days symbolize the tripartite nature of man — soul, spirit, and body.

After his resurrection it was the women who were the first to see him. Just as the first sin was introduced into the world by a woman so it was also women who first announced life to the world. Accordingly they hear the sacred word, *Women, rejoice* (*Matt.* 28, 9), so that the primal sorrow might be absorbed in the joy of the resurrection.

In his brief sojourn he gave proofs in confirmation of his sacred resurrection even to the incredulous so that they might believe that he rose body as well as soul from the dead. And while carrying in himself the complete image, he put off the old man and transformed it into the heavenly man, and then ascended into the heavens, carrying with him man's image assimilated to himself. In view of such a great mystery — man ascending to God — the Powers cried with joy to the hosts above: *Princes, raise your gates, lift up your eternal gates and the king of glory will enter* (*Ps.* 23, 7). Further, when these were asked they replied: *The Lord of powers is the king of glory, strong, robust, and powerful in war.*

Paschal hymn

O mystical choir! O feast of the Spirit! O Pasch of God, who hast come down from heaven to earth, and from earth you ascend again to the heavens. O feast common to all, O universal joy, and honor of the universe, its nurture and its luxury, by whom the darkness of death has been dissolved and life extended to all, by whom the gates of heaven have been opened as God has become man and man has become God. Through him the gates of hell

have been broken, the bars of iron have been loosed, the people
below have been raised from the dead proclaiming the good news;
an antiphonal choir has been formed on earth to respond to the
choir above. O Pasch of God, no longer confined to the heavens
and now united to us in spirit; through him the great marriage
chamber has been filled, and all wear wedding garments though
nobody is expelled for not having one on. O Pasch, illumination
of the new bright day — the brightness of the torches of the
virgins, through which the lamps of souls are no longer extinguished, but the divine fire of charity burns divinely and
spiritually in all, in soul and body, nurtured by the oil of Christ.

Prayer to Christ the King

We call on you, then, sovereign Lord, spiritually eternal,
Christ, Lord and King, extend your wonderful hands over your
holy Church and over your people ever holy; guard and conserve
them, attacking, pursuing and combating all their enemies, and
subjugating all of them to your power, until their invisible forces
are routed and wiped out. Raise now your standard above us
and enable us to chant with Moses the canticle of triumph. For
with you is the victory and the power for ever and ever. Amen.

II
THE SPIRITUAL PASCH[1]

The Pasch is a passover

The Jews celebrate an earthly pasch having denied the
heavenly one. But we celebrate the heavenly pasch having *passed
over* the earthly one.

The pasch which they celebrated was a figure of the salvation
of the firstborn of the Jews; the firstborn of the Egyptians died
without the firstborn of the Jews also perishing; they were symbolically protected by the blood of the paschal victim. But the
Pasch celebrated by us is a cause of salvation for all men beginning with the first-created, who is saved and given life in all.

Things partial and provisory are types of what is perfect
and eternal; they are a shadowy prelude to the Truth which now

---

1. Greek text: PG 59, 723-32, SC 36, 55-75 ed. P. Nautin (Paris 1953).

emerges. But when the Truth appears, the figure is no longer viable. Subjects no longer prostrate themselves before a king's statue when the King himself appears in person.

It is self-evident that the figure is less than the reality; the figure celebrates the fleeting existence of the firstborn of the Jews; the reality celebrates the eternal life of all mankind. For to escape death briefly is a matter of no great importance when one is going to die in any case a little later; but it is of great importance to escape death forever. That is what has happened to us; *for us Christ our pasch has been immolated* (I *Cor.* 5, 7).

The name of this feast only gets its full meaning when used in reference to the Truth: the Pasch means "Passover"; the Destroyer slaying the firstborn passed over the houses of the Hebrews, but with us the passover of the Destroyer becomes a genuine reality; once and for all he passes over us whom Christ has resurrected for life everlasting.

We ought to examine the whole subject of the Pasch in a spiritual manner and believe in it as the apostles have interpreted it. The faithful desires to understand the whole rationale of the figure and its relation to the Truth, and to see spiritual realities that affect him underlying the material things of that time. What pertains to the Law is thus interpreted by him in Christian terms and the invisible is deciphered from the visible.

Why is the lamb immolated in the first month of the year?

When God intended to inflict the tenth plague on the Egyptians — the death of the firstborn — he said to Moses, *This month shall be to you the beginning of months: it is the first to you among the months of the year* (*Exod.* 12, 2). He prescribed in turn the sacrifice of the Pasch and the anointing of the doors with blood, and through this anointing he promised the salvation of the firstborn; but without further ado, what in reference to the Truth is the meaning of defining as *the beginning* of the year that time when the pasch and the salvation of the firstborn took place? It means that the sacrifice of the true pasch is for us also the beginning of eternal life, the year being a symbol of eternity because in its endless cycles it is always turning into itself and never comes to an end and *the father of eternity to come* (*Isa.* 9, 5) has immolated the victim for us, Christ, who wipes out our whole past life and makes us begin another life, by the bath of rebirth, the image of his own death and resurrection. Consequently everybody knowing the Pasch immolated for our salvation should consider as the beginning of life for himself that moment when Christ was found immolated on his behalf. Now the moment when he is sacrificed for a person is that moment when he recognizes grace and understands the life which this sacrifice confers. Knowing this, let him be eager to undertake the beginning of this new life and refuse to return to the old one, whose end he has reached. *For how shall we who are dead to sin still live in it?* (*Rom.* 6, 2).

Why is it kept five days?

Such is the symbolism of the beginning of the year. God also ordains that *on the tenth of the month* a lamb be obtained for each house and that the house should have enough guests seated to consume it all without leaving anything over, and that the lamb be immolated *on the fourteenth day toward evening.*

So, for five days, the victim remains with those to be saved by it; then, when the fifth day is nearing an end, the victim is immolated; death "passes over," and the one who is saved enjoys perpetual illumination, for the full moon shines during the entire night and is succeeded by the light of day. For this is the fifteenth of the month, the day of the full moon.

These five periods indicate the entire duration of the world, divided into five epochs: 1) from Adam to Noah, 2) from Noah to Abraham, 3) from Abraham to Moses, 4) from Moses to the coming of Christ, and 5) his *parousia.* During all these epochs salvation was proposed to every man through that blessed victim, but was not finally realized until, during the fifth epoch, the true Pasch was immolated and the firstborn man was thereby saved and reached the eternal light. And the fact that the Pasch was immolated *toward evening,* not just in the evening, shows that Christ suffered not at the end of this age but toward its end.

The same division of time is manifested in the parable of Christ dividing the day in five, saying that those called to work in the vineyard, i.e., to the works of justice, are called one at the first hour, another at the third, another at the sixth, another at the ninth, and another at the eleventh. And in fact, there were different calls and different works of justice: one in the time of Adam, another in the time of Noah, another in the time of Abraham, another in the time of Moses, and last and most perfect, in the epoch of the coming of Christ when the wages for work are given to the last first, according to the Lord's parable, when first we receive rebirth in baptism we for whom *Christ has been immolated* (I *Cor.* 5, 7) at the time of his resurrection when he infused in us the Holy Spirit for our renewal.

The one place for the sacrifice

Such is the symbolic meaning of the fourteenth day and of the sacrificial victim, and the bright night and the day succeeding the sacrifice. The victim is eaten in its entirety in each house and no flesh is taken outside. This means that only one house has salvation in Christ, namely the Church throughout the world, before this estranged from God, now enjoying unique intimacy with God because it has received the apostles of the Lord Jesus, as of old the house of Rahab, the harlot, received the spies of Joshua, and was the only one saved in the destruction of Jericho.

So, however numerous the Hebrew houses were, they were equivalent to a single house, and likewise the churches throughout town and country, however numerous they are, constitute but a single Church. For Christ is one in all of them everywhere, Christ who is perfect and indivisible. Therefore in each house the victim was "perfect" and was not divided among different houses.

For Paul himself says that we are all one in Christ because there is *one Lord and one faith* (*Eph.* 4, 5).

Unity of Christ

The Law provided a necessary prototype of Christ in the indivisible unity of the victim; this also typified the unity of the Church. For in Christ and in the sacrifice of Christ we have salvation, and we know that everything that preceded his coming was predisposed for his coming, and that this immolation of Christ on behalf of all was laid down from the beginning in the sight of all. But we also know that this salvation is only to be found in the Church and that nobody outside the Catholic Church and the faith can participate in Christ or be saved.

Being aware of this we know further that it is not in observation of the Law but in Christ that the salvation of the whole world is accomplished, and on the other hand we deny all hope to impious heresies putting them completely outside the pale of hope because they have not the slightest participation in Christ but vainly usurp the name of Savior, to deceive and mislead those who are capable of becoming attached to a name and an appearance rather than reality.

Let nobody sunder the bond between ancient things and Christ. Let nobody suppose that any of our ancestors was saved without Christ. Let nobody call Christians those who falsify the truth and fabricate false churches that are far from the truth and alien to Christ. And let nobody have anything to do with such people. This is forbidden, since the victim is not taken outside the sacred house nor offered in communion to those outside.

A perfect lamb

But prefiguring the glory of the Savior is this lamb, *perfect, male, one year old*, as we can see. *Perfect*, for only Christ is without defect in all virtue and without fault in any respect, endowed with all justice from beginning to end, as he himself said, *for so it becomes us to fulfill all justice* (*Matt.* 3, 15).

Why are all these sacrifices offered perfect and without fault? Because all of them have been immolated as a prefiguring of Christ. And God demanded that the priests should be healthy and perfect physically, so that all might be a type of the true Priest.

A male lamb

Furthermore the lamb is *male*, because he is by nature dominant as the male has physical dominance over the female. Christ in nature and truth is leader and king, for he is a celestial being. In his humanity he is a brother to us, but he has dominion over us spiritually in his divinity.

That is why he and he alone is the bridegroom of the whole of humanity which is his bride. Even John the Baptist, the greatest of the prophets, was not the bridegroom. Speaking of Christ and of himself he said of Christ, *He who has the bride is the bridegroom*, and of himself, *the friend of the bridegroom who*

stands and hears him rejoices exceedingly at the voice of the
bridegroom; this my joy therefore is made full (*John* 3, 29).
Nor are the apostles the bridegrooms of the Church; they have
received by grace the likeness of Christ and have become sons
of Christ through the Spirit of Christ, but what does the blessed
Paul say? *For I betrothed you to one spouse, that I might present*
you a chaste virgin to Christ (II *Cor.* 11, 2).

A lamb of one year

The Lord was truly leader, master and king, not only because
he was God among men but also according to his pre-existing
divinity, because he was by very nature king of all creation, not
receiving this kingship as a favor but possessing it in truth and as
a birthright from the Father. Furthermore, the lamb was *of one*
year to indicate that the Lord was new on the earth and had no
part of human decrepitude.

If anyone calls the Lord a mere man and ranks Christ merely
human in nature, such a one cannot see the lamb as *perfect* or
without spot, for such a one the lamb is not *male,* for no mere
mortal has absolute and complete dominion over his fellow creatures. If one counts the Lord as a member of creation and says
that he has divinity as a grace and not truly, he no longer regards
him as a *male* lamb immolated on his behalf. He fails to recognize him as King by nature and turns to one who is neither by
nature nor in truth king. Or if one introduces the marks of
human decripitude into Christ, or dares to say that he admits of
sin, or is bound to the slavery of the law, or subject to the necessity of death, he fails to recognize the lamb of *one year* and the
novelty of Christ.

A lamb and a he-goat

It remains to understand the symbol of the lamb and the he-
goat. The lamb, according to Isaiah, is a symbol of the gentleness of Christ. *As a sheep he was led to the slaughter and as a*
lamb before the shearer is dumb (*Isa.* 53, 7) and a he-goat,
according to the Law, was a victim for sin: *one young buck of the*
goats for a sin-offering (*Num.* 7, 16). Being offered, then, gentle
as a sheep, he was immolated like a young buck for sin, and gave

himself in his gentleness for the salvation of men. To attain which let us pray through the faith and love of him who suffered for us, our Lord Jesus Christ, through whom and with whom is glory to the Father with the Holy Spirit for ever and ever. Amen.

GREGORY OF NAZIANZUS
(† 390)

The essential Gregory can be seen in his first sermon, which he preached at the age of 32 in Nazianzus on Easter Sunday, 362. Personal anecdote is joined to Christian reflection and this is not the least charm of this text, one of the most vivid, perhaps, in patristic literature.

More suited to contemplation than action, Gregory had chosen to live the ascetic life with his friend, Basil, in the province of Pontus. But in the winter of 361, his father, the bishop of Nazianzus, recalled him and ordained him a priest. Irritated by this "violence," and little enamored of the idea of governing a diocese at a time when Arianism was raging, Gregory took flight to his retreat in Pontus. Then some months later, at Easter, stricken by remorse, he returned to Nazianzus and there preached his first sermon where happiness at his return, in spite of everything, was joined by him to the joy of the Resurrection.

What then is the personality revealed here? He is, first and foremost, a human being, sensitive and gentle who admits his weaknesses, and his need for meditation in solitude. Secondly, he is a pastor, concerned to defend his flock against the seduction of Arianism and capable of great firmness (§7); we know the decisive role which he will enjoy at Constantinople where he will liquidate this heresy and speed the triumph of orthodoxy.

Finally, he is a theologian who, in his first sermon, affirms his famous doctrine of imitation: man cannot escape from the nothingness which surrounds him except by conforming himself to the image of God, reliving in him and with him the trials of his life, death and resurrection. "Yesterday I was crucified with Christ; today I will be glorified with him. Yesterday I died with Christ; today I return to life with him. Yesterday I was buried with Christ; today I rise with him out of the sepulchre." Such a doctrine cannot be formulated in the abstract; it is told in existential terms. The old bishop of Nazianzus offers his son to the world, as God offered his, and Gregory relives the very sufferings of Jesus Christ.

Gregory's thought is always expressed in the context of a profoundly lived experience. This preaching is the first chapter of his spiritual autobiography.

The Greek Church uses the present sermon as a trope in its paschal liturgy.

THE SACERDOTAL SACRIFICE[1]
(SERMON I: ON EASTER)

The time of pardon

1. The day of resurrection, an auspicious beginning! Radiantly let us celebrate this feast, giving one another the kiss of peace. Let us greet as brothers even those who hate us, and not merely those souls which in their charity have rendered us some service, or suffered for us. Let us pardon one another in honor of the resurrection, forgetting our mutual wrongs. I pardon you the pleasant violence you have perpetrated on me (it is only now that I find it pleasant) and you who have done me this pleasant violence pardon me for any tardiness that I have displayed. Who knows if God does not prefer the tardiness of some to the speed of others? For it is good to withdraw a little before God; of old this characterized the great Moses (cf. *Exod.* 4, 13) and later Jeremiah (cf. *Jer.* 1, 6); likewise to run in prompt obedience to his call like Aaron and Isaiah. It is only necessary that both attitudes be inspired by piety. The one is a manifestation of our own weakness, the other, of the power of him who calls.

New being

2. A mystery has anointed me. And I withdrew for a little while before the mystery to examine myself.

I return to you in full mystery, bringing with me this beautiful day which helps me to conquer my scruples and my weakness; and I hope that he who today is risen from the dead, will

---

1. Greek text: PG 35, 396-401. This sermon on the Pasch was given in 362 in the presence of his father, Gregory, who was bishop of Nazianzus and had built the church there. It was he who had brought pressure to bear on his son to succeed him.

renew me in spirit, and put on me the new man, giving to this new creation (those who are born according to God), a good worker and a good master, eager to die and be resurrected with Christ.

Former salvation

3. Yesterday, the lamb was immolated; the doorposts were anointed with its blood; Egypt bewailed its firstborn; the destroying angel passed us over, in fear and respect for this seal; the precious blood protected us.

Today, we have fled purified from Egypt, from the Pharaoh, the cruel sovereign, and those pitiless rulers. We are freed from mud and brick and not one will prevent us from celebrating a feast of the Lord, our God, the day of our delivery from Egypt and of celebrating it not with the old leaven of malice and injustice but with the unleavened bread of purity and truth (I *Cor.* 5, 8), with no admixture of the impious yeast of Egypt.

What ought we offer God?

4. Yesterday I was crucified with Christ; today I will be glorified with him. Yesterday I died with Christ; today I will return to life with him. Yesterday I was buried with Christ; today I will rise with him from the tomb.

Let us then carry our first-fruits to him who has suffered and risen for us. Do you think perhaps that I am talking of gold, silver, garments, or precious stones? Insubstantial earthly goods, transitory, tied to earth, owned for the most part by the wicked, the slaves of materialism and the prince of this world? No, let us offer ourselves: it is the most precious and dearest gift in the eyes of God. Give to his image what resembles it most. Recognizing our greatness, honor our model, understanding the force of this mystery and the reasons for Christ's death.

5. Become like Christ, since Christ has become like us. Become gods for him since he became man for us. He has become inferior to make us superior; he has become poor to enrich us by his poverty; he has taken the condition of a slave to procure freedom for us; he has come on earth to bring us to heaven; he has

been tempted to see us triumph; he has been dishonored to cover us with glory; he has died to save us; he has ascended to heaven to draw us to himself, we who lie prostrate because of falling into sin.

Give all, offer all, to him who has given himself for us as a prize and ransom. We will give nothing as great as ourselves if we have grown by the nature of this mystery and have become for him all which he has become for us.

A new Abraham

6. He has given you this pastor here. This one hopes and prays, and asks from you who are subject to him as a good shepherd who lays down his life for his sheep, and he gives himself twice instead of once for you; making the staff of old age the staff of the spirit. He joins a living temple to one that is lifeless; to that illustrious, heavenly temple he adds another which is perhaps mediocre but nonetheless dear to him and costing him much effort and pain. May his efforts prove to have been justified.

He gives you all that he has. What magnanimity is his or, more accurately, what tenderness in regard to his children. He gives you his old age, his youth, a temple, a priest, a testator, an inheritor, and the words which you desired. And these are not vague words scattered in air and unheard by the ear; No, they are written by the Spirit and engraved on tablets of stone or of flesh, in lines not easy to efface or wipe out, but inscribed deeply not by ink but by grace.

The sheep ought to hear their pastor's voice

7. Such is the gift to you of this venerable Abraham, this patriarch, this noble respected chief, this abode of all virtues, this norm of sanctity, this perfection of priesthood. He offers today to the Lord in voluntary sacrifice his only son, the child of promise. And do you offer to God and to ourselves the complete docility of sheep so that we may lead you to pasture, to the waters of refreshment (*Ps.* 23, 1), know your pastor well, and be known to him. Obey his voice as he calls like a pastor and follow him freely through the door. Do not obey the stranger who

comes down the chimney like a thief and a traitor. Do not listen to unknown voices who try surreptitiously to alienate you from the truth, and to lead you to mountains, deserts, ravines and other places not governed by the Lord, separating you from the true faith in the Father, Son, and Holy Spirit, constituting but one divinity and one power. This voice my sheep have always heard; may they still hear it, in place of corrupting words and whatever causes us to be separated from our first and true shepherd.

Let us all, shepherds and flocks, feed and be fed far from poisonous death-bearing herbs and be all one in Christ Jesus today and in the heavenly rest. To him be glory and power for ever and ever. Amen.

GREGORY OF NYSSA
(† 394)

Neglected by posterity, Gregory of Nyssa is just beginning to come into his own, thanks to the deserved attention he is receiving from contemporary scholars. He emerges as one of the most versatile minds of the fourth century. By turns he is philosopher and mystic, logician and pastor of souls, poet and physician. His manifold genius is further enriched by a wide classical culture acquired in the schools of Greece.

The present two sermons bear witness to his complex personality as well as to the deep unity which always characterizes his thought. The first sermon is a demonstration of the reasonableness of the resurrection. The author, in search of proofs. calls on all the resources of his knowledge, taking examples from mysticism, Scripture, botany, zoology, medicine and psychology. The argument is well developed with rigorous logic but the exposition succeeds in remaining vivid, vibrant and at times reaches heights of poetic beauty.

The Christian vision distinguishing these two sermons is already familiar to us.[1] Gregory's reflection is arranged around a need for fundamental unity. The Kingdom announced by the Pasch is the triumph of order and of the unity of creation where all men are assembled in "an adoration without reserve." The

---

1. Cf. A. Hamman, **Riches et Pauvres dans l'Église ancienne**, p. 135.

tableau of eternity etched by Gregory at the beginning of the
first homily is characteristic in this respect.

This demand for order is irresistible: the mystery of Christ's
Pasch, his passion and resurrection, yield place to a single evocation, but how powerful, of the common Pasch of men, which will
elevate all of creation to its creator.

SERMON III: ON THE SACRED FEAST OF THE PASCH AND ON THE RESURRECTION[2]

I. UNIVERSAL JOY

The Pasch, promise of joy for all men

The poor who love feast days and frequent assemblies with
an eager heart and an air of expectancy, even if they have not
as much holiday finery of their own for the occasion as they
would like, borrow from their acquaintances and friends all the
finery that they want so as not to be short of anything on such
occasions. This is the situation in which I find myself today.

I have nothing appropriate and splendid to contribute to the
eulogy which is proposed to us; so I. will resort to the holy
canticle which we have just chanted. I will discharge my debt
from that starting point by interweaving my own words with
those of Sacred Scripture; this way a poor servant can perhaps
find the right words to praise his master.

In the words of David, then, which we have just heard and
have repeated with him, *Praise the Lord all ye nations; praise
him all ye peoples* (*Ps.* 117, 1). He invites without exception all
men born of Adam to this chant; those from the West, the East,
and in between, North and South, he invites each and every
one in this psalm. Elsewhere he invites some men specifically,
calling them "saints" or "sons" (cf. *Ps.* 149, 1; 8, 3), exhorting
them to sing a hymn. In this instance he leads in unison the
nations and peoples, in the psalm.

When then, as the apostle says, *the figure of this world has
passed* (I *Cor.* 7, 31), and Christ has appeared as King and God
to all, and every unbelieving soul is led to the fullness of faith
and certainty of knowledge, and malicious tongues are restrained

---

2. P.G., 46, 652-681.

and bridled, he shall check the vanity of the Greeks, and the error of the Jews, and the uncontrolled tongue-wagging of heretics. Then at last all the nations and the peoples from the beginning of time will prostrate themselves and join in harmonious praise of God, the saints singing their usual praises, the impious making supplication by necessity. And then in truth the song of victory will be sung in harmony by all, victors and vanquished; then even that slave, the author of disorder who has assumed and arrogated to himself the dignity of his master, will be seen admonishing everybody while he is being drawn to punishment by the angels, and all the ministers and allies of this wickedness will be afflicted by suitable punishment and judgments. The one king and judge will appear whom all confess to be the Lord of all. There will be quiet and silence as usually ensues when the herald calls for silence as the praetor takes his seat on the tribunal, and the people, all ears and eyes, wait attentively on the words of his proclamation. *Therefore, praise the Lord, all ye nations, praise him, all ye peoples.* Praise him as powerful, praise him as benign, since he has restored to life those who have fallen and are dead; he has repaired the broken vase, and in his bounty he has changed into incorruptible living beings the dread remains in the sepulchre. As after a long voyage he has led back to its proper domicile the soul which had left the body (four) thousand years before, in no way alienated through time and forgetfulness from its own organism, but returning to it more quickly than a bird to its nest.

Resurrection and redemption

Come, now, to the proper object of this feast, to celebrate it in the appropriate and fitting manner which is called for. Improper and extraneous thoughts will serve no useful purpose; they are out of order and out of place, not only in matters of worship and religion, but also in secular matters and worldly wisdom. An orator becomes a laughable imbecile if he is invited to a distinguished wedding celebration and fails to speak in the complimentary tones called for by the general rejoicing, but instead pronounces something lugubrious in the vein of tragedy and oppresses the festive gathering with his threnody. The same is true, at the other extreme, if one is invited to give the eulogy at a funeral and, forgetting the sorrow of the occasion, appears with a joyful countenance in an assembly that is full of grief. If in worldly affairs propriety and knowledge have their place, they are much more in place in heavenly matters of greater weight.

Today, Christ has risen as God, impassible and immortal. (Pay a little attention now, you pagan, drop that untimely grin of yours until you have heard me out.) He was under no compulsion to suffer or to come down on earth; he did not obtain the resurrection like a completely unexpected favor, but after knowing the end of all things and so making a beginning. In that knowledge gleaned by the eyes of divinity, and before descending from heaven, he saw the disturbance of nations, the obduracy of the Jews, Pilate sitting on his judgment seat, Caiaphas rending his garments, the anger of the seditious people, the betrayal of Judas, Peter fighting in his defence, and shortly afterwards his resurrection and transformation into immortal glory.

Having the whole future telescoped in his mind he did not postpone his favor to men nor delay his divine coming. But just as men who see a helpless creature caught up by a rushing stream know that they may possibly become equally involved in the mud of the torrent and be injured by the stones carried down in the rapids yet nonetheless do not shrink from entering the waters in their sympathy for the one in danger of drowning, so likewise our kind Savior freely underwent what is outrageous and ignominious so that he might save the one who is perishing by deceit. He has agreed to come down on earth, knowing in advance of his glorious ascension. He accepts a human death since he knew in advance of his resurrection. For not like a common mortal has he recklessly exposed himself to dangers, entrusting the outcome to the uncertainty of the future, but as God he directed the undertaking to a certain and preordained end.

The Christian joy of the Pasch

This is the day the Lord has made; let us be glad and rejoice in it (Ps. 118, 24). Not in drunkenness and revelry, not in dancing and debauchery, but in God-like reflection. Today one can see the whole earth like a single household transformed in unity hastening on cue in complete accord to community prayer. There are no travellers on the streets. Today the sea is free of sailors and seamen. The laborer has left hoe and plough aside and dressed up in his Sunday clothes to celebrate. The stores are closed. Riots have disappeared, like winter when summer appears. Disturbances, crowds, and the agitations of life have subsided in the peace of the feast. The poor man is decked out like the rich man; the rich man appears in greater splendor than usual. The elder runs like a youngster to share in the joyous occasion. The man who is ill is strengthened in his weakness; the child by a change of clothes celebrates the feast in external appearance since he cannot yet understand what it is all about. The virgin rejoices exceedingly in spirit, for she sees the remembrance of her own hope so splendidly honored; the married woman rejoices as she keeps festival with her entire household. For now she herself, her husband, children, servants and all join in the festivities. And just as a swarm of bees new and recently born, emerging fresh from the hive or the shelter, fly into the air and daylight and attach themselves in a body to a branch of a tree, so on this feast whole families swarm to the family hearth. And truly by imitation today is rightly compared to the last day: for both are rallying points for men, the last day for the whole world, today for individuals. To speak more truly, in respect to what pertains to joy and happiness, today is more pleasant than the last day, since it will be necessary on the last day to see some weeping because their sins are uncovered. But today's joy admits of no sad faces. For the just man is joyful, and the man whose conscience is not clear hopes for forgiveness from his contrition and all grief sleeps today. For there is no one so overwhelmed with pain that he does not get relief from the splendor of the feast.

For today the prisoner is released, the debtor is liberated, the slave gets his freedom by the good and merciful message of the Church. Nor is the slave forced to submit to the ignominy of a stroke on the cheek, being freed from blows by a blow, nor, as usually happens in the procession, exhibited to the people on a raised platform, beginning his freedom in shame and embarrassment, but he is dismissed in as orderly a fashion as is known. And even he who still remains a slave is done a favor. For though his sins are grievous and numerous, exceeding hope of forgiveness and pardon, the Lord, out of deference for the day's serenity and mercy, receives this renegade even though he is conspicuous among the worthless, as Pharaoh released the cup-bearer from prison (cf. *Gen.* 40, 21). For he knew that at the time destined for resurrection (in the likeness of which we honor the present day) he himself would need the Lord's mercy and goodness, and as if in initial exchange he is giving mercy, expecting it to be paid back when it came to his own turn.

Have you heard, sirs? Keep the word as good; do not slander me to servants as falsely celebrating this present day; dismiss sorrow from your afflicted, anxious souls, as the Lord has dispensed you from bodily mortification. Transform those in infamy to honor, the downtrodden to happiness, those lacking freedom to liberty. Bring out from their corner, as from the tomb, those who are cast down. Let the glory of the festival day shine and reign like a flower in all. For if the birthday or victory-triumph of a human king opens prison gates, will not the risen Christ on his day of victory forgive the oppressed? You poor, embrace the day that is your nurse. You who are mutilated and broken in body, greet the day which heals your misfortunes. For because of the hope of the resurrection, virtue is pursued and evil is an object of hatred. For without the resurrection, one view will be found to prevail over all others, *let us eat and drink for tomorrow we die* (I *Cor.* 15, 32).

Christ's resurrection is the pledge of our resurrection

Looking forward to this day, the Apostle makes light of the passing present life. He looks forward to a future life, making light of the visible world, saying: *If with this life only in view we have had hope in Christ, we are of all men the most to be pitied* (I *Cor.* 15, 19). Because of this day, men are heirs of God and co-heirs of Christ. Because of this day a part of the body eaten by carnivorous birds thousands of years previously will be restored to integrity. And what whales or dogs or sea monsters have devoured will rise in unity with the whole man. And what fire has consumed, or worm eaten in the sepulchres, in a word, all bodies however wasted by corruption will be restored from the earth in complete integrity, and as Paul teaches, *in the twinkling of an eye* (I *Cor.* 15, 52) the resurrection will take place; *the twinkling of an eye* is while you would be blinking. And there could be nothing faster than that. Now in human terms you could not describe the great lengths of time it would take, first for bones that have putrefied and turned to dust to be restored to their former durability and smoothness, reunited after such bending into structural unison and physical harmony.

Then think of the covering of flesh and the separate joinings of sinews, the smooth ducts of veins and arteries fitted under the skin; and the untold, countless multitude of souls emerging from their hidden dwellings and each recognizing his own body as if it were his own coat, and quickly putting it on again, such a multitude of human souls exercising such nice discrimination. Think of the souls since Adam, and the bodies since him; so many houses abandoned and deserted, and their owners returning to them after a long sojourn abroad, and all of them found perfect in an inexplicable manner. For the house is not refurbished in a slow fashion, and the dweller does not wander around and wait outside while he is looking for his things; no, he makes for his home immediately as a dove makes for its own dovecote, however many hover around the same place examining similar signs. Whence returns memory and the recollection of former life, and the perception of each deed, which is so quickly restored to a being whose life had been dissolved so many ages previously? And yet when a man merely awakens from a rather deep sleep, for a short time he forgets who he is and where he lives, and forgets familiar objects, until he gets fully awake and his torpor disappears. Only then are his powers of memory revived. These and similar reflections fill the mind with surpassing wonder and many fail to comprehend and their wonder changes to disbelief. And since their human mind cannot solve their doubts and questionings, and no amount of probing can satisfy their curiosity, they wind up in incredulity because of their failure to understand; and in their failure they reject and reprobate the truth.

II. OUR FAITH IN THE RESURRECTION

The resurrection is conformed to our idea of providence

Since in the course of our sermon we have come to a problem often discussed previously and one that is relevant and appropriate to today's feast, come let us deal briefly with the preliminary question laid down previously and let us try and give assurance to those who remain ambivalent about certainties.

The creator of the universe, when he decided to create man, made him not as a worthless being, but as the most precious of all beings and named him king of the entire earthly creation. With this in mind he made him wise and in God's image, adorning him with every grace. Now surely he did not give him such precedence in nature if he intended him to be born and die and suffer complete extinction? But it is vain and foolish to attribute to God such a plan, such a proposition, such an intention. For it is the way of children to build with care and quickly scatter the building, revealing a mind with no fixed and final purpose. Our teaching points to the other extreme, that God's first creation was fashioned immortal, but that after the fall and the first sin man was deprived of immortality as a penalty for transgression. Then the fountain of goodness overflowed with kindness and, inclining to the work of his own hands, God adorned it with wisdom and knowledge until he thought good to renew us in our former state.

These things are true and worthy of our conception of God. His power testifies to this as well as his goodness. For it is not characteristic of the best and finest type of man to remain unmoved and rigid towards those subject to him and within his care. Thus the shepherd wishes his sheep to be vigorous and almost to be immortal; the cowherd will prosper his cattle by every care. The goatherd prays that his goats may have twin kids; and every herdsman, in a word, wants his flock to be left with him and to endure, with a view to some useful end.

Since this is so and is clear from what we have just said, it would obviously be most fitting for the creator and maker of our human race to reform his impaired handiwork, for it is very clear that those who disbelieve these conclusions are hostile for no other reason than that they think it is impossible for God to raise to life what is dead and dissolved. Now it is a thought of those truly dead and lacking in perception to think that there is anything impossible to God and beyond his power; in this they transfer their own weakness to his omnipotent majesty.

It is no more inconceivable than creation in the first instance

To confound their folly with proofs and arguments, let us show from the past and the present the shape of the future though it is not regarded by them as future. As you have heard, man was fashioned from dust. Tell me, then, I ask you, you who claim everything comes within the scope of your knowledge, how is the thin, rarified dust brought together? How does dust become flesh, and how does the same substance produce bones, skin, fat and hair? How, if the flesh is one, are there different kinds of members, different qualities, different consistencies? How are the lungs soft to the touch, and livid in color? How is the liver solid and red, the heart fibrous and the hardest part in the flesh, the spleen rare and black, the greater epiploon white and fashioned by nature like a fisherman's net.

Let us consider, too, how the first woman from a small part of his rib was formed into as complete a being as Adam; a part sufficed for the whole, a little did for everything, a rib became head, hands, feet, the involved and varied arrangement of intestines, flesh, hair, eye, nose, mouth; in a word, so that I may not protract my talk too much, everything that is marvelous and beyond our puny powers of conception. For with God the reasons of creation are ready to hand and very certain. How, then, can men, who agree that one single rib produced Eve, reasonably deny that from the material of a whole man the same person cannot be reconstituted? For it is impossible, impossible I repeat, for the human mind to comprehend the powers of God. For if everything were comprehensible to us our superior would not be our superior. Why do I speak of God? Even in the case of the irrational animals we do not stand comparison in certain abilities. Even they surpass us. In running, horses outstrip us, and dogs, and several other animals; in strength, camels and mules; in knowing the way, asses; in sight, the roe has keener eyes than we have.

So it is characteristic of reasonable and sensible men to have faith in the words of God and not to seek into the modes and causes of his actions which go beyond our powers. We will say to one of the curious: show me your reason why this visible object has come into existence; tell me by what means God has produced his many-shaped creations. If you discover this you will rightly be at a loss and distressed at not knowing how the world can be renewed, seeing that you know how it came into existence. But if creation is a dream and a fantasy to you and quite escapes your comprehension, do not be annoyed if, not knowing how to account for creation, you do not grasp the restoration of what has perished either, for the artisan of creation

in the first instance is the same as the one who makes the
second transformation. He knows how he will refashion his
original work after its dissolution and restore it to its former state.
If there is a need of wisdom, he is the fountain of wisdom; if there
is a need of power, he has no need of collaborator or assistance.
For this is he, in the words of the wisest of the prophets, *who
has measured the sea with his hand, and the heavens with his
fingers span, and the whole earth with the flat of his hand*
(*Isa.* 40, 12).

Look at those images that afford irrefutable proofs of his
ineffable power, making us despair in our thoughts of imagining
anything that God's nature cannot accomplish. He is and is
called Omnipotent (and perhaps instead of combatting this, you
will grant that it is so agreed); to him who is omnipotent, nothing
is difficult or impossible. There are numerous guarantees of faith
that forcibly impel you to agreement with my words: first of all,
this whole varied and multiple creation which exclaims in terms
clearer than any herald that the great, wise architect has designed
all visible things.

Scriptural examples

Since God exercises providence in regard to this creation and
even looks to the petty souls of the incredulous, he has proved
by deed the resurrection of the dead by restoring life to numerous
corpses. For this reason he rescued Lazarus from the tomb three
days after his death. He restored the widow's dead son to his
mother alive when he was being carried out on a mat for burial.
And there are countless others whom it would be tedious to
enumerate at this point.

But why speak of God and Savior when, the better to confound the skeptics, he endowed his own servants, the apostles,
with the power of raising the dead to life? The proof is obvious.
So why do you contentious give us trouble as if our explanation
lacked evidence? To raise a single one is the same as to raise ten,
and to raise ten, the same as three hundred, and to raise three
hundred, the same as a multitude. The maker of one statue will
easily make a thousand. Don't you know that architects first
fashion beforehand in a little clay the shapes and types of great
enormous buildings. The problems posed in the miniature models
are the same as arise in the large spacious constructions. The

heavens are great. They are God's masterpiece. But since God made man a reasonable being, in order that he might glorify his wisdom and creative ability by the appreciation of his creation, you can see the small sphere of an astronomical being moved in the hand of a scientist as the heavens are by God, thus affording us in microcosm an image of the macrocosm and of what surpasses our comprehension.

What is my object in dilating on this? So that you may know that, if you ask me how will the resurrection of bodies long since dead take place, I can immediately ask in reply: how was Lazarus raised after three days? The prudent man will admit that what is obvious in one instance will be equally obvious in several instances. And regarding God as the creator you will admit that nothing is impossible to him and that you cannot comprehend his incomprehensible wisdom. Nothing is out of bounds for him, but you cannot grasp infinity.

The resurrection is only one of the many marvels of God

We will see this very well if, after what I have said, we examine the manner of man's coming into the world. I do not mean the original creation of Adam by God, which I have already discussed, but subsequent births which take place in the natural way. For this process is inexplicable and incomprehensible to the human mind. For how can the sperm, which is moist and amorphous, solidify into a head, and become hard in the form of limbs and ribs, and make the brain smooth, and the surrounding cranium stout and resistant, and, in a word, bring about the harmonious composition of the entire body, for I do not want to go into everything in minute detail? The sperm, then, in the first instance without form, is formed into shape by the hidden and ineffable handiwork of God, increasing in size and maturity. Likewise, far from being absurd, it is quite logical that matter which is buried should receive back its pristine form and that dust should be made anew into a man, just as man originated from dust in the first instance. Let us grant that God has the same ability as the potter. Examine what the latter can do. He takes a shapeless mass of clay and fashions it into a vase, and exposes it to the rays of the sun to make it dry and solid. What he fashions or forms may be a little jug or a platter or a wine-jar, but if anything happens to make it topple it falls and breaks, losing its shape and becoming a shapeless mass of clay. But the potter if he wishes can refashion it quickly and restore the broken object, and remake the object by his art so that it is just as good as it was. Now the potter is only a minor creation of God's power. And do we refuse to believe God when he promises to restore the dead to life? This is an attitude of pure folly.

Let us examine the example of the blade of wheat which Paul in his great wisdom used for instructing the foolish, saying: *Senseless man, what you sow does not come to life unless it dies. And what you sow is not the body which is to be, but a bare kernel, perhaps of wheat or of some other grain. But God gives it a body as he has chosen* (I *Cor.* 15, 36-38). Let us pay careful attention to the birth of the seed and we will quickly grasp the secret of our own resurrection. The seed is scattered in the ground; it decays in the moist earth, and dies, so to speak, becoming a milky substance which solidifies by degrees, coalesces and becomes white and sharp like a goad. By degrees it grows and puts its head above earth, turning color from white to green. Then appear the grass and hair of the awns. A network of roots which will sustain its future weight can been seen along its surface and spreading out on the underside to nourish it. And just as the sails of boats are extended with many cables on all sides to keep them firm and in equilibrium, so the cord-like offshoots of the root become like holds and fortifications of the grains. When the grain finally rises in the stalk and comes to a head, God protects it with protuberances and knots just as a house is made safe by stays. This is because of the anticipated weight of the grain. Then when its strength has been secured, God splits the stem and causes the grain to emerge. And again there are greater wonders in this, for the grain grows in rows round about the stalk and each seed has its own storehouse. The last stage is when the beards of the corn sharp and smooth emerge. I am referring to the protection against granivorous birds, so that when they prick themselves with the sharp points they do not injure the grain. You see, then, the marvel of one seed falling into the ground, decaying, and rising with so many more. In man's resurrection there is no such multiplication. He merely recovers what he previously had, and so our restoration appears even simpler than that of the grain.

From there let us pass to an examination of trees, noting how winter brings death to them each year. For their fruits are gathered, the leaves fall and the trees remain bare and devoid of grace. But when the moment of spring comes, beautiful flowers cover them and they are clothed again with the shade of the leaves. It is a spectacle to delight the eyes of men, a concert hall for tuneful birds sitting among the leaves, an enchanting scene. So many leave their elaborate homes adorned with Thessalonian and Laconian stone and prefer the delight of living under the shadow of the trees, just as the patriarch Abraham pitched his tent under an oak tree (cf. *Gen.* 13, 18), not that he was in need of a house but because he was delighted by the shade of its branches.

The life of reptiles leads me to the same conclusion, for their spark of movement is dead in winter and they lie completely motionless in their holes for six months. But when the ordained time comes, and thunder reverberates through the world, like some signal of life they hear its sound, quickly leap up and after a long time return to their customary ways. What does this mean? Let the one who criticizes and judges the works of God tell me why he admits that thunder restores the serpents from virtual death, and yet he denies that men are revived when God's trumpet resounds from the heavens as the Scripture says: *For the trumpet shall sound and the dead shall rise* (I *Cor.* 15, 52), and elsewhere more clearly: *And he will send forth his angels with a trumpet and a great sound and he will gather his elect* (*Matt.* 24, 31).

Human life is subject to the laws of change

Let us not refuse, then, to believe in changes and renewals. The life of different animals and plants, and even the life of man himself, teaches us that nothing which is liable to the rules of generation and corruption remains the same, but is liable to change and alteration. But first, if you please, let us examine how we ourselves change from one age to another.

We know the first stage of infancy and lactation; after a short space of time the infant reaches the creeping stage, and is like a little puppy, going around on all fours. About the third year he stands up straight and walks, and begins to talk in stuttering and incoherent fashion. Then he learns correct articulation and becomes a graceful youngster. From that stage he proceeds to puberty and youth. A soft down covers his cheeks, then a beard on his chin, and so forth. Then he reaches the full bloom of manhood, daring and enduring. At the age of forty he begins to decline; his hair slowly turns grey, his strength declines. At length old age comes and causes his strength to disappear. His body bends, he becomes stooped to the ground like over-ripe grains of corn, and his skin turns shrivelled, and again he has become a child who was once a fine youth; he winds up a stuttering fool, back to where he started, creeping on hands and feet. What do you learn from all this? Isn't there change? Are there not manifold metamorphoses? Does not the living being undergo many new forms of life even before death?

Do not our sleep and waking constitute an object lesson of what we are seeking for the wise man? For sleep is an imitation of death, and waking a likeness of the resurrection. Accordingly, some secular philosophers call sleep the brother of death on account of the similarity of the experiences resulting from both. For forgetfulness is a consequence of both and ignorance of the past and future, and the body lies imperceptive, failing to recognize friend or enemy, not looking at those standing around and looking, an exhausted corpse, devoid of any activity, no different from the corpse in tombs and caskets. So, then, you can, if you wish, strip the sleeper like a corpse, you can empty his house, put him in chains, and no perception of what is done reaches him. But a little later, when there is respite and cessation of the experience, like a man lately come to life, he comes gradually to consciousness. He gently recovers his powers of movement as if he had been restored from death to life. If, then, during his earthly existence he is subject night and day to such changes, alterations and cessations of activity as forgetfulness and recovery of memory, it is foolish and contentious not to believe God's promise to us of a final renewal since he has created us in the first instance.

But what especially revolts critics and prepares them for disbelief, in my view, is the consideration that bodies completely disappear. But this is not true. A body does not completely disappear, but is dissolved into its composite elements — water, air, earth and fire. These prototypal elements subsist and the cells which form them remain intact and are preserved in their entirety even after decomposition. If it is easy for God to create something from nothing (for that is how everything had its origin in the first place), it is evidently far easier and less complicated for him to vivify things from principles that already exist.

The hope of a resurrection, basis of morality

Let us not, then, take away this fair hope of men, this remedy for our weakness, this second birth, one might say, which is not liable to death. In our frenzied search for pleasure, then, let us not do violence to the promise of love and kindness God has made to us. Those who are opposed to the present view seem to me to be vicious, the enemies of virtue, lusty and avaricious, with no control of the eyes, or ears, or sense of smell, open to the influence of all kinds of temptation through all their senses. Talk of a resurrection brings up the notion of judgment since Sacred Scripture expressly tells us that our life will have to be accounted for. (When we begin our second life we will all stand before the judgment seat of Christ so that from him as judge we will receive proportionate retribution for our conduct.) In our consciousness of the many sins of our past that merit many punishments, we hate the idea of judgment and reject the notion of resurrection, acting like wicked slaves who have squandered their master's substance, and imagine for themselves the death and destruction of their master, and for their own desire they indulge in their empty speculations.

But no sensible man will follow that reasoning. For what use is justice, and truth, and goodness, and beauty? Why did men strive to acquire wisdom, mastering their passion of gluttony and cherishing temperance, allowing little time for sleep, and being exposed to winter and stifling heat if there is no resurrection? Let us say the words of Paul: *Let us eat and drink for tomorrow we die* (I *Cor.* 15, 32). If there is no resurrection, and death is the end of life, take away from me all accusations and fault-finding, give unimpeded scope to the murderer, allow the roué to plot with complete freedom against marriages, let the self-seeker prey on his neighbors' goods, let nobody rebuke the reviler, let the swearer swear away, for death awaits the man whose oaths are lawful; let another tell lies as he pleases, for truth yields no reward; let nobody pity the poor, for pity does not pay. These considerations create a confusion worse than the deluge, and drive out all sound reason, and excite our inclinations to brigandage and frenzied behavior.

For if there is no resurrection there is no judgment, and if judgment is taken away the fear of God is removed with it. And where fear exercises no restraining influence there the devil dances with evil. And with special application to such people has David written that psalm, *The fool said in his heart, there is no God. They are corrupt; they do abominable deeds* (*Ps.* 14, 1). If there is no resurrection, Lazarus is a myth and Dives and the fearful chasm, and the intolerable flame of fire, and the burning tongue, and the yearning for a drop of water, and the beggar's finger tip (cf. *Luke* 16, 19-31).

For it is obvious that these things prefigure the resurrection to come. For the tongue and finger are not considered limbs of a soul without a body, but are bodily limbs. And let nobody think that these things have just happened in the past: they are a prediction of the future. For they will take place when the restoration shall return their souls to the dead for the reckoning which each man will be called to give of his conduct after getting back his original composition formed of a body and soul.

What was announced in the vision of Ezekiel, that inspired seer of God and of great visions, when he saw this immense plain all covered with human bones over which he was ordered to prophesy? (cf. *Ezek.* 37, 1 f). Flesh was immediately brought upon the bones and all that debris scattered haphazardly was restored to order and harmony. Does this prophecy not give us the clearest indication of the resurrection of the flesh? Those who are in revolt against this idea seem to me to be guilty not just of impiety but of folly. For resurrection, return to life, general renewal, whatever you call it, turns the minds of the hearers to a body liable to corruption. The soul, considered separate and by itself will never rise since it never dies, but is incorruptible and indestructible. Being immortal itself, it has an associate in every action that is liable to death. Then, when the time will come to render an account to the judge it will rejoin its associate so that it can jointly receive rewards or punishments.

Resurrection unites body and soul

Or rather, that our discussion may proceed more logically, let us reason thus: What is our definition of "man"? Soul and body together, or one or the other? But it is plain that the union of the two is the hallmark of a living being. There is no point in being sidetracked over what is incontrovertible and well-known. Since this is so, let us ask again if the actions of men, such as adultery, murder, theft, etc., or the opposite virtues, temperance, moderation, and everything that is opposed to vice, are regarded by us as proceeding from both soul and body, or do we define them as activities proper to the soul? Here also the truth is obvious. The soul is never separated from the body when it commits theft or housebreaking; nor when it gives bread to the poor, or drink to the thirsty, or goes without hesitation to prison to bring help to the prisoner languishing there. In every action, soul and body are riveted together and share equally in what is done. In the face of this, how can you say that they will be separated from one another when you agree that there will be a judgment of their actions? And how can you confine judgment to the soul when you admit that their actions are common to soul and body? For if anyone would judge exactly the faults of men and examine carefully the origin of the prime causes of sin he would undoubtedly find the body primarily responsible for disorder. For often when the soul is enjoying peace and calm the eye passionately observes something which it would be better not to look at, and communicates this disorder to the soul, thereby changing its peace into storm and disturbance. Likewise the ears grant passage to the soul of words that are unseemly and provocative, thus introducing the mud of disorder or disturbance into the reasoning. Sometimes the nose by its inhalations and scents causes unendurable evils to the inner man. The hands by certain contacts know how to enervate the resolution of the stoutest soul. And as I proceed in my detailed examination I find the body responsible for many faults.

It also endures toils for virtue and struggles in the contests for what is good; mutilated by the sword, scorched by fire, and threshed by rods, and weighed down by grievous chains, the body endures every outrage to avoid a betrayal of sacred philosophy as it is besieged like a fortified city by the assaults of vice. If, then, it joins the soul in its struggle to be good and does not desert it under the pressure of evil, what is your basis for bringing the incorporeal part of man to judgment on its own? Such reasoning is neither just nor sensible. If the soul was alone and naked in sin let it be alone in punishment, but if it had an open accomplice a judge who pretends to be just will not exonerate the latter. But I hear the Scriptures telling us that the just chastisements of the condemned will be fire, darkness and the worm. All of which are punishments of bodies that are composite and material. Fire will never reach the soul on its own, nor will

darkness bother it since it has no eyes or organs of sight. And
what can worms do which are destructive of bodies but not of
souls? Therefore, by all these logical considerations we are forced
to accept the idea of the resurrection of the body which God
will accomplish in its own time to confirm his promises by acts.

Let us have faith, then, in the words: *For the trumpet shall
sound, and the dead shall rise* (I Cor. 15, 52). and again: *The
hour is coming in which all who are in the tombs shall hear his
voice. And they who have done good shall come forth unto resurrection of life; but they who have done evil unto resurrection
of judgment* (*John* 5, 28-29).

He does not merely promise. By the deeds which he ac-
complishes daily he shows clearly that he is Omnipotent. Neither
has he grown weary after his original act of creation, nor will he
decline in wisdom by transforming it.

Have confidence in God

Let us look to the present and not lose faith in the future.
Every act of God has its place for causing us astonishment. It
is a matter of great and unspeakable wonder when we behold
the resemblances of fathers and great-grandfathers faithfully
reproduced in the appearances of their descendants, and the
children being the image of their ancestors. I marvel even more
at the all-wise art of the supreme artist, God and Savior, how
in an ineffable mystery he fashions and produces imitations of
archetypes that are non existent and invisible so that the dead
seem to be restored to life.

Often, too, the particular traits of many individuals are found
reproduced in one body, the father's nose, the grandfather's eye,
the uncle's walk, the mother's voice. And one individual looks
like a tree which has received the impressions of many trees and
offers many kinds of fruits to the harvesters.

All these things are marvelous and we do not know how they
are done, but they are easy to the creator and accomplished, as
we know, without the slightest difficulty. It would be very absurd
and stupid to hold that resemblances to beings already dead and
corrupted arise in our infants who are born every day, and that
extraneous qualities pass to others, while at the same time to
deny that what is proper and special to these is resurrected and
granted a new lease of life, maintaining the opposite and con-

tending that God's promise is not genuine but a myth, yet God
has created the whole of this visible universe and adorned it as
he wished. But we believe in the resurrection and render glory
to the Father, Son and Holy Spirit, now and forever and ever.
Amen.

THE PROMISE OF GOD[1]

The liturgy of the paschal night invites us to joy

The true Sabbath rest, that which has received God's blessing,
in which the Lord has rested from his works on behalf of the
world's salvation spending the Sabbath in the inactivity of
death, is now at an end. It has manifested its grace to our eyes,
our ears and our heart through all these things which the feast
has accomplished in us — in our eyes, our ears, and our joyful
heart. What have we seen? A light like a cloud of fire of the
candles burning during the night. All night our ears have re-
sounded with psalms, hymns and spiritual chants; it was like a
river of joy running through our ears to our soul and filling us
with blessed hopes. And our heart, delighted by what we heard
and saw, was marked with ineffable joy, conducting us by means
of the visible spectacle to the invisible. Those blessings *which
eye has not seen, nor ear heard, nor have entered into the heart
of man* are shown to us in replica by the blessings of this day of
rest; they are a guarantee for us of the ineffable blessing we hope
for.

Since then this night is aglow with lights which mingles the
brightness of its lights with the first rays of the dawn making
one day with no interval of darkness, let us reflect, brethren, on
the prophecy that says: *This is the day which the Lord has made*
(*Ps.* 118, 24). This proposes to us nothing difficult or hard, but
joy, happiness, rejoicing, as it goes on to say, *Let us rejoice and
be glad in it.* O wonderful instructions! O sweet order. Who can
be slow to carry out such instructions? Who does not feel guilty
even at a slight postponement of carrying out these orders?
Joy is our task and rejoicing is our instruction. By this the judgment pronounced on sin is effaced and grief is turned into joy.

---

1. Greek text; PG, 46. 681-684; Jaeger, **Gregorii Nysseni Opera Sermones
I** (Leiden 1967), IX. 309-311.

The paschal mystery, promise of redemption

It is a saying in *Wisdom* that evils are forgotten on the day of joy (cf. *Ecclus.* 11, 25). This day makes us forget the first sentence brought against us; or rather it eliminates its very existence and not just its memory. For it has completely erased the memory of our condemnation. At that time birth took place in travail; now our new birth is painless. At that time we were flesh born of flesh; now it is a spirit that is born of spirit. At that time we were sons of men; now we are born children of God. At that time we were relegated from heaven to earth; now the one in heaven has made us sharers of heaven with him. At that time death reigned because of sin; now thanks to Life it is justice which has taken over the power. At that time one man opened the gate of death; now through one man the gate of life is opened in its place. At that time we fell from life through death; now death is abolished by life. At that time we were hidden under the fig tree by shame; now by glory we approach the tree of life. At that time through disobedience we were expelled from paradise; now through faith we are admitted into paradise. Once again the fruit of life is offered to us to be enjoyed by us freely. Once again the fount of paradise with its four rivers of the Gospels irrigates the whole face of the Church, so that the furrows of our souls are inebriated which the sower of the word has ploughed with doctrine, and the seeds of virtue increase and multiply. What else then should we do because of this except to imitate the mountains and the hills of prophecy? *The mountains, we are told, skipped like rams, and the hills like lambs* (*Ps.* 113, 4). Come, then, let us exult before the Lord who has broken the enemy's strength and power, and raised up the great trophy of the cross for us to destroy our adversary. Let us exult. For exultation or jubilation is the cry of victory raised by the victors over the vanquished. Since then the battle line of the enemy has collapsed, and the one who once held sway over the force of devils has been vanquished and disappeared, annihilated, let us say that God is a great Lord and a great King over the entire earth. He has crowned the year with his kindness (cf. *Ps.* 64, 12) and has assembled us in the spiritual choir, in Jesus Christ our Lord, to whom is glory rendered for ever and ever. Amen.

JOHN CHRYSOSTOM
(† 407)

The sermon on the Feast of Easter is a model of its kind. In it we find the traditional cathechesis: the parallelism of the two Adams and of the tree in the Garden of Eden and the tree of the cross. The presence of the neophytes like spring suggests to the preacher the image of trees and fields in bloom pre-figuring the new creation.

John of the Golden Mouth is preoccupied with the persever-ance of the neophytes and their readiness for every temptation, because there will be no let-up in the struggle. Once more he returns to the theme of poverty. Christ has abolished social dis-tinctions: rich and poor are equally invited, equally served. God does not make distinctions except in our interior dispositions.

The second sermon published here has often been discussed by historians. Its authenticity has been questioned, but the arguments advanced have not won universal acceptance.

At the present time this discourse is still read in the Byzantine rite at the Easter Vigil. With good reason, since it is an appeal to all those invited by God, and sings of the hope of a universal resurrection.

I. VICTORY OVER DEATH[1]

The Pasch, a victory over death

1. Today we must all exclaim with blessed David: *Who can utter the mighty doings of the Lord or show forth all his praises?* (*Ps.* 105, 2). Today we have come to a longed-for and salutary festival: it is the day of the resurrection of our Lord Jesus Christ, a day which has seen the end of the war and the conclusion of peace, a day when our reconciliation has been sealed, a day when death has been destroyed and the devil vanquished. Today is the day when men are united to angels and mortals join in chanting hymns with the angelic powers. Today is the day that the devil's tyranny is abolished, the bonds of death are broken, and the triumph of hell is annihilated. Today is the day that the

---

1. PG 46, 65-681.

word of the prophet can be repeated: *O death, where is thy sting? O death, where is thy victory?* (I *Cor.* 15, 55)

Today Jesus Christ our Lord has broken the gates of brass and has caused the very person of death to disappear. Did I say "the very person of death"? He has even changed its name. Death is no longer called "death" but "repose" and "sleep." Before the coming of Jesus Christ and the economy of the cross the name death had a fearful ring. The first man Adam heard his condemnation in the sentence: *On whatever day you eat of the fruit of this tree you will die the death* (*Gen.* 2, 17). And blessed Job called it by this name saying, *Death is rest for man* (*Job* 3, 23). The prophet David also said, *The death of sinners is worst* (*Ps.* 34, 22). Not only is this separation of the soul from the body called death, but even hell. Listen to the words of the patriarch Jacob, *You will lead with sorrow my white horses to hell* (*Gen.* 42, 38). And again, hear another prophet: *hell has opened its abyss* (*Isa.* 5, 14). And another prophet: *he will deliver me from the depths of hell* (*Ps.* 86, 13). And you will find many other passages of the Old Testament calling departure from this life "death" and "hell." But since Jesus Christ our God was offered for us in sacrifice and rose from the dead, our loving Lord has removed these names and introduced a new and extraordinary convention into human life. For departure from this life is no longer called death but "repose" and "sleep."

What is the proof of this? Jesus Christ himself says, *Lazarus, our friend, sleeps. But I go that I may wake him from sleep* (*John* 11, 11). Just as it is easy for us to awaken and rouse a sleeping man, so it was easy for the Lord of us all to raise a man from the dead. And since his remark appeared novel and strange, and the apostles failed to comprehend it, he put it in clearer terms in deference to their weakness.

And the blessed Paul, the teacher of the world, writing to the Thessalonians said: *But we would not, brethren, have you ignorant concerning those who are asleep, lest you should grieve, even as the others who have no hope* (I *Thess.* 4, 13). Elsewhere he says, *Hence they also who have fallen asleep in Christ have they perished?* (I *Cor.* 15, 18). And again, *we who live, who survive until the coming of the Lord shall not precede those who have fallen asleep* (I *Thess.* 4, 19). And further, *For if we believe that Jesus died and rose again, so we ought also believe*

*that with him God will bring those who have fallen asleep
through Jesus* (I *Thess.* 4,13).

A virgin, a tree, and death

2. You see death everywhere called "repose" and "sleep," and
what was dreaded before Jesus Christ is become easy to accept
since his resurrection. You see the illustrious triumph of this
resurrection? By it we have received a host of blessings. By it
the wiles of the devil have lost their effectiveness. By it we laugh
at death. By it we overlook the present life. By it we hasten to
the prospect of future blessings. By it, though still clothed in a
mortal body, we can, if we wish, enjoy the same privileges as
the incorporeal angels.

Today we celebrate a great triumphal victory. Today our Lord
has erected a trophy over vanquished death, destroyed the
tyranny of the devil, and opened to us through his resurrection the
the way to salvation. Let us all then rejoice, exult and be glad. For
though our Lord alone was victor and erected the trophy we
should share in his joy and happiness. It is for our salvation that
he has accomplished all these things. And he has triumphed over
the devil by the devil's own devices. He has taken the devil's own
weapons and waged the contest with them. Listen to how he did
this.

A virgin, a tree, and death had been the instruments of our
defeat. For Eve was a virgin; she had not yet known Adam when
she was seduced by the devil. The tree was the tree of knowledge,
and death was the penalty it imposed on Adam. You see how a
virgin, a tree and death became the instruments of our fall?
Now see how they next became the instruments of our victory.
Mary takes the place of Eve. The tree of the Cross replaces the
tree of knowledge of good and evil. The Lord's death replaces
the death of Adam. Do you see how the devil is defeated by the
very weapons of his prior victory? The devil had vanquished
Adam by means of a tree. Christ vanquished the devil by means
of the tree of the Cross. The tree sent Adam to hell. The tree of
the Cross has recalled men from there. The tree had shown Adam
laid prostrate, naked and low. The tree of the Cross manifested to
all the victorious Christ, naked and nailed on high. Adam's death
sentence passed on to his successors. Christ's death gave life

even to his predecessors. *Who can utter the mighty doings of the Lord or show forth all his praises?* (*Ps.* 105,2) Through death we men have become immortal. Through a fall we have risen. Through a defeat we have emerged as victors.

The joy of heaven and earth

3. Such are the signal blessings of the cross. Such are the striking proofs of the resurrection. Today the angels exult, and all the heavenly powers rejoice, delighted at the salvation of mankind. For if there is joy in heaven and upon the earth at one sinner doing penance, that joy is multiplied at the salvation of the whole world. Today the Son of God has delivered the human race from the tyranny of the devil and reestablished it in its former dignity.

When I see my first-fruits triumph in this way over death I no longer fear; I no longer tremble at the combat. I no longer think of my own weakness, but look instead to the immense strength of the One who would champion my cause. For he who has overcome the tyranny of death and removed all its power will stop at nothing in the future for his fellow beings, for he though. it to assume our nature in his wondrous goodness, and to wage war in human form against the devil. Today there is joy everywhere on earth and spiritual rejoicing. Today the host of angels and the choir of heavenly powers exult because of man's salvation. Consider, then, beloved, the greatness of the joy, seeing that the heavenly powers join in our celebrations. They join in celebrating our blessings, though it is we who benefit from the Lord's favor. They are not ashamed to share in our celebration. Why do I say, "are not ashamed," fellow-slaves of ours that they are? Their Lord and ours is not ashamed to join in our celebration. Why do I say "is not ashamed?" For he actually longs to celebrate with us. Hear his own words: *with desire I have desired to eat this Pasch with you* (*Luke* 22, 15). If he desired to eat the pasch with us it is clear that he wants to join in our celebration. So you see, not merely the throng of angels and heavenly powers, but also the Lord himself of the angels joins in our festivities. Hence why should you too not enter into the spirit of the feast? So on this day let indigence not be a matter for feeling humiliated since this is a spiritual feast. Nor let opulence be matter for pride since riches are no help to the present feast. In secular feasts, in worldly celebrations which are celebrated with such ostentation the poor man is sad and mortified while the rich man is contented and self-satisfied. Why? Because the rich man can deck himself out in splendid apparel and enjoy a sumptuous repast, but the poor man is forbidden by his indigence from sharing in the splendor.

On the present occasion by contrast it is quite different. There is no class distinction. Poor and rich, slave and master, share the same table. If you are rich you have no advantage over the poor man. And if you are poor you are no less privileged than the rich man; your indigence in no way diminishes the joy of participation in the spiritual feast where heavenly grace predominates, a grace which knows no distinction of persons. What did I say? Poor and rich share the same table? The same table is shared by the prince wearing a crown on his brow and dressed in purple and by the poor man who depends on public charity, for such is the nature of spiritual gifts that they are not distributed according to dignity of rank but according to the sentiments of the heart. The poor and the prince participate in the divine mysteries with the same confidence and the same advantage. The poor man often bears himself with greater confidence? Why? Because the prince is engrossed in countless distractions and is filled with cares and preoccupations; in the midst of a tempestuous sea he is buffeted by many temptations. The poor man, however, free from all these attachments, is only concerned about his daily food and enjoys a tranquil, peaceful existence, at anchor, as it were, in a calm port and approaches the sacred table with deep fervor.

There are other sources of pain and humiliation in secular feasts for the poor man. Not only the abundance and luxury of his table, but also the luxury of his way of life are a source of satisfaction for the rich man, and this is an embarrassment for the poor man. The poor man is distressed when he sees the expensive dress of the rich man; it makes him unhappy and causes him to bewail his lot constantly. He does not experience this kind of unhappiness in our spiritual feast, for the Christians are all dressed in the same spiritual sacred dress: *all of you*, exclaims St. Paul, *who are baptized in Jesus Christ have put on Jesus Christ* (*Gal.* 3, 27).

Let our joy be spiritual

4. Do not, then, dishonor this feast, I beg you, but assume sentiments worthy of the favors bestowed on us by the grace of Jesus Christ. Let us not give ourselves up to excesses of drinking and eating, but considering the liberality of our common Mother who gives equal honor to rich and poor, slaves and freemen, who confers her gifts equally upon all, let us strive to recognize the blessings of God who bears us testimony of so much love. We cannot recognize them better than by a life which is agreeable to him, by increased carefulness. There is no need, then, on this feast which we solemnize, of riches and great expense, but only of a right will and a pure heart. Today there are no physical advantages: all is spiritual — the preaching of the word, the hallowed prayers, the priests' blessings, participation in the divine mysteries, peace and concord, and finally all the spiritual gifts worthy of the generosity of God. Joyfully, then, let us celebrate the day on which the Lord has risen. Yes, he has risen and with himself he has raised up the whole earth. He has risen after breaking the bonds of death; he has raised us after having broken the bonds of our crimes.

Adam sinned and died. Jesus Christ did not sin and died: a strange, extraordinary thing. Now why did Jesus Christ die, seeing that he had not sinned. It was in order that he who had sinned and died might be delivered from the bonds of death by him who died without having sinned. We often see this happen between debtors. A man owes another man money and when he fails to pay him he is sent to prison. Another man, who is not in debt, in his generosity pays the debt for the man in prison and has him released. The same thing took place with Adam and Jesus Christ. Adam was under penalty of death and was detained in prison by the devil. Jesus Christ who owed no indebtedness and was not in prison came into the world and paid the ransom price of death for the one in prison to deliver him from the bonds of death.

You see the benefits of the resurrection. You see the bounty of our divine Master and the excess of his goodness. Do not then be ungrateful to such a benefactor. Do not grow slack now that we have come to the end of the fast. Let us take even more care of our souls than before for fear that the soul may grow weak as the body grows fat, and that the soul, our master, might be neglected as we dance attendance on its slave, the body. What use is it, I ask you, to distend your stomach and exceed the limits of propriety? For intemperance destroys the body and degrades the soul. Adhering to the laws of sobriety let us take just enough nourishment so as to pay equal attention to the health of the body and the dignity of the soul, thus avoiding the loss of any of the fruits of the fast.

I do not forbid you from using nourishment or from the legitimate pleasure of a frugal board. I am not opposed to these pleasures. What I am calling for is to avoid all excess, to keep to what is necessary and to contribute to your own peace of soul and health of body by observing moderation. The one who exceeds the limits of moderation will find no real satisfaction in eating and drinking. This is only too well known to those who have experienced it for themselves, whose intemperance has led them into a host of painful infirmities causing disgust and weariness.

Baptism, the gift of new life

5. Since this is so, coming to the end of my exhortation I turn to those who in this blessed night are having the grace of baptism conferred on them: I address myself to those fair off-shoots of the Church, those spiritual flowers, those new recruits of Jesus Christ.

Two days ago the Lord died on the cross. Today he has risen from the dead. In the same way two days ago these neophytes were held in the bondage of sin. But today they rise along with Christ. He died in the flesh and rose in the flesh. They likewise were dead in sin and have risen from sin. The earth in the present season of spring produces for us roses, violets, and every type of flower. Today the waters of baptism show us a field much more pleasant than the earth. And do not wonder, beloved, if the waters produce fields bedecked with flowers. For the earth did not spontaneously produce growths of herbs from the beginning, but rather in obedience to the orders of the Lord. And the waters produced living creatures when they heard the words, *Let the waters produce creeping creatures having life* (*Gen.* 1, 20). And it was so done. This inanimate substance has produced living beings. So also the divine command can effect everything. For then it was said, *Let the waters produce creeping creatures having life.* But today it is not creeping things but spiritual charisms that are produced. Then the waters produced irrational fish. Now they produce rational, spiritual fish for us, thanks to the fishermen, the apostles. *Come, follow me,* he said, *and I will make you fishers of men* (*Matt.* 4, 19). An absolutely new method of fishing! For fishermen normally take the fish out of the water and kill what they catch. But we cast the fish into the water and what we catch is given life.

The Jews once had a pool of water. But learn the limits of its power so that you can compare the poverty of the Jews with our affluence: *For an angel used to come down and disturb the water. And the first to go down into the pool after the troubling of the water was cured* (*John* 5, 4). The Lord of the angels descended into the waters of the Jordan, sanctified the nature of all water, and cured the whole world. Formerly the one after the first person to descend into the waters was not cured, for that was the limited grace given to the Jews in their weakness and worldliness. But now the second, and third, and fourth, and hundred thousandth to descend into these spiritual waters — even the whole world — does not exhaust the supply of grace, does not diminish the gift, does not disturb the waters or lessen the generosity.

Brethren, you see how great this gift is. Pay particular attention, you who this night have been received among the citizens of the heavenly Jerusalem. Show vigilance in proportion to the excellence of the graces which you have received so that they may ever abound; for the Lord increases his liberality to those who show gratitude for his gifts. He does not allow you, dear brethren, to live haphazardly; you should direct your lives according to his laws and rules so as to live correctly paying the closest attention even to what seem to be the most unimportant details. This life is an unending struggle and it is necessary that those who once enter this arena of virtue should always maintain a scrupulous temperance. *Every athlete that strives for the prize practices great self-control* (I *Cor.* 9, 25). In athletic contests you see how the athletes take care of themselves, although their contest is only with fellow human beings. Notice how austere is their discipline in training their body. We should imitate them, all the more so since our contest is not with mere men but with spirits of wickedness circulating in the air. Our discipline and our exercises ought to be spiritual since the arms we have received from the Lord are spiritual. Our eyes ought to be restrained and regulated to avoid lighting indiscriminately on every object. Our tongue should be guarded to prevent speaking without prior reflection. Our teeth and lips should be placed as guards on our tongue, keeping it from violating these barriers and confining it to sounds which are regulated and timely, speaking with discretion only such words as would instruct and edify the audience. Immoderate laughter should be completely avoided; our walk should be peaceable and orderly, and our clothes decent and respectable. Whatever is prescribed for the arena cannot be too detailed or too correct in matters relating to exterior modesty, for bodily decorum is an index of the sentiments of the soul.

If we quickly contract these good habits we will walk without effort in the path of virtue and reach the end of our journey without mishap. The ways will be made more and more level before us and we will obtain great help from above. So we will be able to weather the storms of this life without fear, triumph over all the wiles of the devil and attain to eternal blessings by the grace and bounty of our Lord Jesus Christ with whom is glory, honor and power with the Father and Holy Spirit, today and always, for ever and ever. Amen.

II. THOSE INVITED[1]

The joy of Easter, the Lord's reward for good works

If anyone is pious and loves his God, let him enjoy this beautiful feast. If anyone is a faithful slave let him enter with joy into the joy of his Lord. If anyone has endured the hardships of fasting, let him now receive his penny reward. If anyone has labored from the first hour let him receive today his just recompense. If anyone has come at the third hour let him join with gratitude in the feast. If anyone has come after the sixth hour let him not be upset; he will not be penalized. If anyone has delayed until the ninth hour let him come without hesitation. If anyone has come just at the eleventh hour let him not be perturbed at the lateness of the hour.

For the Lord is liberal and receives the last as the first. He

1. PG 52, 765-772.

gives to the one coming at the eleventh hour just as to the one working from dawn. He takes pity on the last to arrive just as on the first; the latter receives in justice the former in charity. He rewards both good actions and good intentions.

Let all, then, enter into the joy of the Lord. Let first and last receive their reward. Let rich and poor sing in unison. Let the abstemious and the careless celebrate today's feast. Whether you have observed the fast or not, rejoice today!

The festive board is laden; let you all feast yourselves. The fatted calf is served; let no one go away hungry. Let all of you enjoy the wealth of his kindness.

Pasch, Promise of Resurrection

Let no one bewail his poverty; the kingdom is opened to all. Let no one deplore his offenses; pardon has come from the tomb. Let no one fear death; the death of our Savior has freed us from the slavery of death. He has been overcome by death and thereby has in turn overcome it. He has descended into hell and rebuked it. He has cast down in terror those who touched his flesh and Isaiah has foreseen this, exclaiming, *Hell below was in an uproar at thy coming* (*Isa.* 14, 9). When it ran to you below it was made bitter. It was dejected for it was overturned. It took flesh and received God. It seized earth and found heaven. It received that which was visible and fell into that which was invisible. *O death where is your victory? O death where is your sting?* (I *Cor.* 15, 55).

Christ has risen and death has been cast down. Christ has risen and the devils have fallen. Christ has risen and the angels rejoice. Christ has risen and there are no corpses left in the sepulchre. For Christ in rising from the dead is *the first-fruits of those that sleep.* To him be glory and power for ever and ever. Amen.

ASTERIUS OF AMASEA[1]
(† 410)

Asterius, Bishop of Amasea in Pontus, has left us about fifteen homilies imbued with fervor and poetry.

This Father, who had a predilection for preaching on martyrs,

---

1. PG 59, 721-723.

sees the Christian faith as an inner experience replete with emotion and joy. This did not prevent him from undertaking an investigation on his own of the typological origins of the redemption in the Old Testament. Joseph in particular occupied his attention and he was the first to establish the parallelism between Joseph and Christ.

This comparison is developed with great vividness, moral exhortation alternating with lyrical transports. His celebrated *Hymn to Night* and the magnificent prayer with which he closes this meditation deserve particular attention.

JOSEPH AND JESUS
(Homily 19 on Psalm 5)

Joy of the Church, as heir

Today let the Church as heir rejoice. For Christ, her spouse, who has suffered has risen from the dead. She wept at his suffering, and now rejoices at his return to life. Let the heirs rejoice; for disinherited people are covered with confusion because of killing the heir and losing the inheritance. The bridegroom has risen, and the Jew, his adversary, is ashamed. What is the cause of his shame? Because of the denial of the resurrection in saying, *The disciples have stolen the Lord (Matt.* 28, 13). If they had removed him from the tomb, how could the apostles cure the lame man in his name (cf. *Acts* 3, 6). A dead man does not cure a lame man; a dead man does not restore the use of legs; a dead man does not teach walking. One cannot give to others what one does not know oneself.

The Bridegroom is risen and, like advocates at the bar, the holy prophets and apostles approach him for the inheriting Church.

Rejoice, O Church, spouse of Christ! The resurrection of your spouse has raised you also from the ground where you lay and were trampled upon. No longer the altars of demons distract your children, but the temples of Christ embrace the newly baptized. No longer does the tyranny of idols persist but the altars of Christ reign in triumph. No longer do flutes compel adoration of the golden statue (cf. *Dan.* 3, 5), but the psalms teach honor to God. No longer do the feet of the harlot dance for the death of John, but the feet of the Church trample upon death. Apostasies have come to an end, and genuflections have increased. The tragic stage is neglected and the psalmody flourishes. The smoke of sacrifice does not rise, but the incense of prayers: *Let my prayer be directed like incense in your sight* (*Ps.* 140, 2). The sacrifices of irrational animals have no more efficacy. For the lamb that takes away the sins of the world is immolated.

A night of happiness

O miracle! Hades has swallowed Christ the Lord and has not digested him. The lion has devoured the lamb, and has not stomached him. Death has swallowed life and has vomited in nausea, even those which it has previously devoured. The giant could not bear the dead Christ. The corpse was dreadful to the giant. It struggled with the living but has fallen, vanquished by a corpse. If the devil had been vanquished by a living being, he could have alleged, "I was unable to wrestle with God." But he wrestled with a living being and fell victim to a dead one and completely lost his alibi.

A single grain was sown and the whole world is nourished. As man he was slaughtered and as God he became alive, and gave life to the whole world. As an oyster he was trampled upon, and as a pearl he has adorned the Church. As a sheep he was slaughtered and as a shepherd with his cross for a staff he has expelled the flock of demons. As a light on a candelabrum he was extinguished on the cross, and as the sun he arose from the tomb. A double wonder could be seen: when Christ was crucified the day became dark, and when he arose the night became bright as day. Why was the day darkened? Because it was written concerning him, *he made darkness the cloak about him* (*Ps.* 17, 12). Why did the night become bright as day? Because the prophet said to him, *for you darkness itself is not dark and night shines as the day* (*Ps.* 138, 12).

O Night brighter than day;
O Night brighter than the sun;
O Night whiter than snow;
O Night more brilliant than torches;
O Night more delightful than paradise;
O Night which knows not darkness;
O Night which has banished sleep;
O Night which has taught us to join vigil with angels;

O Night terror of demons;

O Night most desirable in the year;

O Night of torchbearing of the bridegroom in the Church;

O Night mother of the newly baptized;

O Night when the devil slept and was stripped;

O Night in which the Inheritor brought the beneficiaries into their inheritance;

An inheritance without end.

Joseph, figure of Christ

The synagogue had conspired against Christ as Egypt conspired against Joseph; it was compliant to the law, which covered it with the smoke of sacrifices, like the chief cook. (For the Jewish law resembled the chief cook in that it delighted in the fumes of meat.) It wished to be united with Christ against the law of the Gospel and wanted to drive away the virgin Assenetha, that is, the Church, so that it might plunder the riches and beauty of the husband and leave the wife without an inheritance. So, when Christ came forth from the tomb, as Joseph from prison, and sat on his royal chariot above the cherubim, *the chariots of God are myriad, thousands on thousands (Ps. 67, 18)*, then the saints implored him on behalf of the heiress.

In this Joseph is a figure of Christ. Let that not surprise you. The texts teach as much. Of Joseph we are told, *Jacob loved Joseph more than all his sons (Gen. 37, 3)*, and of Christ, *the Father loves the Son, and has given all things into his hands (John 3, 35)*. His father made a colored tunic for Joseph. And Christ says, *My soul shall be joyful in my God for he has clothed me with the garments of salvation; and with the robe of justice he has covered me, as a bridegroom decked with a crown (Isa. 61, 10)*. It is written about Joseph, *Joseph was well formed and handsome (Gen. 39, 7)*. And the prophet said about Christ: *Fairer in beauty than the sons of men (Ps. 44, 3)*. His brothers heaped bitter vituperation on Joseph, and the Jews said, blaming the Lord, *We have not been born of fornication (John 8, 41)*. Instead of him, put yourself, you son of an unwed mother! Joseph was sent to his brothers as a visiting physician, and was found like a scheming enemy. Christ was sent as a merciful pastor, and was seen crucified like a thief.

Joseph was sold for twenty golden pieces, and Christ for

thirty pieces of silver. One of the twelve brothers sold Joseph to
the Ismaelites, saying: *Let us sell him to the Ismaelites (Gen.
37, 27)*. And one of the twelve disciples sold Christ to the
Israelites. In one case Judas consented, in the other Judas sold.
Joseph was in the cistern, Christ in the tomb. The calumny of
Egypt sent Joseph to prison, the false testimony of the synagogue
sent Christ bound before Pilate. Joseph was in the presence of
two eunuchs, the royal cup-bearer and the baker, and Christ was
crucified along with two thieves, one on the right and the other
on the left. Joseph sent one of the two eunuchs to the Pharaoh,
Christ brought one of the two thieves into his kingdom: *this day
you shall be with me in paradise (Luke 22, 43)*. Joseph, seized
by the Egytian woman, let go his clothes to her and departed.
Christ seized by death departed, and the garments which he
wore he left in the tomb. The Egyptian held the clothes of Joseph
but could not hold Joseph. The tomb had the winding sheet, but
did not detain the Lord, for one could not be held by the other.

Joseph, model for new Christians

Therefore, I exhort you, who have heard me speak of Joseph,
become imitators of his chastity. Joseph was sold into slavery by
his brothers and was freed by God. And you, newly baptized were
formerly sold to the slavery of sin, but have been freed by the
grace of Christ, *in virtue of the freedom wherewith Christ has
made us free (Gal. 4, 31)*. Joseph was wandering in the desert
and was led by God to the King; but *he who led Joseph like a
sheep (Ps. 79, 2)* has also found you wandering like a sheep and
carried you, as a shepherd might, and offered you as a gift to
his father in the kingdom of God.

Imitate this pure man. Joseph was sold to a cook, and turned
away Putiphor's wife like smoke. The pure man felt his eyes
harshly affected by the smoke, and the wanton woman's mind
was clouded by the fumes of passion. She seized his garment,
but did not take away his purity. She struggled with his garments,
but did not despoil the athlete; she bit his garments in her mad
passion, but the young man did not become infected with her
madness. Attend! when a mad dog has torn someone, immediately
that man strips and throws away his clothes lest the poison make
its way through them and become the seed of death to the wearer.
So Joseph threw away the garments which were touched by the

rabid Egyptian, and escaped the lethal poison of adultery. And if the mistress of a house could not subject her slave to the slavery of sin, neither can a harlot enslave you, recently baptized, nor can meretricious fornication become the bedfellow of a free man. For the mistress of your house is nothing more than a harlot seeking to enslave free men. O contradiction!

The mistress did not subjugate the slave Joseph, to sin; yet the free master becomes the slave of his slave through passion.

Joseph at the last Judgment

But Joseph will contend with such a one on the day of Judgment, saying: I was sold in a foreign country, but did not sell out to sin. I did not make myself an exile from God, and that without receiving the Law, without learning the Prophets, or reading the Gospels, nevertheless before these writings I wrote myself beforehand a book of chastity for life. But you, newly baptized, after the Law, after the Prophets, after the Gospels, after doctrine and catechisms, after the anointing of athletes, after the bath of the spouse, after the spiritual anointing, after the putting on of the shining robe, you have become the slave of a female slave, reduced to salvery by passion. Flee the female slave of sin, and receive the inheritance of sonship. An inheritance without end.

Roman law does not permit a slave to inherit. He who is a slave to sin is thrown out from the inheritance by the laws of God. You have the gate of the law; flee the false gate of iniquity. He who does not come through the gates but goes in another way is a thief and a robber. He is a thief in that he fornicates in secret, a robber in undermining somebody's else's marriage. He who enters through the door of a legitimate marriage is the shepherd of the sheep, the father of legitimate children. And even below he enjoys the inheritance, and in the world above he is made to inherit the Kingdom of Heaven, to which may we all attain by the grace and generosity of our Lord, Jesus Christ, to whom be glory and power, now and forever and ever. Amen.

PROCLUS OF CONSTANTINOPLE
(† 446)

Consecrated bishop of Cyzicus in 426, Proclus became second successor of Nestorius in 434 in the patriarchal see of Constantinople. He had combatted Nestorianism in his famous Marian sermon. Under his name have come down to us seven letters and twenty-seven homilies, a large part of which are apocryphal.

Sermons 13 and 14 on the Pasch reveal inspiration of different sort: the first is lyrical — a sort of hymn where the author exalts the miracle of the resurrection and the renewal of all things. The special sensibility of the Greeks to nature can be seen here. With Proclus nature becomes a living person, which comes to witness, in his final personification, the divinity of the one who has come.

Homily 14 takes its inspiration from the tradition of Hippolytus of Rome. It contains the parallelism of the two paschs, and the passage from figure to reality. This text is characterized by sobriety and great good will toward the Jews. All invective has disappeared. The Father simply tries to show them that they have ceased to be reasonable.

THE COMING OF GOD[1]
(Sermon 13)

A unique event

1. Reverential awe should be the prevailing mood on this feast when our salvation is accomplished. Let every loquacious tongue be silent, realizing its impotence to proclaim in adequate terms the resurrection of Christ crucified. What event has ever occurred of similar magnitude as that which we now witness by faith? When has mind imagined, or heart contemplated, or thought conceived, or word expressed, or eye seen, or ear heard such a grace as Christ has now donated to the world by his incarnation? Never before has sun viewed on the cross the devil branded in dishonor. Never has cross ransomed human nature from the curse under which it had fallen. Never did thirty pieces of silver buy the redemption of the world. Never did innocent suffering bring about the confounding of sin. Never did a living being crucified on a cross triumph over the tyrant. Never did a monument of death announce the death-knell of death. Never did the heavens become dark at noon so as not to witness the drama daringly

---

1. PG 40, 433-444.

attempted against divinity though it only affected his humanity. Never did hell shake in carrying off its prey. Never was earth adorned by a tomb which sheltered actual life, or rather by a tomb which proved to be a wedding chamber. For the one entombed was not liable to death, and he descended to the tomb to celebrate a marriage. Never after three days and three nights has nature brought about a resurrection. But he who fashioned his own body in the virgin's womb has united his separated soul to his flesh after three days and manifested himself in his resurrection. Then time bore witness to his birth that he was man. Now the tomb bears witness to his power, that he is God. For the lamb who takes away the sins of the world was never placed on the altar until God took the form of a servant. He who created the dust inexplicably assumed the dust of his own making. His flesh is life, his blood is redemption. His spirit is the seal. His divine nature is without beginning.

The renewal of the world

2. The blessed Paul has well said: *the former things have passed away; behold they are made new* (II *Cor.* 5, 17). The heavens are made new for he who came down from them consecrated them by his ascension. The earth is made new for it was sanctified by his human birth in the stable. The sea is made new since it kept afloat on its surface the footsteps of him whom neither flesh conceived nor sin had rendered heavy. The earth is made new since he freed it from war and filled it with a great calm. Mankind is made new since it was washed by him in water and moulded in the fire of the spirit. The worship of God is renewed since sacrificial fumes and circumcision have disappeared and now faith is resplendent, praising and adoring three persons in one substance.

The splendor of God

3. The prophet Isaiah in announcing this blessed renewal said, *On that day God will be resplendent in wisdom and glory throughout the earth* (*Isa.* 4, 2. LXX). On what day, O prophet? That day, he means, on which God assumed flesh from a woman in defiance of all the laws of nature. For a virgin without man's intervention begot this mystery. He was born man, the friend of

mankind, but he was not subject to change. Death disgorged him whom it swallowed unknowingly. The tomb became the treasury of life and resurrection. The prison was the mother of freedom. Why dilate? When God the Word became man and was crucified on the cross his flesh suffered but his divinity triumphed.

But tell us, O prophet, how did God illuminate those on earth? Was it without his humanity, without his flesh? No, no. Eye does not withstand the ray of divinity. The devil shrinks from the contest. For death trembles before the creator and does not dare to swallow an incorruptible nature. Hell trembles before God who is stripped of his flesh. Hell also trembles before him at whom the cherubim do not gaze.

Christ's divinity needed covering, not to conceal it but to conceal our infamy. It needed not the veil of Moses because that was darkness and cloud. Nor did it need the variegated veil, which was flowered with many tints; nor the golden veil of propitiation because that was material beauty, nor the finely-wrought cherubim, the masterpiece of all art. Divinity assumed the form of a lamb to bring about the destruction of the wolf who was devouring men.

The witness of nature

4. But the Jew, always resisting the Holy Spirit, tramples these words underfoot and carps at the eloquence of the prophet. And what does he say? I do not believe that God has appeared on earth or that a human being can form any notion of God who is not reducible to form. But, O Jew, even if you are wrong about the Law and mistake the Prophets, even if you reject the Gospels, and look with suspicion on the apostles, let us invoke the elements and see if they do not bear witness to the Lord who suffered in the flesh. And it is but right that we first call on the sun. Tell us, sun, why did you darken your rays when the Lord was crucified? Was it that the crucified one was a mere man? Should you not have done the same when Abel the Just was put to death? Now let us call on the heavens. Tell us, O heavens, why did darkness descend at noon when the Jews pierced the side of the Lord? Was it that the crucified one was a mere man? Why then did you not weep when Naboth the Just was stoned? Let us ask the earth too. Tell us, earth, why did you tremble when the enemies of God made bold in this way? Was it that the crucified

one was a mere man? Why, then, did you not tremble seeing Isaiah cut by Manasses with a wooden saw? Let us also ask the temple. Why, O temple, was your veil rent in two at the crucifixion of Christ? Was it that the crucified one was a mere man? Why were you not rent when the blood of Zechariah was poured out in your midst?

All of creation answers (not with a human voice of course), saying, we have proclaimed the Lord in our distress. We did not lament the suffering of a fellow slave, but we deplored the dreadful treatment of the Lord. The heavens exclaim: he who assumed human nature was God. He was crucified in the flesh. He it was who as God inclines and descends. The sun exclaims: My Lord was crucified in the flesh. Terrified by the splendor of his divinity I withdrew my rays. The earth exclaims: My maker in his incarnate state was crucified in the flesh. For although I encompassed his flesh in the crib I could not circumscribe the might of his divinity. The sea also exclaims: He who was crucified in the flesh was not my fellow slave; for the footsteps of my fellow slave Peter weighed down my back, but the feet of the Lord sanctified my waters. The temple also exclaims: The God who was formerly worshipped in me is now severely afflicted in the flesh, but I cannot endure such a deed of daring and therefore I rent my veil. Hades also exclaims: it was no mere man who descended here. I know from experience. The one I received as a prisoner I have discovered to be the omnipotent God.

Do you now disbelieve the elements? Then let us also ask the heavenly powers. Tell us, angels, archangels, and all ye heavenly powers: Who is it who has appeared on earth and is crucified in the flesh? And they will all answer through the prophet David, saying: *It is the Lord, the God of powers, it is the king of glory* (*Ps.* 23, 10). To him be glory and power for ever and ever. Amen.

THE MODEL AND THE STATUE[1]
(SERMON 14)

Universal Joy

1. How beautiful is the Paschal celebration! Beautiful too is the present assembly. The mysteries contained so much that is

---

1. Greek text: PG 65, 789-796.

both old and new! Our week of feast or rather of joy contains so much community that it is not just men on earth that rejoice but also the powers above join in our activities and celebrate with us because of the resurrection of Christ. For now the angels join in the feast, and the hosts of archangels celebrate the king of heaven, Christ our God received as victor returned from earth to heaven. The choirs of saints keep festival too: they proclaim Christ *risen before the dawn* (*Ps.* 110, 3). The earth celebrates the feast: it has been washed in the divine blood. The sea celebrates; it has been honored by Christ's footsteps. And let every man celebrate, born again of water and the Holy Spirit. Let our first parent, Adam, celebrate, made free of his first transgression.

From the Law to the Resurrection

2. Such is the joyous grace with which Christ has filled us by his resurrection. He not only provides us with a festival but also grants us salvation from suffering, immortality from death, healing from wounds and resurrection from a fall. Formerly, dearly beloved, the mystery of the Pasch was mystically accomplished in Egypt through the Law, and symbolically revealed through the slaughter of the lamb. But now through the Gospel we spiritually celebrate the solemn paschal day of the Resurrection. Formerly the lamb from the flock was sacrificed according to the Law. But now Christ himself, the Lamb of God, is led forth. Formerly a sheep from the fold was taken, now, in place of a sheep, it is the Shepherd himself, the good shepherd who lays down his life for his sheep! Formerly, it was the sign of the sprinkled blood of an irrational animal that provided protection for the whole people. Now the precious blood of Christ is poured out for the salvation of the world that we may receive the remission of sins. Formerly the firstborn of the Egyptians were put to death. Now the numerous offspring of sinners are purified by confession. Formerly, Pharaoh and his fearful host were submerged, now the spiritual Pharaoh with all his force is submerged by baptism. Formerly the Hebrews after crossing the Red Sea sang the hymn of victory to their benefactor, crying, *Let us sing to the Lord, for he is gloriously magnified* (*Exod.* 15, 1). Now those initiated in baptism mystically sing the hymn of victory, saying, *There is one who is holy, one Lord Jesus Christ, in the*

glory of God the Father. Amen.[2] The prophet also exclaims, saying, *the Lord has reigned, clothed in majesty* (*Ps.* 92, 1). The Hebrews ate manna in the desert after crossing the Red Sea. Now those who have come from the font of baptism eat the bread which has come down from heaven. For it is his voice which says, *I am the bread which comes down from heaven* (*John* 6, 31).

What should the Jews do?

3. Rightly has the blessed Paul exclaimed: *These things happened to them in figure and were recorded for our benefit as a warning* (I *Cor.* 10, 11). For plainly the Jews transgressed, failing to recognize the truth. *For if they had known they would never have crucified the Lord of glory* (I *Cor.* 2, 8). The unfortunate people did not recognize that oracles in type could only last until the reality should become manifest. For when an artist intends to make a statue of a king in gold, silver, or bronze, he first fashions from clay the outline of the statue that he is planning; he is careful to keep this type made of clay until the real one — gold or silver — is finished for it is necessity in his creative work. But when the real statue is completed the clay model is destroyed, since it is now of no use and serves no artistic purpose.

It is the same with the Jews. Before the truth appeared to men, they carefully retained the types; but after Jesus Christ, our Lord, appeared saying: *I am the light of the world* (*John* 8, 12) *and the truth and the life and the resurrection* (*John* 14, 6; 11, 25), they continued to retain the types to no purpose, for these are no longer even types.

Let the pugnacious, God-resisting Jews cease slaughtering irrational sheep for the redemption of the people. For the rational lamb, the Son of God, has been immolated who takes away the sin of the world and ransoms us from the Destroyer. Let them bid adieu to the old ferment and receive the new leaven of truth. Let them stop eating bitter herbs for Christ has drunk gall for us to mix for us a sweet drink as a fountain of healing. Let us then invite them to feast with us, *not in the leaven of perversity and malice but with the unleavened bread of sincerity and truth* (I *Cor.* 5, 8). So that at the end of this life we may all together praise the Lord of glory in company with the angels, saying: *The*

---

2. From the liturgy of St. John Chrysostom.

Lord reigns. clothed in majesty (*Ps.* 92, 12). To him be glory, honor and adoration for ever and ever. Amen.

BASIL OF SELEUCIA
(✝ 468)

Included among the spurious works of Athanasius, this homily, which has also been attributed to Nestorius,[1] should undoubtedly be restored to one of his contemporaries, namely Basil, Metropolitan of Seleucia.

Under a rather exaggerated and gradiloquent form springs a preaching that is vigorous and vehement of the composition that is clean-cut and balanced. The homily is addressed to the newly-baptized whom it enlists in the combat. In this discourse the author in the first place strives to increase their faith, which draws him to speak on the character of Thomas, who survives in all those who are skeptical and lukewarm; here we are presented with a fine analysis of his hesitations. Secondly, he tries in anticipation to arm the will of his neophytes against the temptations which will assail them just as they assailed Christ.

The Pasch is here a call to trial, solicitation of all our energies, to continue and bring to a successful conclusion the war which God conducts with men, in a "waiting filled with hope."

THE CHRISTIAN COMBAT[2]

The return of a great king

1. Jesus Christ, risen from the dead, has made one continuous feast of the life of men. Thanks to him men live no more on earth but in heaven, a gracious starting point of joy. St. Paul, the mouthpiece of Christ, testifies, *But our citizenship is in heaven from which also we eagerly await a Savior, our Lord Jesus Christ* (*Phil.* 3, 20). And who does not celebrate this day in his expectant hopes? Who, reflecting on the coming of the Savior, does not joyfully anticipate the experience of the reality? Who, hearing of the approach of an earthly king, does not become alert in mind, and joyful in soul in anticipation of the joy of actually

---

1. Cf. Battifol, **Revue biblique,** 9 (1900), p. 329 ff.
2. Greek text: PG 28, 1081-1092.

seeing him? On such an occasion the people are moved, children exult, old men try to forget that they are old, since their hopes give them new life. The king's coming stirs everybody to joy.

But what will one say when the one coming is the immortal King Christ, and he comes not to adorn cities and raise towers, or to distribute gifts that wear away with time, but to clothe man with immortality and to establish him, once the prey of death, in the security of heaven.

I. THE GIFT OF THE FAITH

The gates broken down

2. Today Christ risen from the dead has appeared again to the disciples and this second appearance strengthens their faith in his resurrection. He appears although the doors are closed. For he who had seen the gates of hell gaping wide open did not need open doors to enter. God's will suspends all the usual laws. Once he walked on the sea and liquid water was able to sustain his feet of flesh; his footsteps trod on the waves and the sea to assist him became as hard as the ground.

So Jesus entered although all the doors were closed. And yet at his resurrection the stone at his tomb was rolled back and the entrance to the sepulchre was opened. But there it was shown that what happened to the visible tomb also happened to invisible Hades; with the opening of the tomb death is also shown to be without doors. It was only fitting then that the sepulchre should be emptied along with hell, and that the visible should become blighted with the invisible. He entered, then, although the doors were closed so that those who were skeptical about the resurrection should be astounded at his entry and should be led by the hand to a miracle by a miracle.

From Eve to Mary

After his resurrection Christ appeared to the women before he appeared to the disciples. And it is the women who announce to the apostles that Christ has risen. This is no accident. The curse which fell on Eve boomeranged on the devil. The source of evil becomes its remedy. Resurrection appears from the originator of death. For a woman was both the cause of the transgression and the herald of the resurrection. Woman who caused the first Adam to fall testifies that the second Adam has risen.

The impatience of Thomas

3. Christ, then, appeared to the apostles huddled in a room. He entered, although all the doors were closed. But Thomas, absent at the time, remained incredulous. He wanted to see Jesus with his eyes and refused to believe his ears. He closed his ears and wanted to open his eyes. He was struck with the desire and wounded: *Unless I put my finger into the place of the nails, and put my hand into his side, I will not believe* (*John* 20, 25).

Longing to see, Thomas protests his disbelief in the hopes that he may be allowed to see. "You will dissolve my lack of faith" he says, "by appearing. I will put my finger in the place of the nails. I will embrace the Lord whom I love. Let him blame my lack of faith and grant the grace of appearing to me. As an unbeliever I will see him, and as a believer I will embrace and enjoy him. Let me see the wounds in the hands which restored health to the prevaricating hands of Adam. Let me see the side by which death, which came from a side, was taken away. I want to see the Lord, not to hear about him. Hearing of him only inflames my desire. You increase my sorrow by the news you bring. My malady will be cured only by taking the cure into my own hands."

The faith of those who have not seen

4. But the Lord appeared again and dispelled both the sorrow and the doubt of his disciple. What did I say? He did not dispel his doubt, but he satisfied his desire. He enters closed doors. This unheard-of exploit confirms the unheard-of resurrection. He finds a new subject of astonishment to convince Thomas.[3] *Put your finger in the place of the nails,* he said to him. You looked for me when I was not there; now take advantage of my presence. I knew your wish in spite of your silence. Before you spoke to me I knew what was on your mind. I heard you speak and although invisible I was in your presence, to witness your doubts

---

3. In Greek Thomas means "marvel."

and without seeing me. I was waiting on you, witnessing your impatience. *Put your finger in the mark of the nails, put your hand in my side and do not be incredulous but believe.* When Thomas touched him, all his defiance ceased and filled with a sincere faith and divine love due to his God he exclaimed: *My Lord and my God.* And the Lord said to him: *Because you have seen me you have believed, Happy are they who have not seen and have believed.*

Thomas, preach my resurrection to those who have not witnessed it. Draw the whole world to belief not by seeing but by hearing. Go around foreign countries and cities. Teach them to take up the cross instead of armor. Only preach and they will adore and believe. They will not ask you to show me to them. Tell them of the call and witness their faith. Truly *"blessed are they who have not seen and have believed."*

Such is the newly chosen army of the Lord, such are those born of the spiritual bath, the products of grace, the spirit's harvesting. They obey without seeing. They have desired and believed. They have known Christ not with the eyes of the body but with the eyes of faith. They did not put their fingers into the place of the nails, but they became attached to his cross and embraced his sufferings. They did not see the open side of the Lord but by grace they became united to his members, confirming in themselves the words of the Lord: *Blessed are they who have not seen and have believed.* Those who have not seen have become incorporated in Christ.

II. THE VICTORY OF THE BELIEVER

The combat of the newly baptized

5. Today you took off the garments you were wearing. But do not lay aside the secret seal. Take off the outward signs but do not lay aside your soldier's badge. Soldier of Christ, lay aside your white garment, but do not strip off the armor of faith. For now increasingly there is need of armor. For now the enemy is more actively hostile to you than before and the war has been escalated.

While you were a prisoner and slave of the Adversary, he was winning and took no thought of combat. But when you fled the enemy and joined Christ, running away from the wolf and drawing near to the shepherd, he follows you like an old object of prey, weaving many subtle traps for you. To this camp Bl. Paul enlists and invites us, saying: *For it is not against flesh and blood that we have to struggle, but against the sovereignties of this world of darkness and the evil spirits* (*Eph.* 6, 12). Do you see an enemy line, and a heated battle? For whose sake then is the war being fought? What are the spoils of battle? The leader himself continues, *in the heavens*, that is, for heavenly possessions. He arms us for incorruptibility, and fights for indestructibility. He draws up his battle line to be with Christ. All these are heavenly possessions. That is what the devil wants to take away. Paul does not allow you to fight unarmed. He arms you with the armor of the Father. And look, I beg you, at the menacing gleam of this armor to the enemy! For he says: *Stand, therefore, having girded your loins with truth, and having put on the breastplate of justice, and having your feet shod with the readiness of the gospel of peace, in all things taking up the shield of faith with which you may be able to quench all the fiery darts of the most wicked one. And take unto you the helmet of salvation and the sword of the spirit, that is, the word of God* (*Eph.* 6, 14-17). Paul arms us with invisible armor against our invisible enemy —

The temptation in the desert

6. Such is the strength in these arms. Notice how they defend us, although they are invisible. If the devil has dared to tempt Christ, if in his impudence and folly he has had the nerve to make trial of the Lord, do you believe that he will cease to attack you? Look at Christ at his baptism (and pay particular attention here, newly baptized), then behold him being exposed to the temptations of the devil. See him hungry in the desert. Hunger is an evil collaborator and the devil makes use of it to inflict his wiles. He approached him and tries to tempt him saying: *If you are the Son of God command that these stones become loaves of bread* (*Matt.* 4, 3). Only another way of saying: You are called Son of God in your pride and intoxication. But the name you boast of is devoid of meaning: I see you hungry and will I call you Son of God? Such an honor is ruled out by this experience. Attend to your need by a miracle. Let the stones obey your command,

and I will believe in your name. Let them show reverence to your order and I will go along with the miracle. I will accept your divine name and do it honor. But he was answered by the words of the Scripture: *Not on bread alone will man live but on everything that comes from the mouth of God* (*Deut.* 8, 3).

Shamed in the first contest he proceeds to the second: *Cast yourself down. For scripture says: he will give his angels charge concerning thee and upon their hands they shall bear you up* (*Matt.* 4, 6). But again he heard: *You shall not tempt the Lord your God.* Nor did he accept defeat by this second repulse, but hoping for victory mounted his third attack, as an enticement to fall. *All these things I will give you if falling down you will adore me.* Do you see the tenacity of the devil? Do you see the subtlety of his deceit?

Christ has triumphed over all temptations

7. But perhaps you thought that there were only three kinds of temptations, following the numerical pattern. Every type of temptation is contained within these three categories. He would never cease tempting until he had emptied his quiver of arrows. For he brought all the devices of pleasure to bear on him in the appetite for food, marshalling all kindred appetites in a single assault. And when he said, "Cast yourself down," he stirred up all the resources of pride. When he said, "All these will I give you," he introduced the worst root of sins, avarice. Now from this single root every type of sin grows. There is not a single sin among men that does not come by way of these. Sin either wounds through pleasure, or strikes by way of love of glory, or allures to crime because of avarice. When his quiver was empty he ceased bending the bow. And Christ left him stripped of weapons against us, and blunted his attacks; when his wiles were exposed it was easier for us to deal with them.

Men have become members of Christ

8. Let us award the victory to Christ in his struggles. Let us erect our own trophies for Christ's warfare. Let us not soil the tunic of faith which grace has woven. Do not dishonor the gift which you have received from Christ. Recognize the Giver and

protect the gift. If you were guarding a pearl or royal purple, would you not exercise custody until death? But now you are not merely entrusted with custody of pearls, or royal purple, or property; the Lord's body itself has been entrusted to you. More than that, I say you have become the body of the Lord, you are a member of Christ. Put on Christ, in Paul's words: *You have been baptized in Christ, you have put on Christ* (*Gal.* 3, 27). Do not betray Christ's members. You have become the dwelling place of the Spirit and a member of the King of the heavens. Let us, then, honor the gift with virtues! Let us practice temperance; let us exercise generosity. Let us practice almsgiving. Let us shake off the poison of lack of faith; let us avoid guile, the devil's friend; let us hate lies, the weapon of our enemy. Let us imitate the blessed Paul who after his baptism preached Christ whom he had persecuted beforehand. Let us imitate the Ethiopian eunuch who was baptized along the road and himself became a road to baptism for the Ethiopians. Let us multiply the talent of grace, so that we may hear the longed for voice of our Lord, saying: *Well done, good and faithful servant, you were faithful over a few things, I will place you over many. Enter into the joy of your Lord.* To him be glory and power for ever and ever. Amen.

GREGORY PALAMAS
(✝ 1359)

At the time when Scholasticism flourished in the West, Byzantine theology produced one of its most illustrious stars in the person of Palamas. He completed his classical studies at the emperor's expense. He became a monk at Mt. Athos and later become archbishop of Salonica. The Greek Church has canonized him and named him a doctor of the Church.

The name of Palamas is linked with the theological discussions which put the East in conflict with Western thought. Faithful to the thought of the Cappadocians he developed a theology of divine powers and deifying grace which was in the East admired and controverted in the West. Its influence, however, has remained profound, especially on Russian theology.

Palamas was an admirable preacher as this paschal homily shows. He has bequeathed to posterity sixty-three homilies which constitute an almost complete cycle for the liturgical year. We

5

are happy to enrich the present collection with this clear, simple exposition which has no literary pretensions but successfully weds doctrine to keen psychological perception.

MARY MAGDALENE[1]
(HOMILY 20)

The Resurrection narrative in John

John, the virgin, who by a singular grace received as a treasure the only virgin mother, the beloved disciple of Christ, the son of thunder, that thunder which reverberated when the Lord ascended into heaven, more deserving of the appellation "son" than any of the other evangelists in that his witness was more resounding than theirs, recounts for us the events of the resurrection of the Lord from the dead, and the manner of his subsequent appearances, read on last Sunday and heard in church in his Gospel pericope. These are his words: *Now on the first day of the week, Mary Magdalene came early to the tomb while it was still dark, and she saw the stone taken away from the tomb. She ran therefore and came to Simon Peter, and to the other disciple whom Jesus loved (John 20, 1).* It is to himself that he refers. We have also heard his words: *But Mary was standing outside weeping at the tomb.* For when John himself and Peter heard from her, they ran to the tomb from which he had proceeded alive, saw what they saw, verified it through witnesses and departed home marveling.

Mary is slower to believe than the apostles

But Mary stayed. She stood at the tomb weeping outside. It is plain that she had not yet received any clear testimony of the

---

1. Greek text: PG 151, 265-273. Sermon on the eighth morning Gospel according to St. John. This means the eighth of the eleven Gospel narratives of the resurrection which, according to the usage of Jerusalem are read at the Sunday office of Matins (**Orthros**), accompanied by the chanting of a trope commenting on them, a poem attributed to the emperor Leo VI, the Wise. This eighth Gospel is the narrative of the apparition to Mary Magdalene (**John** 20, 11-18).

Lord's resurrection. And yet she had come to the tomb twice with the others, first with the Mother of God as Matthew narrates in the words: *Now late in the night of the Sabbath as the first day of the week began to dawn, Mary Magdalene and the other Mary came to see the sepulchre. And behold there was a great earthquake (Matt.* 28, 1,2). Secondly, she came with Peter and John who believed what they had seen and departed in a state of wonder and admiration. Twice, then, she came to the tomb with others and they all went away filled with faith and awe. But she alone, as if she got no reassurance, wept inconsolably.

Like Mary Magdalene, the Christian is not always prompt to believe

One can see that this thing happens also in the struggles to be virtuous. For some get the help of grace immediately in their struggles, and the recognition of pledges is granted to them, giving them a foretaste of the promised rewards, as if a kindly hand were outstretched to receive them and anoint them for the future combat. The end of the contest finds others waiting, but the rewards of their patience have been fully prepared for them. One of the Fathers puts it like this: "Some receive their just recompense without pain, others in pain, and others only at the end." These things happen as a result of the complex disposition of our affairs by an all-wise Providence, which in its kindness allocates what is fitting and profitable to each in the practice of virtue and the mysteries of faith. It is then in accordance with his wise and providential disposition of Mary Magdalene's affairs that the Master has preferred to delay her recognition of the certainty of his resurrection and at the same time he converts through her those coming after by inspiring them to perseverance.

Mary Magdalene is rewarded by a vision of angels

Hear now how her patience and constant perseverance were subsequently rewarded. *So as she wept, she stooped down and looked into the tomb and saw two angels in white sitting, one at the head and one at the feet where the body of Jesus had been laid (John* 20, 11). The stooping down and looking intently into the tomb mark her intense concern. But first we should inquire how, since it was dark, as the evangelist tells us earlier, she was able to see everything, wholly and individually, outside and inside the tomb. It is obvious that it was still dark outside, and the brightness of day had not yet manifested itself completely. But this sepulchre was full of the light of the resurrection which was divinely seen by Mary and kindled her soul to a greater desire for Christ and gave her angelic vision not merely to see, but even to converse with, the angels. Such was the light with which she saw. She saw the angels sitting, dressed in white, not only because of the purity and splendor of the angelic nature but also as it were clarifying and illuminating the mystery of the resurrection, while at the same time celebrating with us the truly illustrious day of the Lord's resurrection. They were sitting, which makes me think that they had not just entered but were there for some time, and that they who, though present, were not seen might so give an indication of their rank. I think, too, that they were sitting from a desire to approach nearer the place where the Lord's body had lain. Since they were bound in charity to sit at the tomb, one at the head and the other at the feet, they showed that the angels hold in equal honor and love Christ's divinity, symbolized by the place of the head, and his incarnation, symbolized by the place of his feet. They said to Mary: *Woman, why do you weep?* You see heaven in the tomb, or rather a heavenly temple in the place of an earthly tomb, one filled with heavenly angels instead of earthly guards, whose great glory it is to guard the place of the living God, and who graciously announced that the tomb is empty. But you, *woman, why do you weep?* They do not ask her this as if they did not know what she was seeking, but to cure her grief and to share with her their own thoughts, thus getting a chance to fulfill their task. For the task of the angels sitting at the tomb of the living God was simply to announce the glory of his resurrection.

The Vision of the Lord

When the angels ask her why she weeps she answers: *Because they have taken away my Lord and I do not know where to find him. And saying this she turned back.* What moved Mary to turn back suddenly? No doubt the servile adoration and profound respect of the angels of the Lord. For she called him her Lord, and called the transfer of his body theft, and showed devotion of body and also complete devotion of soul thinking nothing divine in him. But the angels showed by their attitude that this Lord was also Lord of the angels themselves.

As he had not yet appeared the angels were sitting by the tomb but at the Lord's appearance they promptly stood to attention in their own appearance they showed their devotion and awe of him, keeping their eyes fixed on him.

Mary turning to see what imperceptible influence had acted on the angels saw Jesus standing. She did not know that it was Jesus, since his resurrection was to her unheard of and incredible. Darkness still obscured the daybreak and the Lord did not reveal his divine splendor which made him known even in the midst of suffering.

Mary did not recognize him, but thought that he was the gardener, he who was the cultivator of souls, the founder of the universe. When he spoke and called her by name "Mary" she changed her mind and replied "Rabboni" which means "teacher." Yet even though she saw him alive she did not conceive of anything divine about him, but simply as a man of God, speaking of him as teacher of divine mysteries. And so she rushed not just to fall before him but to touch his feet, impelled by her love. But she hears the words *"Do not touch me"* as if he said, "Since your mind has not risen to the exalted concept of the mystery that I am God, I am seen by your eyes in a body that more than ever resembles the divine. Accordingly, do not touch me." This honor had to be reserved for the Mother of God; she was the only woman to touch his body after the Resurrection, for he had become incarnate for us through her. That is what happens according to the account in the evangelist Matthew. On Mary's account it says: *They came and clasped his feet (Matt. 28, 9).* But to Mary Magdalene he says: *Do not touch me, for I am not yet ascended to my father.*

The mission of Mary Magdalene to the apostles

This accords with what he then said to his disciples: *I go to my Father.* In fact, I am not yet ascended. He says that to stimulate their zeal and eagerness, and excite in them a desire to see him and recognize him. But for Mary Magdalene he adds, *Do not touch me,* because the body in which I am now fitted is more buoyant and mobile than fire; it can rise to the heavens and even close to my Father to the highest heavens. I am not yet ascended to my Father, because I have not yet appeared to my disciples after my resurrection. Go, find them. They are my brethren. For we are all children of the same Father, but not under the same aspect. I am his legitimate son and partake of his nature. They are sons because I have procured for them adopted sonship of God.

Go to my brethren and tell them: I ascend to my Father and your Father, to my God and your God. As he is our Father by grace and by virtue of the spirit of adoption and his own Father by nature by reason of his divinity, so he is our God in that he is the author of our nature and he is his God at the time that he has taken on human nature. See why he has spoken separately of himself and of us so that we might perceive the difference which exists on both sides. By this indication *I go to my Father* he gives them to understand that his body is no longer a human one capable of movement on the earth as it was beforehand during his stay with them.

As to Mary Magdalene, the only one of the women carrying perfumes to the tomb of Christ whose memory we celebrate, she from whom Christ expelled seven demons to make place for the seven gifts of the Holy Spirit, her perseverance in remaining near the tomb enabled her to see the angels and to converse with them and then when she saw the Lord himself she became his apostle next to the apostles.

Instructed and assured by the mouth of God himself, she proceeds to announce to them that she had seen the Lord and to report to them his message. Consider, my brethren, how Mary Magdalene though yielding in dignity to Peter, chief of the apostles, and John, the divine interpreter whom Jesus loved, was nonetheless more favored than they. For they, when they ran to the sepulchre only saw the linen bands and the winding sheet. But she, because of her perseverance and her constancy, sticking to her determination to stay at the entrance to the tomb, saw before the apostles not just the angels but the Lord himself of the angels resurrected in the flesh. She heard his voice and was named by the voice of God himself as the minister of his commandments.

The Church and the tomb of Christ

The Church in which we now are is a figure of the rock-hewn sepulchre. It is even better than a figure. It is, so to speak, a second tomb. It contains the place where the body of the Lord is laid, at the back of the veil here and in this place, the sacred table. He who runs with all his heart to this tomb, the real tomb of God, he who clings to it and remains attached to it for ever, in recollection and devotion, will understand there the words of the inspired Scriptures which will instruct him after the manner of the angels on the divinity and humanity of the Word incarnate and will also see without any possible doubt the Lord himself with the eyes of the mind — I might almost say with the eyes of the body.

For he who looks with the eyes of faith on the mystical table and the bread of life reposing on it sees there really present the Word of God become incarnate for us and determined to dwell among us. And if he proves himself worthy of receiving he not only sees him there but particpates in his being. He receives him so that he may abide in him, being filled with the divine grace which emanates from him, and just as Mary saw what the apostles desired to see, so he merits to see and enjoy that which the angels, in the words of the apostle, Peter, *aspire to contemplate* (I *Pet.* 1, 12). By this contemplation, by this participation in the mystery he is completely divinized.

Final exhortation

So, my brethren, *make strong your weary hands and strengthen your tottering knees* (*Isa.* 35, 3). Make straight your paths and enter into the straight ways of the Lord — justice, modesty, charity, humility, and truth. The crooked and twisted ways, on the other hand, are hatred, falsehood, deceit, envy, avarice, anger and the other vices. If these vices result in sinful acts or even if they only succeed in giving us pleasure or sinful thoughts, they incur the wrath of God. For man only views the surface but God sees deeper. *It is he who searches the hearts and the reins* (*Ps.* 7, 10). So you who are assembled *gird your soul like men stripped for action,* says Peter, the chief of the apostles, *Be vigilant. Fix your hopes on the gift of grace which is to be yours when Jesus Christ is revealed* (I *Pet.* 1, 13).

It is impossible when one is in the holy Church of God, rec-
ollected in spirit and directed toward God, with thoughts occupied and filled with the sacred chants from beginning to end,
not to be transformed by a divine transformation in proportion as
one applies one's thoughts to God and to his message. This fervor
warms the heart, chases away bad thoughts like flies, brings peace
and spiritual consolation to the soul and sanctifies the body, as
it said: *My heart burns in me. By continual reflection the fire will
flame* (*Ps.* 39, 3).

That is why one of the holy Fathers has given us this instruction: "Commit all your ardor to act interiorly according to the
will of God and you will overcome the passions from without."
And the great St. Paul exhorts us in these terms: *Be guided by
the Spirit and you will not fulfill the desires of your lower nature*
(*Gal.* 5, 16). That is why he elsewhere advises us, *Buckle on the
belt of truth* (*Eph.* 6, 14). And so our mind, occupied by the
things of God, attached to truth as God desires will keep subject
and under surveillance the part of our soul which is subject to
passion and repulse the enticements of the flesh. Then we will see
an end to carnal thoughts. The grace of God will find our soul
pacified and will give us a foretaste of those ineffable blessings of
the future which the human eye, in its negligence and dissipation,
has not seen, nor ear heard, nor has the heart conceived. In tast-
ing those blessings we will also receive a pledge, and the heart
which receives such a pledge becomes sanctified and receives
an assurance of its salvation. If anyone then wishes to receive
this assurance and recognize with exactness this spiritual pledge,
let his conduct be in accordance with the prescriptions of the
word of God. He will thus become a fellow citizen of the saints
of God and will partake with them of those eternal and ineffable
blessings which have been promised to us.

Let us all strive to obtain them by the grace and bounty of
our Lord Jesus Christ to whom, as to his eternal Father and the
Spirit who gives life, are due glory, power, honor and adoration
now and always for ever and ever. Amen.

PART TWO

The Latin Church

CHROMATIUS OF AQUILEIA
(† 407)

Among the great writers of the fourth century, Chromatius, bishop of Aquileia in Italy, has passed with relatively little notice. This man of integrity and of shrewd theological acumen, was closely linked to the events of his time: the liquidation of Arianism, the vindication of John Chrysostom, and the settlement of the Origenist controversies. As a moderate he mediated the dispute between Rufinus and Jerome.

Most of his literary work has disappeared. Today some of it is reappearing, thanks to the indefatigable studies of Dom LeMarié. He has discovered in the collections and edited a series of sermons of Chromatius, one of which, a short one of Easter, we publish here in its first English translation. This sermon is at once a song of recognition and a prayer. The author eulogizes the power of God who has vanquished death and brought joy to the three stages of creation: heaven, earth and hell. Furthermore, this joy touches the divinity itself in its three persons, Father, Son and Spirit. On the earth three peoples participate in the celebration, Christians, and Jews and Pagans also, almost in spite of themselves. The sermon ends with an appeal to God's mercy which God has already shown is unfailing.

THE UNIVERSAL VIGIL
(Sermon 16[1])

The Sleep and Vigil of Jesus

All the days that are kept holy by the Catholic Church in the Lord's honor are believed to be pleasing and acceptable to him.

---

1. For text see **Revue bénedictine, 72** (1962) 273-274, ed Dom LeMarié.

But this day in particular is called and believed to be *"the* day of the Lord" beyond all others. For about today it has been written: *This was a night of vigil for all the Israelites (Exod. 12, 42).* And the night preceding this day is rightly called *the vigil of the Lord* because he kept vigil on this night during his lifetime so that we should not sleep through it in death. The Lord undertook for us the sleep of death through the passion of the cross. But, behold, that sleep of the Lord has become the vigil of the whole world, because the death of the Lord has driven far from us the sleep of that eternal death to which we were all subject. This he himself declares through his prophet saying: *When I lie down in sleep, I wake again, and my sleep has been sweet (Ps. 3, 5).* Clearly that sleep has become sweet for Christ the Lord because he has recalled us from the bitterness of death to the sweetening of life. Therefore, this night is called the Lord's vigil, because in it he also has awakened from the slumber of his passion and death in which he has clearly declared the mystery of his own divinity and of our humanity. For in the sleep of his passion he slept in the flesh, but in his divinity he journeyed to the depths of hell to lead out forcibly mankind therein detained. Therefore our Savior wished to come from heaven to earth to visit the world; and to descend from earth into hell to illuminate it. He visits all places with his works of mercy to show mercy to all. Rightly, therefore, this night is called the Lord's vigil because it illuminates hell as well as earth.

Joy in heaven, on earth, and in hell

2. Angels in heaven, men on earth, and the souls of the faithful in hell celebrate this Lord's vigil. The angels in heaven celebrate this vigil of the Lord because by his death Christ destroyed death, stamped out hell, saved the world, and liberated mankind. Rightly then they celebrate it because the salvation of the world is the joy of angels. For if there is joy among the angels over one sinner repenting (*Luke* 15, 7, 10) how much more joy is caused by the redemption of the whole world? Men celebrate on earth because Christ underwent death for the salvation of the human race, so that by dying life might triumph over death. The souls of the faithful celebrate in hell, because Christ's purpose in descending to hell was to end death's sway among them. And why wonder if this vigil of the Lord is celebrated by the angels in

heaven, humanity on earth, and the souls of the faithful in hell when he has risen from the dead on this day, he who is creator and lord of heaven, earth and hell, and has not refused to die that we might live.

Joy of the Father, Son and Holy Spirit

3. There is a further reason why Father, Son and Holy Spirit should celebrate the vigil of the Son of God. According to the will of Father and Holy Spirit, the Son died for us that by rising from the dead he might confer life on us. This day, then, is not just the celebration of angels and of men. It is also sacred in virtue of Father, Son and Holy Spirit because the whole Trinity collaborated in the redemption of the world and the liberation from captivity causes joy to all three divine persons. Therefore, we should solemnize with all devotion the celebration of such an important night, because on this night the world was redeemed. On this day, death was vanquished and life became victorious. Today the captives of the world are set free.

Victory of heaven, earth and hell

4. Rightly, then, this night is called *The Lord's Vigil*, because it is celebrated most devoutly throughout the whole world in honor of his resurrection. Rightly, too, this day is called *the day which the Lord made* because today Christ the Lord arose in the flesh from the dead and his flesh became immortal forever. There are as many individual prayers on this holy day as there are individual desires; as many lights on this holy night of the Lord's resurrection as the gifts of blessing which he poured down. The dark days of the devil's domination have been overcome by the light of Christian devotion.

5. The angels rejoice in heaven in celebrating the most glorious expectation of this holy night. Men rejoice on earth, redeemed by the precious blood of Christ celebrating the resurrection of the same Lord Jesus Christ. Even the infernal powers rejoice, because today a light has risen for them, because they too have been reached by the glorious celebration of this holy night. And even though Jews and Gentiles seem estranged from the celebration of this holy day they are nonetheless not without joy

because they are somehow inspired by the mysterious grace and blessing of the name of Christ — he who is blessed in him on earth will be blessed in him in heaven. Amen — For he is the Lord of all. Finally, not a few of the Jews and even Gentiles celebrate as their own the solemnity of our vigil at least in joy of heart, if not liturgically.

Prayer to God

6. And since this is the night on which the firstborn of the Egyptians long ago perished and the sons of Israel were delivered, let us pray the Lord with all our heart and all our faith that he deign in his clemency to rescue and deliver us from any domination by our enemies. May he not look to our merits, for we are but sinners, but rather to his own unlimited mercy by which Israel has already been delivered by him in view, not of its merits, but of his own mercy. May he safeguard with his customary mercy, may he repel from the Christian people redeemed by his blood, the yoke of Satan's domination. May he accomplish for us what Moses promised the sons of Israel: *The Lord himself will fight for you; you have only to keep still* (*Exod.* 14, 14). May he join personally in the battle. May he be victorious. May he show mercy, and grant forgiveness of our sins. For always his clemency has shown mercy even to the undeserving. For he himself, says through the prophet: *Call upon me in time of distress; I will rescue you and you shall glorify me* (*Ps.* 49, 15).

JEROME
(† 419-420)

In his lifetime Jerome compared the obscurity of his own preaching — uttered in a corner of a monastery for the benefit of a few hearers — with the widespread fame of the sermons of Augustine. Posterity has insolently taken him at his word. At Jerusalem Jerome preached daily to the monks: the preacher breaks through the exegete. On the whole he is more concerned to instruct than to move.

Jerome prepared for baptism candidates destined for the monastic life. His commentary on Psalm 42 was addressed to them. He explains the text; when its literal meaning is clear he searches for its spiritual meaning. The faith is made concrete in the person of Christ. This is the Christ of the baptismal confession in his humanity, humble and humiliated, poor and persecuted, crucified and risen.

Psalm 42 formed part of the ancient baptismal liturgy. It is still chanted today when the clergy go to the baptismal font. Jerome takes from it a meditation on the Christian's fast during Lent and the joy which awaits him at the Lord's banquet, the Eucharist.

The second sermon, with the same skill, and what perhaps is the consummation of art, the same simplicity, proceeds to discover the meaning of the Scriptures which Jerome possessed at his finger-tips and recounts the history of salvation recounted in the Psalms and the other books in a language still mysterious.

AS THE HIND LONGS FOR THE RUNNING WATER[1]
(ON PSALM 42, TO THE NEOPHYTES)

As the Hind longs for the running water

I have gone through the whole Psalter very attentively and I nowhere find the sons of Korah singing any sad song: always their hymns are joyful and pleasant. Always they rise above the lowly and the earthly and yearn for heaven and eternity. They are true to their name, for Korah (Latin, *calvities*) is translated "bald skull." Because then our Lord was crucified and buried on Calvary (skull-place), whoever believe in his cross and resurrection are called the sons of Korah, that is the sons of Calvary. On Calvary our Lord, the true Elijah, ascended after his resurrection to the kingdom of heaven. He is scoffed at by the children of the Jews. But bears devour those that scoffed (II *Kings* 2, 23-24). Let that brief comment on the title suffice; let us now return to the beginning of the Psalm.

The hinds kill the serpents

As the hind longs for the running waters, so my soul longs for you, O God. The hinds by nature are insensible to snake poison. In fact they exstirpate them from their holes with their nostrils to kill them and tear them to pieces; and when the poison begins to burn internally (for although it cannot prove fatal it causes a burning thirst) they yearn for the waters and quench the burn-

---

1. Latin text: PL 40, 1203-1206.

ing of the poison in the clear waters. Just as those deer yearn for the water fountains, so do our deer who have withdrawn from Egypt and the world and killed the Pharaoh in their deeds, slaying his whole army in Baptism; after the slaying of the devil they long for the fountains of the Church, namely the Father, the Son and the Holy Spirit. The Father is described as a fountain in Jeremiah: *They have forsaken me, the fountain of living water and have dug to themselves broken cisterns that can hold no water* (*Jer.* 2, 13). Of the Son we read elsewhere *you have forsaken the fountain of wisdom* (*Bar.* 3, 12). And finally of the Holy Spirit, *the water that I will give him will become in him a fountain of water springing up into life everlasting* (*John* 4, 14), and the text immediately goes on to explain that the Savior was speaking of the Holy Spirit. This is the clearest proof that the three fountains of the Church are the mystery of the Trinity.

The ascesis of the baptized

The soul of the believer yearns for the Trinity, the soul of the baptized yearns saying: *My soul thirsts for God, the source of life.* It is no ordinary desire to see God, it is a desire full of ardor, like a burning thirst. Before receiving baptism they say to one another: *when shall I go and appear before the face of God?* And, dearly beloved, their prayer has been heard; they have come and they are before the face of God, and they are at the view of the altar and before the mystery of the Savior. Alone they merit to contemplate it those who repeat in all conscience and from the depths of their heart this word: *I have eaten of the bread of tears, day and night.*

During this Lent, they have devoted themselves to prayer and fasting, they have slept on sackcloth and ashes, and seek the future life in confession of their sins. And because they have shed their tears and are sorry, he says to them, *who sows in tears reaps in joy* (*Ps.* 126, 5) and *Blessed are they who mourn, for they shall be comforted* (*Matt.* 5, 5).

Their reward

For all these reasons the devil has insulted them saying: *where is your God?* But today they have been admitted to the body of Christ; reborn in the source of life, they exclaim, full of fervor: *I will go to the admirable tent, to the house of God.* The Church is the house of God, it is his *admirable tent.* In it resound the words of joy and praise, and the murmur of those who participate in the banquet. Yes, their faith and the gift of eternal life which our brothers have today merited to receive, rejoice the angels in the heavens and all the virtues. Because if there is joy and gladness among the angels on high for a sinner who repents, for a sick lamb which the shepherd hoists on his shoulders, how much more will there be for so many of our brothers born again and purified in the waters of life; will not the entire kingdom of the heavens rejoice in seeing these men cleansed of the stain of sin and all coming ready to dwell in it.

Nature transformed

Beloved, you have today put on Christ and march under our direction, you are raised up by the word of God, like a fish on a hook, from the ocean of the world. With us normal life is transformed, for fish die as soon as they are taken from the water. But as for us, the apostles have taken us from the seas of this life and we sinners although dead return to life.

As long as we were in the world we remained in the depths and our life was submerged in the mire. But since we have been rescued from the waters we have begun to see the sun, we have commenced to look on the true light. With joy we have said to our soul: *Hope in God.* And *I will remember you from the land of the Jordan and of Hermon, from the humble mountain. Deep calls unto deep.* And we *from the land of Jordan,* that is, from the river where the Lord was baptized, and *from Hermon* that is from the curse cast on the earth (Hermon means anathema), and from the humble mountains of this world; never was there a saint living in this world climb a great high mountain but a low and *humble* one. We cry, I say, to the Lord, and let us interpret the profound mysteries of the Scripture by other witnesses of the Scripture. Everything which we cannot discover in the abyss of the Old Testament we will find revealed in the New in the roar of God's cataracts, that is to say in his prophets and apostles. All the lofty wastes of the Lord, his seas and his impetuous rivers which gladden the city of God (*cf. Ps.* 45, 5) have been broken under us in Christ Jesus, to whom be glory and power forever and ever. Amen.

THE GATES OF HEAVEN[1]
(On Easter Sunday)

The brightest day

1. I cannot put in words the thoughts of my mind, and my tongue cannot express the joy of my heart. And I am not alone in my suffering, this longing to communicate my sentiments, but you suffer too with me, for your joy is more in your inner souls than in outward expression. This day seems brighter than others to me. The sun shines brighter on the world, the stars and all the elements rejoice. At the death of Christ they had ceased to shed their light and had gone into hiding. They could not look on their creator crucified. But now that this is his day of victory, after his resurrection from the dead, they perform their proper task attending upon him by their own brightness (if one can call it that). Heaven believes, earth believes. And the net let down for the whole world cannot contain the Jews.

This is the day the Lord has made; let us be glad and rejoice in it (Ps. 117, 24). Just as the Virgin Mary, Mother of God, holds first place among all women, so among all other days this day is mother of all. A novel thought, perhaps, but one confirmed by Scripture. This day is one of seven and one outside of seven. This is the day called the octave, and that is why certain psalms are entitled "For the Octave."[2] This is the day on which the synagogue ended and the Church began. This is the day, *the octave day,* the souls were saved in Noah's ark. *Likewise,* says Peter, *the Church also saves you also* (I *Pet.* 3, 21). But why go on *ad infinitum?* It would take the whole day to list everything significant in regard to this day.

Jewish and Christian Pasch

2. I confine myself here to telling you that today's solemnity has transformed the whole dispensation of the Sabbath, that ancient feast of the Jewish people. They did no servile work on the Sabbath day. We do no servile work on the Lord's day, that is the day of resurrection, because we are not slaves to sin and vice: *Every one who commits sin is a slave of sin* (*John* 8, 34).

---

1. Latin text: PL 39. 2058-2059.
2. For example Psalm 7.

The Jews did not leave their houses, and let us not leave the
house of Christ for we are in the Church. The Jews did not light
a fire on the sabbath; let us, by contrast, enkindle in ourselves the
fire of the Holy Spirit and let us burn out every vice and every
sin. The Lord said of the fire, *I am come to bring fire to the earth,
and how I wish it were already kindled* (*Luke* 12, 49). The Lord
desires this fire to burn in our hearts, that is, in the words of the
apostle, *to be fervent in spirit* (*Rom.* 12, 11), so that our love of
God should not grow cold. The Jews on the Sabbath do not
undertake journeys, for they have lost him who said, *I am the
way* (*John* 14, 6), but we say: *Happy are they whose way is
blameless, who walk in the law of the Lord* (*Ps.* 118, 1), and
Teach me the way of your commandments (*Ps.* 30, 26).

The Jews crowned our Lord with thorns; let us be a crown
for him, if we are precious stones. Diadems adore the head of
princes of this world; let us place ourselves on the head of our
king so that we may be adorned by the head. The Jews did not
receive Christ and were prepared to accept anti-Christ. We have
received the humble Son of God so that we may afterwards
possess him in triumph. Finally our he-goat is immolated on the
altar before the Lord; their he-goat anti-Christ, spat on and
accursed, is cast into the desert (a scape-goat for sin). Our thief
entered into paradise with our Lord. Their thief, a homicide and
blasphemer, died in his sins. For them the thief Barabbas gets his
freedom; for us Christ is put to death.

The gates of heaven

3. For all these reasons, dearly beloved, let us chant in unison,
*This is the day the Lord has made; let us be glad and rejoice in
it.* Today Christ with the thief has set aside the sword of fire
and opened the gate of paradise which had remained unyielding
to all. Today Christ has said to the angels: *Open to me the gates
of justice; I will enter and speak to the Lord.* And once opened
they never more close to believers.

From the time when the Lord suffered until today this gate
is both closed and open. It is closed to sinners and unbelievers; it
is open to the just and believers. Peter entered through it. Paul
entered through it. All the saints and martyrs entered through it.
The souls of the just throughout the whole world daily enter
through it. For there are two gates: the gate of paradise and the

gate of the Church; and the gate of the Church opens the gate of paradise for us.

Our life should be such that we be not expelled from that house, and once expelled be devoured by wild beasts which the prophet recalls in his fear elsewhere: *Deliver not to beasts the soul that trusts in you* (*Ps.* 74, 9).

Behold today the Lord standing in the gate of paradise speaks to us congregated in his house and says: *This is the gate of the Lord, the just shall enter by it* (*Ps.* 117, 20). May he grant us this grace who lives and reigns for ever and ever. Amen.

AUGUSTINE
(✝ 430)

Augustine gets the lion's share. No preacher has left us such a volume of sermons, several hundreds in all. The paschal homilies of the bishop of Hippo could easily fill a volume.[1] There are at least seventy four authentic ones, not to mention countless imitations. Augustine's entire theology is encountered in his preaching. The selection which we publish draws upon the sermons collected by the Benedictines of St. Maur (PL 38). Dom Morin had the good fortune to discover a manuscript containing a series of other sermons of exceptional quality which greatly enriches the corpus of Augustine's preaching (PLS). The sermon on Genesis is one of those published by M. Denis, S.J., in 1792.

We have arranged these texts in the following order: three sermons on the paschal vigil, two sermons on the day of the resurrection, four sermons on scriptural pericopes (appearances narratives), and three sermons on liturgical texts.

Like his predecessors Augustine insists on the universal character of the paschal vigil. The Christians are not alone this evening in fighting off sleep and feverishly keeping vigil for the paschal dawn. Their enemies also keep vigil for different reasons: hatred, jealousy, and fear keep them on the alert, and also shame, sadness, and the fear of God, because some are already "walking towards faith." Both the friendly and hostile worlds, then, keep watch. But what is the meaning of their watch? Why the vigil?

For Augustine the vigil is an ordinary Christian exercise.

---

1. Cf. S. Poque, **Augustin d'Hippone, Sermons pour la Pâque**, (SC 116, Paris 1966).

Just as sleep is an image of death, so the vigil is an image of
eternity. It is defined as the state of the angels and the Christian
who aspires to salvation will not claim to abolish death if he
cannot at least lessen its image.

But this exercise invests this evening with a special character.
Why is this vigil "the mother of all vigils"? Because this image of
eternity coincides with the eternal resurrection of Christ. It is
to bring out this twofold aspect of the paschal vigil that Augustine
takes time to show that Saturday night belongs to Sunday: the
vigil and Easter Sunday are part of the same day.

The vigil naturally invites us to meditate on the eternity of
God. The second sermon of our series outlines the spiritual ascesis
required to think and conceive of that which is invisible, immutable, and beyond time. The spectacle of creation is the first
stage of a knowledge of God. But the Christian ought to go
beyond all representations of the senses. He ought to go beyond
his own soul which, though invisible, is subject to change whereas God is immutable. Beyond himself does man arrive at the
perception of the one who is? Does he know how to reach him
who is? The compassion of God, who is become man will help
him to perceive this.

The paschal vigil, then, is for Augustine not only a watch;
it is truly a preparation for eternity, a symbolic preparation in
refusing to sleep, and a mystical preparation in searching for
God. The resurrection does not call for the same mental gym-
nastics. It leaves for longer to the Christian his liberty which is
unfolded in joy. But not for too long. Here is where Augustine becomes restless once more: what is the meaning of "resurrection,"
he asks. Is it simple survival? The salvation announced moves
him to return to the question of man's very condition.

Man is subject to birth and death. Each instant of his life
approaches the final term in spite of all illusion and in spite of
all anxiety. And in comparison with this life which is whittled
away every day what is eternal life? A life which is the death of
death, in Jesus Christ, and which is not subject to any of the
accidents of earthly existence. The preaching of Easter Sunday
exorts man to be aware of these two orders of existence and to
prepare himself for the second; it endeavors to communicate to
him the only fruitful disquiet which he has a right to have — to
live the good life where he will have access to eternity.

The next four sermons are devoted to commentaries on

pericopes: Mary Magdalen, the two disciples met on the way, the question put to Peter. On the strength of the weaknesses which mark the witnesses of the risen Christ Augustine employs a pastoral rather than a spiritual approach; the true Christian touches Christ by faith. We ought to recognize the Lord in the breaking of the bread; we ought to recognize the voice of the stranger and share our meal with him. Thus we will see the invisible Christ whom the disciples have not seen. The demand made on us is to believe without seeing. That is the definition of true faith. Several of the Fathers have insisted on this point, as we have pointed out in passing in the Introduction (p. xx). This effort on our part will find its reward in the Lord's coming.

These first two texts, then, are an invitation to faith. The next two constitute a strong appeal for unity of faith. This unity is a bond of love. In loving one another Christians love Christ, that is to say they participate in the same community, in the one flock of which he is the one shepherd. All shepherds whatever their name belong to the body of the one Shepherd. Augustine puts his faithful on their guard against the bad pastors who usurp the name of Christ to cause them to stray from the true faith and then from the Church. His homily ends with an edifying example of a heretic whom the good word has brought back to the fold!

Finally, the last group of sermons gives a commentary on liturgical texts: the New Day, the New Chant, and Alleluia. Here these liturgical figures are integrated in a personalized conception of the Christian faith. The "new day" does not awaken in the bishop of Hippo the image of a renewal in the cosmos in the midst of unfailing brightness: rather this theme is charged for him with an entirely interior significance. The glory of God shines forth not so much in the splendor of the universe as in the perfection of man. In each of these sermons he develops the same point: in his works of justice the Christian becomes himself the new day, the new chant, the Alleluia. But how can man become day, chant, or Alleluia? By living the good life, of course. But that is not all. The chant he sings is the expression of his love. It is in loving then that man becomes a chant. In loving God, or his neighbor, which comes to the same thing. And in leaving nothing in himself which permits of self-love. In rejecting the human which is the prey of sin and perdition.

It is then when he becomes depersonalized, stripped of himself, that man arrives at the transformation into chant or day, in delivering himself from himself, which is nothing but sin, in existing in God alone. This is the conclusion, a moral one this time, which the liturgy of the Pasch inspires in him. These five groups of sermons, then, in their different ways reveal five aspects of Augustine's genius to us. These aspects, far from being independent, offer us a synthesis of Augustine's paschal thought: this feast is a privileged time when man becomes aware in the center of his sinful being of eternity and of God whom he seeks; the withdrawal from himself is what leads him in his upward journey to God; by faith and love he enters into a relationship with the Spirit and already experiences a foretaste of the eternity which awaits him, which is God himself.

THE WORLD KEEPS VIGIL[1]

Our vigil is a struggle

St. Paul the Apostle, in exhorting us to imitate him, among other traits of his virtue mentions his *many sleepless nights* (II *Cor.* 11, 27). How much more fervently ought we to remain sleepless on this vigil, the mother, as it were, of all holy vigils, on which the whole world keeps watch. Not that world of which it is written: *If anyone loves the world, the love of the Father is not in him, because all that is in the world is the lust of the flesh and the lust of the eyes and the pride of life; which is not from the Father* (I *John* 2, 15-16). Such a world is under the rule of the devil and his angels, namely, the children of unbelief against whom we have to struggle as the same apostle exhorts us: *Our wrestling is not against flesh and blood, but against principalities and powers, against the rulers of this world of darkness* (*Eph.* 6, 12). Yesterday we too were ourselves darkness, but today we are light in the Lord. And so, by the light of our vigil, let us resist the rulers of darkness. It is not, then, their world that keeps watch this evening, but the watch is kept by that world of which the Apostle says: *For God was truly in Christ, reconciling the world to himself by not reckoning against men their sins* (II *Cor.* 5, 19).

Nevertheless the fame and prestige of this vigil are so great throughout the world that they compel those to keep watch in body at least whose hearts are, I do not say asleep, but buried in

---

1. Latin text: PL 38, 1087-88: sermon 219.

abysmal wickedness. Those also keep watch on this night when the ancient prophecy is fulfilled before their eyes: *And night shall be light as the day* (*Ps.* 139, 12). This is realized in the hearts of devout people of whom St. Paul says: *For you were once darkness, but now you are light in the Lord* (*Eph.* 5, 8). This is also true of all who are partisan, both those who believe in the Lord and those who do not.

The different watches of men

On this night all the world keeps vigil, the hostile and the reconciled worlds. The reconciled one does it to praise the Healer; the hostile one to pour insult on the judge who had passed the unfavorable verdict. The one keeps vigil all vibrant and resplendent in tenderness; the other's vigil is with trembling and gnashing of teeth. Love inflames the one, injustice the other. Love keeps the one from falling asleep, diabolical jealousy the other, on this feast. So our very enemies teach us in spite of themselves how we ought to keep watch since it is in envy of us that they keep watch. Many of those who in no way are sealed with the name of Christ keep vigil this night because of pain; many, too, because of shame, and some, already close to the faith, because of fear of God. Thus various reasons inspire man to keep this vigil.

Ought not the friend of Christ watch in joy when the pagan watches in pain? Ought not the Christian be fervent in observing the vigil when even the pagan is ashamed to sleep? Ought not he keep vigil who has already entered this great house (the Church) when the one who is only preparing to enter it keeps vigil?

Watch, I tell you, and pray. Let us celebrate this vigil internally and externally. Let God speak to us in these readings. Let us speak to him in our prayers. If we hear his words obediently, he whom we pray to will dwell in us.

THE VIGIL OF VIGILS[1]

Our vigil enlightens the darkness

Since our Lord Jesus has made the day glorious by his resurrection which he had made doleful by his death, let us recall both

---

1. Latin text: SC 116 210-221, PLS 2, 549-552: sermo Guelferbytanus 5.

days in solemn memorial, keeping vigil in recollection of his death
and rejoicing in celebration of his resurrection. This is our annual
feast, and our pasch, not in prefigure by the sacrifice of a lamb
as for the people of the Old Law, but for us, the new people,
fulfilled by the death of our Savior. For *Christ our Passover has
been sacrificed* (I *Cor.* 5, 7) and *the former things have passed
away; behold, they are made new* (II *Cor.* 5, 17). For us our
only distress is caused by the weight of our sins, and our only
cause for joy is our justification by grace: *he was handed over for
our sins and raised up for our justification* (*Rom.* 4, 25). Re-
gretting our sins and rejoicing in the resurrection, let us rejoice.
We do not let the occasion go by in ungracious forgetfulness but
celebrate with grateful remembrance Christ's sufferings on our
account and behalf, and the gladness he presaged.

Let us keep vigil, then, dearly beloved, because Christ's
burial was prolonged until this night; so that on this very night
the resurrection of the body should take place, a body which on
the cross was a butt of derision but is now adored in heaven and
on earth. This night, of course, is understood to be part of tomorrow which we call the Lord's Day. And his resurrection had to
take place at night because by his resurrection he also enlightened
our darkness. Nor was it in vain that the psalmist of old sang to
him: *Thou shalt enkindle my lamp, O Lord, my God; thou shalt
enlighten my darkness* (*Ps.* 18, 28).

Accordingly our piety confronts us with this great mystery,
so that just as our faith fortified by the resurrection continues to
keep vigil, so also this night, enlightened by our vigil, may shine
forth in splendor so that we may worthily think with the Church
spread throughout the world today lest we be found in the night.
For all these people — and what people! — congregated in the
name of Christ on all sides for this solemn festival the sun has
set, but day has not ended since it has been succeeded by an
earth resplendent with the light of the heavens.

A vigil among all vigils

2. Furthermore, if one should inquire about the reasons why
we keep such a vigil, the answer is easy to find and give. For
he who has granted us the glory of his name has illuminated this
night: he to whom we say: *Thou shalt enlighten my darkness*
enlightens our hearts, so that just as our eyes rejoice at this

splendor of lighted candles so our mind may be enlightened and shed light on the meaning of this resplendent night.

Why, then, is it that Christians keep vigil on this anniversary night? For this is our greatest vigil and no other vigil of similar proportions is known. In answer to our eager query: when do we keep vigil? we reply: several other vigils are kept by us, but nothing comparable to this vigil. The Apostle has urged the faithful to frequent fastings and vigils recalling his own practice in the words: *in fastings often, in many sleepless nights* (II *Cor.* 11, 27). But tonight's vigil is so special that it deserves to appropriate to itself the common title of vigil. First, then, with God's help, let us say a few words about vigils in general, and then about this special vigil.

Vigils prepare us for eternity

3. In the life to come, whose rest we toil to obtain, which is promised to us in the Gospel after the death of the body or at the end of this life, we shall never sleep just as we shall never die. For what else is sleep except a daily death which does not completely take man away from this life nor take hold of him for too long a period? And what else is death except a deep and lasting sleep from which man is awakened by God? There death shall be no more and sleep, the image of death, shall be no more. Sleep is the lot of mortals only. Angels do not need sleep, for they are eternal and do not need to replenish their strength by sleep. Life for them is without end and so is their vigil: for to live in heaven is nothing else than to keep vigil, and keeping vigil is nothing else than to live.

But we who live in a body, *the corruptible body that oppresses the soul* (*Wisd.* 9, 15), are in need of sleep to repair our strength and our life is regularly interrupted by this image of death so that we can protract our lives gradually and by stages. And so all those who keep vigil chastely, in innocence and fervor, undoubtedly are preparing for the life of the angels. The more the infirmity of the flesh oppresses us on earth, the more it lessens our heavenly desires. But if constant vigils are utilized against this deadly burden of the flesh, then one obtains merit for life everlasting. But it would be inconsistent for a man to aspire to eternity and to fail to embrace extended vigils. He is not willing to die at all, but he is unwilling to curtail death's image, sleep.

Such are the reasons and motives which prompt the Christian to exercise his spirit in protracted vigils.

The Paschal Vigil

4. And now, brethren, let me briefly bring to your attention the special significance of tonight's vigil. We have already said why sleep should frequently be set aside and vigil kept. Now we must explain why we keep vigil with special solemnity on this night.

Every Christian unquestionably believes that Christ, the Lord, rose from the dead on the third day. The holy Gospel testifies that it was on this night that it took place. Everybody knows that a complete day begins on the preceding night, and is not computed according to the order of days in *Genesis,* although even there night took precedence: *Darkness covered the abyss* when God said, *Let there be light, and there was light (Gen. 1, 2-3).* But this darkness was not night yet, for no day had yet preceded it. *God separated the light from the darkness (Gen. 1, 4),* and first called the light day, and then called the darkness night. From the creation of light to the following morning was called one day. It is clear that those days began with light and ended the following morning.

Afterwards, however, when created man lapsed from the light of justice into the darkness of sin (from which the grace of Christ has delivered him), days began to be computed from nightfall. For we strive to come not from light to darkness but from darkness to light, and that is the object of our hope, aided by God's grace. As the Apostle says: *The night is far spent; the day draws near. Let us cast off deeds of darkness and put on the armor of light (Rom. 13, 12).*

Therefore the day of our Lord's passion, on which he was crucified, already had succeeded the night of which it was part, and was terminated by the Parasceve which the Jews also call the "unblemished supper." The observance of the Sabbath began at nightfall. Likewise the Sabbath beginning at night ended at the following sunset which was the beginning of the Lord's Day, so called because the Lord consecrated it by the glory of his resurrection. And it is this night which begins the Lord's Day that we now spend in recalling the memory of that solemnity. We spend that night in vigil on which the Lord rose and on which he began in his own flesh that life of which we have already spoken where death is no more and sleep no more. He raised up his own body from the dead so that *he dies now no more; death shall no more have dominion over him* (*Rom.* 6, 9).

For when the women who sought him lovingly did not find his body when they arrived at the tomb *at daybreak,* they were told by the angels that he had risen. This is a clear proof that he arose during the night prior to that *daybreak.*

Therefore, may the risen Christ to whom we sing in a vigil more protracted than usual grant us to live with him in his kingdom without end. And even if his body were still in the tomb in the hours of our vigil and had not yet arisen, our vigil is not in vain. For he slept that we might keep vigil; he died that we might live.

GOD THE CREATOR[1]
(On Genesis 1, 1 f.)

God created all by his Son

1. We have been listening to many readings from Sacred Scripture. Their length will prevent our speaking at our usual length, and even if we could you would not be able to keep the thread. With God's help, then, we wish to speak to you, beloved brethren, on the first verse of the Bible in the reading you have heard: *in the beginning God created heaven and earth.* Consider attentively the creator. I am well aware that you cannot consider him in himself. So at least consider his works and praise the creator.

In the beginning God created heaven and earth. Yes, his works are visible to all; we rejoice at seeing them. The works are visible, but the creator is hidden; the object of our view is visible, but the object of our love is invisible. So when we behold the world and love its creator our love transcends our view. We see with our eyes, but love with our souls. Let us proclaim the superiority of love to the senses, because he whom we love without seeing him surpasses his works which we see with our bodily eyes.

But let us seek, if you please, what instruments God used when he produced his magnificent work. The Artisan's instrument was the Word of the master. Why are you astonished? His work

---

1. P.L., 46, 821-826.

expresses his omnipotence. Who created it? God. What did he create? Heaven and earth. By what means did he create it? By his Word, which was not created. His Word by whom heaven and earth were created was itself not created. For if it had been created, how was it created? *All things were made by him* (*John* 1, 3). If every created thing is the work of the Word, then certainly the Word itself was not created since it is the origin of everything.

Besides, Moses, the servant of God, in describing creation says: *In the beginning God created heaven and earth.* How were they created? By his Word.

Did he not also create the Word? No. And why? *In the beginning was the Word* (*John* 1, 1). The Word, by whom he created, was already in existence; and he only created what was not already in existence.

We can grasp, and rightly understand, that it was through his only begotten Word that he created heaven and earth. They were created in him and by him. The Word, then, can be conceived as the beginning in which God created heaven and earth. For this Word is the wisdom of God of whom it is said: *in wisdom you have wrought all things* (*Ps.* 103, 24). God has made all things in wisdom. But it is certain that God's only begotten Son is the wisdom of God. We cannot doubt then that these works which were created by the Son, were also created in the Son. For the Son himself is the beginning. When the Jews demanded of him, *Who are you?* he replied, *I am the beginning* (*John* 8, 25). *So, in the beginning God created heaven and earth.*

How to reach God

2. When the elements of the world were separated, disposed, and ordered, when the non-existent in heaven and earth was created, God spoke *and so it was. And God said, let there be ... and so it was. For he spoke and it was made* (*Ps.* 32, 9). What language did he speak? And to whom did he address his words? Do not go on for ever feeding on milk. Elevate your minds with us, directing them to more solid nourishment. Let no one imagine God as having a body. Let no one think of God as a mere man. Let no one think of him as an angel, even though he saw fit to appear to our ancestors, not in his own substance, but in that of one of his creatures. For the invisible could not make himself visible in any other way to human eyes.

Let us find out, what is the superior part of man. Then we can try to discover what is superior to all.

What is superior in man? The soul.

What is superior to all? God.

Why seek the superior through the inferior? In you, the body is inferior to the soul. And in creatures nothing is superior to God. Elevate, then, that which is superior in you to reach, if you can, what is superior to all. In my words to you I addressed myself to your mind. It is your human faces that I see just as I myself am a visible human being. But my visible being enables me to speak of what is invisible. I carry within myself a word conceived in my heart, which I wish to transmit to your ear. This word which my heart has conceived I wish to speak to you. I want to reveal my soul's secret to you. But how can a secret reach your spirit? First, I try your ears, which are the gates so to speak of your mind. Since I cannot communicate the invisible word born in my heart I use the vehicle, so to speak, of the voice. I charge an organ of sense with an invisible message and so I reach your ear. So the word goes from me to you without ever having left me.

Now if you let me compare what is small to explain what is great, the ordinary to explain the sublime, the human to explain the divine, I will say that such was God's mode of action. The Word was hidden in the Father. To reach us it used a sort of vehicle, it became incarnate; it came to us without leaving the Father. But before the Incarnation, before the existence of Adam even, who was father of the human race, before heaven and earth and everything they contain — *in the beginning was the Word* and *in the beginning God created heaven and earth.*

In the beginning were the Father, Son and Holy Spirit

3. When God created the world it had no beauty or form: *it was waste and void; darkness covered the abyss.* Darkness prevailed where there was no law. For light[2] was not created as yet. *The Spirit of God moved over the waters,* and the creator himself was not separated from the Father and his only-begotten Word. In these words *at the beginning God created* one can discern the essence of Father and Son: "the beginning," the Son, calls

---

2. In Latin there is a play of words on **lex** and **lux**.

for the Father. There remains the Holy Spirit to complete the Trinity. *The Spirit of God moved over the waters.*

And *God said.* To whom did he speak? Before the existence of creation was there anyone who could hear? Yes, Scripture tells us. Who, may I ask? The Son himself. God spoke to his son. What was his Word to his Son? Because if the Son already existed (as Christians are convinced he did) he was also the Word. The Son was the Word and the Father spoke to the Word. Did God and the Word, then, exchange words? No. Brethren, get rid of such merely human concepts, and think in abstract terms about abstract notions. Do not let physical images flutter before your mental eyes. Transcend everything merely sensible. Reach out to what is abstract in you. The body is visible, the soul is not, however changeable it is. For by turns it desires and does not desire, it knows and does not know, it remembers and forgets, it progresses and retreats. God is not like that: he does not have such a nature, and the soul is not a part of God's nature. Everything in God is immutable goodness, incorruptible goodness. God cannot be seen, neither can the soul. But the soul is changeable, God is unchangeable. Reach out, then, beyond not only everything that is visible in you, but everything that is changeable. Transcend everything, even yourself.

From human spirit to God's essence

4. The lover of invisible beauty, the lover of the invisible and the eternal, exclaimed amid his groans and sighs of love, *My tears are my food day and night as they say to me day after day,* *"Where is your God?"* (*Ps.* 41, 4). How could it be otherwise than that his tears should be his food? He made them his repast as if they were delicious nourishment and let his sobs accumulate as long as he did not see the object of his love and as long as they said to him day after day, *Where is your God?*

I say to a pagan, where is your God? And he shows me his idols. If I break the idol, he shows me a mountain, a tree, a worthless pebble from the river. This rock which he takes from a pile, which he places in a reserved place, and to which he genuflects, is his God. There, he says pointing his finger, there is my God. And if I scoff at his stone, or throw it away, or break it, or shatter it in pieces, or ridicule it, he points his finger at the sun, or moon, or one of the stars. He calls it Saturn, or

Mercury, Jupiter or Venus. I ask him where he is pointing his finger. He answers, there is my God. I see the sun, but I cannot break it, I cannot overturn the stars, or turn the heavens upside down; this makes him bold to show me those visible objects, to point his finger at what he wants me to see, and to say, there is my God.

And he turns to me and says: *Where is your God?* When he puts that question to me I have nothing to show his eyes. I find them only proud and scoffing. To his eyes which he owns for sight I have nothing for my part to show. And what I have to show him this he has no eyes to see. That is why *my tears are my food* and I want to weep. Because my God is invisible, but the one speaking to me calls for what is visible when he demands *where is your God?* Now I, in order to reach my God, as it says in the Psalm, *I reflected and poured out my soul within me.* My God is not lower than my soul, but higher. How am I to reach him who is higher than my soul, if I do not first pour out my soul?

Now as for this insolent fellow who seeks only for visible objects, and gloats on what he points out, I will try to answer him, with God's help. You ask me, *where is your God?* I will ask you, where are you yourself? That is my answer, and a reasonable one, I think. You asked where is God. And I ask, where is my questioner. He will say, "Here I am. You are looking at me. I am speaking to you." But I will answer him: I am looking for my questioner. What I see is his body, his face; I hear his voice, I perceive his tongue. But I am seeking him who focuses his eyes, moves his tongue, makes his voice audible, and submits me to questioning. For it is his soul that does all of the things I mention.

But to be brief. You say, show me your God. I say to you: show me your soul. You are pained and at odds with yourself and reduced to silence when I say, where is your soul? I know that you cannot show me. And why? Because your soul is invisible. It is higher than your body. And my God is higher than your soul. How then can I show you my God when you cannot show me your soul, which my God surpasses, as I will show you.

But if your reply is, "recognize my soul from its works, I open my eye for seeing, my ear for hearing, I move my tongue for speech, I produce words to be heard, and that, in my opinion, is how you ought to recognize my soul." You see, you cannot show me it, you can only make me recognize it through its works. Well I too can show you God from his works. But I need not labor the point; I might expose your incredulity to a mystery beyond your powers of comprehension. I do not submit all the works of God to review. He made invisible objects and visible objects — heaven and hell, the sea and everything in it. I will not overwhelm you with the details of this mystery — I return to yourself. You are a living being. You are composed of a body and soul, a visible body and an invisible soul. Your body is a dwelling, your soul a dweller. Your body is a chariot, your soul a charoioteer; the former is driven, the latter is the driver. Your senses are obviously the doorways of your body through which messages reach your soul which dwells within. Eyes, ears, nose, taste, touch, the external senses generally, fulfill that function. But what is that interior principle which makes you know and animates your members? All that which is so marvellous to you — that is God for me.

God in his mercy reveals himself as the source of eternal life

5. Therefore, brethren, if I have somehow penetrated to your minds, your inner souls, with such words as are at my command, if my words have reached your souls which inhabit the frail abodes of your bodies, I ask you not to try and think of the things of God in merely human terms. God transcends everything on earth and in heaven. Do not try to visualize him as some great Artisan, arranging, disposing, fashioning, twisting and turning the universe. Or as some emperor sitting on his ornate throne issuing orders and creating. You must be iconoclastic with such images. Consider what was said to Moses when he asked what was God's name: *I am who am* (*Exod.* 3, 14). Ask yourself what else *is*. In comparison with God nothing *is*. He who truly *is* is not liable to change. Everything that is liable to change can be spoken of in terms of *was* and *will be* — and therefore is not *is*. *Is* is unchangeable. *Was* and *will be* are not applicable to God. *Is* and *was* are incompatible; so are *will be* and *is*. What is going to happen *will be*, but is not *is*.

Grasp, then, if you can, the words: *I am who am.* Do not be distracted by passing thoughts, by a train of images. Concentrate on *who am*. Where are you going? Stop, so that you too can call yourself *who am*. But when can we check our imagination and fasten on to *who am?*

God takes pity on us. He who is has said: *You will say this to the sons of Israel: He who is sent me to you....* He first gives the name that is his by nature, and then his name in virtue of his compassion. What is his name by nature? *I am who am. You will say to the sons of Israel: He who is sent me to you.* Moses was a mere man. He was in the world, on the earth, in human flesh, his soul clothed in human frailty, at an incomparable distance from God. How did he react to: *I am who am?* The invisible had spoken to him through the visible. The hidden God revealed himself by means of the visible. What Moses saw was not the whole God, anymore that what a man says aloud is his whole word. His word exists in his heart apart from its utterance. The utterance is transitory, but the word itself is abiding. Likewise when the invisible God spoke to man under the form in which he chose to manifest himself — the eternal in the transitory, the immutable too in the changeable, He said to him: *I am who am. You will say to the sons of Israel: He who is sent me to you.* As if man could not comprehend this name: *I am who am,* he adds *He who is sent me to you.* Or perhaps even though he might comprehend it we would fail to do so in reading his words. So immediately after his name of substance he added his name of mercy. As if he were to say to Moses: you did not grasp the meaning of *I am who am.* Your heart is not stable, you are not stable like me. Your mind is not unchangeable. You have heard what I am. Hear now what you can grasp, hear what you can hope. God said again to Moses: *I am the God of Abraham, the God of Isaac, and the God of Jacob.* You cannot grasp the name of my substance, grasp the name of my mercy. *I am the God of Abraham and the God of Isaac and the God of Jacob* (*Exod.* 3, 6).

But what I am is eternal. Abraham, Isaac and Jacob are eternal. I do not mean are eternal, but they have been made eternal by Him. Thus the Lord himself convinced the Sadducees who calumniated him in denying the resurrection by giving them the scriptural testimony: *Read what the Lord said in the bush to Moses: I am the God of Abraham, and the God of Isaac and the God of Jacob. He is not the God of the dead but of the living* (*Matt.* 22, 32; *Mark* 12, 26, 27), for all these are alive. Accordingly God did not add: This is my name forever when he said *I am who am,* for no one doubted this. For that which is is so because it is for ever. But when he says, *I am the God of Abraham, the God of Isaac and the God of Jacob* he there added:

this is my name for ever. As if He were to say, why do you fear human mortality? Why are you apprehensive about ceasing to exist after death? *This is my name for ever. The God of Abraham, the God of Isaac and the God of Jacob* could not be a name for ever if Abraham, Isaac and Jacob did not live for ever.

THE DEATH OF DEATH[1]

Faith that saves

1. You have heard the reading from the holy Gospel on the resurrection of Christ. Our whole faith is founded on this resurrection. Pagans, sinners and Jews have all believed in the Passion of Christ; Christians alone have believed in his resurrection. The Passion of Christ recalls the miseries of this life; the resurrection of Christ announces the happiness of the life to come. For the present let us labor and hope for the future. Now is the time for work; the future is the time of reward. The man who is lazy in doing his work here, is he not ashamed to demand recompense? You have heard what the Lord said after his resurrection to his disciples. He sent them to preach the Good News and they obeyed his command. The Good News has been preached and has been announced to us. *Their sound has gone forth into all the earth: and their words unto the ends of the world* (Ps. 18, 5). Step by step the Gospel has come to us and to the farthest limit of the world.

In a few words spoken to his disciples the Lord has outlined for us what we are to do and what we are to hope for. As you heard in the reading of the Gospel: *he who believes and is baptized shall be saved.* Faith is demanded from us and salvation is offered to us: *he who believes and is baptized shall be saved.* So precious is the gift promised to us that faith makes little or no demands.

Man's two salvations

2. *He who believes and is baptized shall be saved.* What then? Were not those who heard these words safe? Do not many believe who are already safe? Are they not safe before they believe?

---

1. Latin text: PL 38, 1112-1115: sermon 233.

It is clear that they are safe, but *vain is the salvation of man* (*Ps.* 59, 13). What is the nature of that *salvation of man?* What is that salvation, common to man and beast? Where does it originate if not from him of whom Scripture says: *Man and beasts you will save, O Lord* (*Ps.* 35, 7), and the passage continues, *according to the multitude of your mercies, O God!* Yes, your loving mercy is great: salvation comes from you to the flesh of beast as well as to the mortal flesh of man. Yes, your love is great. But what have you given to your sons? Listen: *Man and beasts you will save, Lord.* Will there be nothing more for us? Will you merely reserve to us what you allot to beasts and the commonality of man? By no means. What, then, do you give us?

Christ, the source of life

Listen: *The children of men take refuge in the shadow of your wings. They have their fill of the prime gifts of your house, and from your delightful streams you give them to drink. For with you is the fountain of life* (*Ps.* 35, 8-10). Christ is the fountain of life. We were *saved* in common with the beasts until the fountain of life came among us. The fountain of life came among us; the fountain of life died for us. Will he not leave us his life, he who has died for us? This is the salvation which is not in vain. Why? Because it has no end.

Man and the Son of Man

3. Note well the distinction made: *Men and beasts you will save, O Lord,* and *Men* here means mankind. *The children of men take refuge in the shadow of your wings,* that is men who belong to the son of man. Visualize the two men. Arouse your faith. Prepare your soul. Recall the man in whom we have been deceived. Recall the man in whom we have been redeemed. Was the former the son of man? No, Adam was man, but not the son of man. Christ the Lord constantly speaks of himself as the son of man in order to remind us of the man who was not the son of man, so that Adam would remind us of death and Christ of life, Adam of sin and Christ of remission of sin, Adam of conviction and Christ of liberation, Adam of condemnation and Christ of pardon. These two men are invoked in the psalm: *Men and beasts you will save, O Lord,* men, which means man-

kind, you will save as you save the beast. For *man when he was in honor did not understand; he is compared to senseless beasts and is like them* (*Ps.* 49, 13). So, *men and beasts you will save,* men who through lack of understanding have become like beasts and who have been created to rule the beasts but have come to resemble them.

The salvation of Jesus Christ

4. Is that the salvation of which the Scripture says: *He who believes and is baptized shall be saved?* No, indeed, it is not this salvation. The angels possess it; do not search for it on earth. It is great but it is not here. Such a blessing is not allotted to this world; this salvation is not here on earth. Lift up your hearts. Why seek for this salvation here below. This salvation came here but here it encountered our death. When our Lord Jesus Christ came here did he find salvation here below among us? Coming like a merchant from his own country he brought here a great blessing, but he only found here the fruits which abound here. What are earth's fruits? Birth and death. The earth abounds in birth and death. Christ then was born and he died. And in what way? He came to our country but by a way unknown to man. He came from heaven from his Father, yet he was born subject to death. He was born of the Holy Spirit and the Virgin Mary. Were Adam and Eve born to us in this way? No, we are born from carnal desire, but not he. Mary was a virgin who knew not man nor the fire of passion. It was to withdraw her from the ardor of passion that the promise was made to her by the angel: *The Holy Spirit will come upon you and the power of the Most High will overshadow you.* So Mary conceived without knowing man. She believed and she conceived. And Christ was born a mortal for us mortals. Why was he a mortal? Because he was *in the likeness of sinful flesh.* He was not attired in sinful flesh but in the likeness of sinful flesh. And what are the attributes of sinful flesh? Death and sin. What does *the likeness of sinful flesh* mean? Death without sin. If he were a sinner he would have assumed sinful flesh. If he were not to die he would not be in the likeness of sinful flesh. That is how he came, the Savior. He died but he vanquished death. He has perfected that which he threw to us in terror. He has taken death and put it to death as a mighty hunter confronts and slays a lion.

The death of death

5. Where is death? Seek it in Jesus Christ, for it exists no longer. It was in him but it exists no longer. O life, the death of death! Take courage and it will die also in you. What has begun in our Head will continue in his members. Death will die also in us. When? At the end of the world. At the resurrection of the dead in which we believe without the slightest doubt. *He who believes and is baptized will be saved.*

Read what follows — it is formidable: *He who does not believe shall be condemned.* Death will die in us but it will be victorious in those who are condemned. There will be everlasting death where death itself does not die because the torments will be everlasting. In us, however, death will die and will exist no more.

I am going to cite some words of those who have vanquished death. Reflect on them, sing them in your heart, and they will provide an objective for your hope and a meaning to your faith and good works. Hear the victorious words to be repeated when death will be no more, when death will perish in us as it has already perished in Christ our head. *This corruptible body,* says St. Paul, *must put on incorruption and this mortal body must put on immortality. Then shall be fulfilled the Scripture saying, Death is swallowed up in victory* (I Cor. 15, 53). As I have said already, death will die in us. *Death is swallowed up in victory.* That is the death of death. It will be swallowed up in eternal nothingness. What do we mean by "eternal nothingness"? It will have no existence, within or without. *Death is swallowed up in victory.* Let the triumphant rejoice. Let them rejoice and repeat the following words in the quotation: *O death, where is your victory? O death, where is your sting?* Where is death? You have seized it. You have taken possession of it. You have vanquished it, you have subdued it, you have struck and killed it. *O death, where is your victory? O death, where is your sting?* Has not my Lord destroyed it? O death, when you threw yourself on him you ceased to live in me. That is what salvation means for the one of whom we say: *He who believes and is baptized shall be saved. But he who does not believe shall be condemned.* Flee from this condemnation. Love and hope for eternal salvation.

SURVIVAL AND LIFE[1]

The risen Christ

1. The resurrection of our Lord Jesus Christ is the seal of the Christian faith. That he was born man from man at a given time, but also God from God, and God outside of time; that he was born in mortal flesh and in the appearance of our sinful flesh; that he passed through infancy, proceeded to boyhood and arrived at adulthood, and continued until death, all this contributed to his resurrection. For he could not rise without dying; and he could not die without being born. In being born and dying he prepared for his resurrection.

(The text) goes on: *Christ our Lord is man born of man.* Pagans and infidels! If they do not know that he was born of a virgin, his enemies and his friends believed that Christ was crucified and died. But only his friends knew of his resurrection. And why?

Christ the Lord did not want to be born and die apart from the plan of his resurrection, and that is the seal of our faith.

In our condition, the human condition I mean, we know two moments: birth and death. But to teach us to apprehend also what we do not know, he has taken that which we know. The law which rules our earthly state, our mortal state, I mean, is that of birth and death; it is a law which is ceaselessly observed on earth so that it will cease to be observed in the heavens. But who ever knew of resurrection and of life for ever?

Such is the revolution which he brought on earth, who came from God. He has become man, for man. O immense compassion: He who made man has become man. It was not great enough for Christ to be what he was. He aspired to be greater still by becoming that which he had already made. What means: to become what he had made? To become man, he who had made man. Such was his compassion.

The country of birth and death

2. All the events of this life, where men aspire to happiness and without success. . . . Because they are right to hold it so

---

1. Latin text: PLS 2, 568-572: Sermon Guelferbytanus 12.

strongly, but they do not seek happiness where it is to be found. All the earth's benefits do not appear except at certain definite points. The earth does not in all places produce gold, silver, or lead. These products flourish in their proper places. And each area is rich or sterile in various products; such a fruit here, such another one there: different good things in different places. And nothing at all exists everywhere apart from birth and death. Now this law of birth and death does not constitute the law of the entire universe, but holds sway only in this tiny corner where we dwell. In the heavens birth and death have no place, because there everything is definitive. Doubtless the prince of the angels was able to fall from there with his own; but in place of those who fell, men will come from here and occupy the places of those who fell. Now the devil saw that man would rise to the place from which he had fallen. He saw it and was jealous. He fell and made man fall. Now what means, the devil fell? And what means, he made man fall? He who did not fall but descended won a complete victory. Man fell. God descended and became man.

Therefore the place where birth and death abound is a region of misery; men seek to be happy in this region of misery, seeking eternity in the region of death. The Lord says to us, truth says to us: What you seek is not here, because it is not from here. You seek a good thing which every man wants: you seek a good thing, for to live is good, but we are born for death. Do not look at what you wish for, but examine the condition of your coming. We are born to die. Men desire life but it is not obtained by those destined to die, and so they are more miserable. For if we died and had wished to live, we would not be very miserable; we are so miserable, however, because we wish to live and are forced to die. Don't you know that no man can stay awake but also longs for sleep? It is not against his will that he sleeps, for to keep awake is not possible: his sleep is voluntary. Both staying awake and sleeping are part of being a man.

In life every man says: I want to live, and no one wants to die. And although he does not want to die, death comes to him. Insofar as he can, he acts, by eating, drinking, sleeping, providing for his necessities, sailing, walking, running, minding himself. Often he lives free from many dangers; but let him hold on, if he can, to his middle age; let him avoid reaching old age. The day of danger passes and a man announces: I have avoided

death. How have you avoided death? Because the day's danger
is past. But you have only added a day: you have lived a day
longer, or rather a day less if my calculation is accurate. For if
you still had to live, say, thirty years, when this day is gone, it is
subtracted from the sum of what you have to live and is added
to the burden of approaching death. And yet they say: "Years
add up for man." I say, however, that they recede, for I attend
to the sum that remains, not to what has passed. They add up,
how? Because he who has lived forty years is already forty-one.
How many years does he live or, better, how many should he?
Eighty years, for example, was his life expectancy, fifty of which
are gone and thirty remain. He lives one: that makes fifty-one
lived, and twenty-nine left to live. One is added to what is
lived, one taken away from what is left to live. But when you add,
you do not keep what has been taken away. In fear a second
year is lived; there remain twenty-eight. A third year is added;
that leaves twenty-seven. In living we draw on the span of life,
and life is shortened in the process and finally is no more. For
there is no way of avoiding the last day.

The necessity of death

3. But our Lord Jesus Christ came to tell us in some such
words: "O men, what are you afraid of; I have created you and
have not abandoned you. O men, ruin is from you, creation from
me; O men, why did you fear death? Behold, I die; behold, I
suffer. Behold, you should not fear what you do, because I show
you reason for hope." Behold, he did so; he showed us resurrection for eternity. The evangelists have described it in their
Scriptures; the apostles have preached it throughout the world.
Because of faith in this resurrection the holy martyrs did not fear
death, and yet they feared to die: they would have died more,
if they feared to die, and denied Christ in their fear of death.
For what is to deny Christ except to deny life? What folly it
is to deny life in one's love for life!

Therefore the resurrection of Christ is the characteristic work
of our faith. Therefore it is written, in both the Old and New
Testament, to do penance and receive remission of sins, *through
a man he has appointed, one whom he has endorsed in the
sight of all by raising him from the dead* (*Acts* 17, 31). This
is the endorsement of faith — the resurrection of our Lord, Jesus

Christ. You live, on condition that you wish to live. I mean to say that if you live the good life, you will live for ever. Do not be afraid to die badly. Fear to live badly.

A strange paradox! Every man fears what no one can evade and does not do what he can do. You can do nothing about avoiding death, but you can do something about living well. Do what you can and you will not fear what you can do nothing about.

For nothing is so certain for man as death. Begin at the beginning. Man is conceived in the womb: perhaps he is born, perhaps he dies before birth. Next he is born: perhaps he grows up, perhaps he doesn't. Perhaps he goes to school, perhaps he doesn't. Perhaps he marries, perhaps not. Perhaps he has children, perhaps not. Perhaps they turn out good, perhaps bad. Perhaps his wife is good, perhaps bad. Perhaps he becomes rich, perhaps poor; perhaps ignoble, perhaps honorable. But among all these alternatives can one ever say: Perhaps he will die, perhaps not? Everyone at birth contracts an evil from which no mortal can escape. He dies from it, whatever its name. It is dropsy: death is inevitable; it is inescapable. It is leprosy: death is inevitable; it is inescapable.

Because death is inevitable, then, and life is nothing less than a passage by degrees from birth to old age, however decrepit, nothing remains but to seek refuge with him who died for us and gave us hope by his resurrection; let us fly to him who promised us eternal life, since we can do nothing to make life which we love so much eternal, destined as we are to run our mortal course and die.

Brethren, consider what our Lord has promised us — a life of eternity and happiness. Certainly this life is miserable. Who does not know and admit as much? What wretchedness; what suffering, what unwanted trials in this life! Quarrels, dissensions, temptations, ignorance of another's disposition so that we sometimes embrace an enemy and fear a friend! Hunger, nakedness, cold, heat, weariness, sickness, jealousies — certainly this life is miserable.

Nevertheless if somebody could make this wretchedness of ours eternal, who would not congratulate us? Who would not say, "I want to stay as I am, I only do not want to die." Now if you are willing to settle for this miserable life, what must that one be like which can make you eternal and happy? But if you wish to come to the eternal and happy life, be good in this fleeting life here below. If it is good in works, it will be happy in reward. If you refuse good works, however, how can you expect reward? If you cannot say to Christ "I did what you ordered," how will you dare to say, "Give what you promised?"

BELIEVE AND TOUCH[1]

A strange contradiction

1. It is good that you recall to mind what you are in the habit of hearing every year. It is not enough to read a text once, nor is it enough to give a simple explanation of the difficult passages. You, then, who have already heard and understood them, who keep them in mind and follow them faithfully, listen patiently; some are now being instructed who have perhaps forgotten; others, perhaps, are hearing these words for the first time.

Is it possible to touch Christ who is in heaven?

It is strange, when the woman, ever faithful, comes to see the body of her master in the tomb and cannot find where it has been laid. The Lord said to her, "*Do not touch me for I am not yet ascended to my Father*" (*John* 20, 17). If he did not wish to be touched before ascending to the Father, he had not yet ascended to the Father when he said to the disciples: *see my hands and my feet — feel me and see* (*Luke* 24, 39). He does not wish to be touched, but he wants to be felt. This, then, is the question to be solved; for nobody has ventured to say, Christ wished to be touched only by men before his ascension; women were allowed to touch him only after his ascension to the Father. Who touched him while ascending or rather after ascending to the Father? Did he reserve until that time being touched by women when in fact he could not be touched even by men at that time? And yet, moved by love, he not only allowed Saul, the persecutor, to touch him but even to cast him to the earth, making Christ exclaim from heaven: *Saul, Saul, why do you persecute me?* (*Acts* 9, 4). Christ the Lord is both in heaven at the right hand of the Father and toils here on earth. He is in

---

1. Latin text: PLS 2, 572-574. Sermon Morin Guelferbytanus 13; first homily on Holy Thursday.

heaven in person, and is on earth in his members; in heaven he is going to judge the living and the dead, and simultaneously he is here on earth among his own concerning whom he will one day say: *As long as you did it for one of these ... you did it for me* (*Mark* 25, 40).

The woman in the crowd

What, then, do these words mean: *Do not touch me for I have not yet ascended to my Father?* It is better to contact Christ by Faith than in the flesh, for contact by faith is real contact.

The woman with the hemorrhage approached Christ full of faith and touched his garment with her hand and his majesty with her faith. See, that is what touching means: the Lord, pressed by the crowds though he was, was touched only by this woman. He asks: *who touched me?* The disciples who saw the crowd pressing were amazed at the question and answered him: *the crowds press you and do you ask who touched me?* And Jesus replied: *someone has touched me.* Yes, the crowds merely press on you, they do not really touch you. Then how has this woman touched you except through her faith?

To touch is to believe

2. Today, brethren, Jesus is in heaven while he remained among his disciples, clad in visible flesh, and in possession of a palpable body. He could be seen and touched. What of today when he sits at the right hand of the Father, which of us can touch him?

And yet woe betide us if we do not touch him. All of us touch him who have faith. He is far away in heaven at an immeasurable distance from us. But believe and you touch him. What did I say? Touch him? If you believe you already possess him in whom you believe.

If then to believe means to touch or rather if to touch is to believe what is the meaning of: *Do not touch me for I am not yet ascended to my Father?* Why does he say this?

Mary did not know how to touch the Lord

Why do you seek to touch my body, when you do not yet know my divinity? You know how this woman wished to touch him? She sought him as dead and did not believe that he was to arise. *They have taken away my Lord from the tomb.* She wept for a mere man. If only she could touch him! Since he saw her completely engrossed with him in the form of a slave and incapable of knowing, believing and understanding his divinity which made him equal to the Father, he refused to let her touch him before this made sense.

Do not touch me, he said, *for I am not yet ascended to my Father.* Should you touch me prior to my ascent to the Father then you only see the man in me. What has this faith given you? Let me ascend to my Father. I have never left him but for you I will ascend to him if you believe me to be equal to the Father.

Our Lord Jesus Christ has never left his Father when he descended from him. No more has he abandoned us in returning to his Father. For in the moment of departing and sitting at the right hand of the Father he said to his disciples: *I am with you even unto the consummation of the world (Mark* 28, 20).

THE PRESENCE OF CHRIST[1]
(Sermon 235: On Luke 24, 13-21)

Diversity of Gospel accounts

1. Yesterday, that is last night, the reading from the Gospel was the resurrection of our Savior; that reading, however, was according to Matthew. Today's, as you heard from the lector, was an account of the Lord's resurrection for us according to the evangelist Luke. As you have often to be reminded and should remember, it should not disturb us if one Gospel gives an account of something that another omits, because even if it omits what the other says, it also tells us something that the other has omitted. Some things are told in all four Gospels, some are omitted in three, some in two, some in one. But so great is the authority of the holy Gospel that because it is the one spirit that speaks in them, even what one evangelist records is true.

What you have just heard about our Lord Jesus after rising from the dead finding two of his disciples in the way talking to one another about what had happened and Jesus saying to them:

---

1. Latin text: PL 38, 1117-1120.

What are these discussions which I hear, etc., is only found in the evangelist Luke. Mark makes a brief allusion to it, telling us that he appeared to the two in the way, but he does not say what the Lord said to them.

The disciples fail to recognize Christ

2. What is the message of this reading for us? Something great, if we understand it properly. Jesus appeared. He was visible to the eyes but not recognized. The Master was walking with them in the way, and he was the Way. And they were not yet walking in the way; he found them out of their way.

For when he was with them before his passion, he foretold all things to them, that he would suffer, die, and rise on the third day. He had foretold everything but they forgot when he died. They were so perturbed when they saw him hanging on the cross that they forgot his teaching, and did not expect his resurrection nor hold to his promise. *We were hoping,* they said, *that he would redeem Israel.* O disciples, you *were* hoping! Therefore you are no longer hoping? Behold Christ is alive. Has hope died in you? Assuredly Christ lives. But the living Christ finds that his disciples' hearts are dead. He was seen and not seen by their eyes. He was visible and hidden. For if he was not seen, how did they hear him asking, or answer him questioning? He was walking as a companion with them in the way and yet he was their leader. Of course they saw him but they did not recognize him. For *their eyes were held,* as we have heard, *so that they might not recognize him.* They were not held so that they might not see him, but that they might not recognize him.

Jesus present at the breaking of bread

3. And when, brethren, did the Lord wish to be recognized? At the breaking of bread. With us it is easy. We break bread and we recognize the Lord. He delayed recognition until then for our sake, we who would not see him in the flesh and yet would eat his flesh. And you, individual member of the faithful, if you are no mere nominal Christian, if you are no casual arrival in the Church, if you hear the word of God with fear and hope, you are consoled in the breaking of bread. The absent Lord is

not absent for you. Have faith and he whom you do not see is present with you. But these two, when the Lord spoke with them, because they had not faith, they did not believe that he had arisen, and they had no hope that he could rise. They had lost faith and lost hope. They were dead men walking with a man alive, they were dead men walking with life itself. Life was walking with them but in their hearts there was no life yet.

And you, if you wish to have life, do what they did to recognize the Lord. They offered him hospitality. The Lord looked bent on continuing his journey but they detained him. When they reached the end of their journey they said: *Stay with us here for the day has turned to evening* (*Luke* 24, 29). Take in the stranger if you wish to recognize the Savior. Hospitality restored to them what lack of faith had taken away; the Lord manifested himself in the breaking of bread. Learn where to seek the Lord, where to get him, where to recognize him; in eating bread. For the faithful know something that gives them a better insight than the uninitiated into this text.

From faith to possession

4. The Lord made himself known to them, and after he was recognized he was seen no more. He was taken from them in body when he was grasped by faith. And so our Lord has bodily departed from every Church and ascended into heaven to fortify our faith. For if you only know what you see, where does faith come in? However, if you believe what you do not see, you will rejoice when you see it. Fortify your faith and your seeing will be restored. What we do not see, brethren, will come, it will come. See how it will come. For it will come because men say: where is he, when, how, when will it be? When is he going to come? Be certain, he will come. Not only will he come, but he will come even in spite of us. Woe to them who have not believed and great the joy of those who have believed. The faithful will rejoice, the infidels will be confounded. The faithful will say, "Thanks to you, Lord. We have heard the truth, we have believed it, we have hoped for it, we have seen it." But the infidels will say, "Why is it that we have not believed. Why is it that we have regarded as lies those truths which were read." [Those[2]

---

2. Latin text: PL 38, 1117-1120.

then are to be praised who do not see and yet believe; for they will rejoice when they see. To save us the Lord has assumed our flesh, thereby taking on death. He rose the third day, now to die no more. In recovering the substance of flesh which had left in death he gave us for the first time a precedent of an incorruptible resurrection. Ascending to the Father in the same body, he sits at the right hand of God, and shares with the Father the power of judgment; we hope in his coming to judge the living and the dead. We believe too that we will assume the same body from the dust of our remains, the same bones, and the same members in danger of no further dissolution. We are all destined for resurrection but not all for joy. *For the day is coming in which all who are in the tombs shall hear the voice of the Son of God. And they who have done good shall come forth unto resurrection of life; but they who have done evil unto resurrection of judgment (John 5, 28-29).*] And so it will be that punishment will be added to confusion, and reward to joy: *And these will go into everlasting punishment, but the just into everlasting life (Matt. 25, 46).*

THE ONE SHEPHERD[1]

To love Christ

Behold the Lord appearing another time after the resurrection to his disciples. He questions the apostle Peter and compels him to confess his love three times, just as three times he had denied him through fear. Christ had risen in the flesh, and Peter in the Spirit. Christ died by suffering, Peter by denying. Christ the Lord is resurrected from the dead. By his love he resurrected Peter. He asked him to confess his love, and confided his sheep to him.

What did Peter offer Christ in loving him? If Christ loves you, it is you and not he that gains. The Lord Christ willingly shows man how he ought to manifest his love, when he should do so himself: in loving his sheep. This is clearly revealed in *"Do you love me? Yes. Feed my sheep."* This happens once, twice, thrice. Peter's only reply is that he loves him. Christ's only question is: Do you love me? And he entrusts nothing else to him except his sheep.

---

1. Latin text: PLS 2, 579-582: Sermon Guelferbytanus 16.

Let us love ourselves and love Christ, God from eternity was born man in time. As man born from man he appeared as man among men. As God in man he rose from the dead. He remained on earth forty days as man with men. As God in man he ascended into heaven before their eyes. And he sits at the right hand of the Father.

We believe all this without seeing it. We are bidden to love Christ, the Lord, without seeing him. And we all exclaim: I love Christ. *How can he who does not love his brother, whom he sees, love God, whom he does not see?* (I *John* 4, 20). In your love for the sheep testify to your love of the shepherd. For the sheep are the Shepherd's members. He condescended to become a sheep so that the sheep might be his members. That the sheep might be his members *like a sheep he was led to the slaughter* (*Isa.* 53, 7). That the sheep might be his members it was said of him: *Behold the lamb of God who takes away the sins of the world* (*John* 1, 29). But this lamb has great strength. Would you like to know what strength appeared in that lamb? The lamb was crucified and the lion was vanquished. See and consider with what strength Christ the Lord governs the universe, when by his death he has vanquished the devil.

We are the successors of Peter

2. Let us love him, then, so that nothing is dearer to us. Or do you think that the Lord does not address his question to us also. Did Peter alone deserve to be questioned, and not us? At this reading each Christian is being questioned in his heart. When you hear the Master saying: *Peter, do you love me?* imagine a mirror and see in it your reflection. For what else was Peter but a figure of the Church? Therefore when the Lord questioned Peter it was us that he was questioning, it was the Church. To know that Peter was a figure of the Church just recall that passage of the Gospel: *You are Peter, and upon this rock I will build my Church, and the gates of hell shall not prevail against it. And I will give you the keys of the kingdom of heaven* (*Matt.* 16, 18, 19). Only one received them. And what the keys of the kingdom of heaven are he has told us: *Whatever you shall bind on earth shall be bound in heaven; and whatever you shall loose on earth shall be loosed also in heaven* (*Matt.* 16, 19). If these words were only addressed to Peter he alone

accomplished them. He is now dead and departed. Who binds now, who looses?

I make bold to assert that we too possess the keys. What do I mean? Do I mean that we also bind and loose? Yes, you bind, you loose. For whoever is "bound," is separated from your community; and when he is separated from your community he is bound by you. And when he is reconciled he is "loosed" by you, because it is again you who pray to God on his behalf.

The One Shepherd

3. We all love Christ. We are his members. And when he commends his sheep to his shepherds, all shepherds are incorporated in the one shepherd. To understand how the whole number of shepherds is incorporated in the one shepherd consider that Peter is certainly a shepherd, clearly a shepherd. And likewise Paul. John was a shepherd, James was a shepherd, Andrew was a shepherd, and all the other apostles were shepherds. All the holy bishops are shepherds without a doubt. How then is it true that *there shall be one fold and one shepherd* (*John* 10, 16)? If it is true that there is one fold and one shepherd, then the whole countless number of pastors are all incorporated in the body of one pastor. And you are that one body, you are its members. These very members Saul was persecuting, when the head was calling for the members, Saul who was a persecutor first and later a champion, breathing threats of slaughter.

But one word dissipated all his anger. What word? *Saul, Saul, why do you persecute me?* (*Acts* 9, 4). Now surely Saul could not throw a stone to heaven, where Jesus sat? Maybe Saul was in the crowd when Jesus was hanging on the cross. Perhaps he joined his voice to the crowd which said: *crucify him, crucify him* (*Luke* 23, 21). Perhaps he was among those who were wagging their head in taunts and saying: *If he is the son of God, let him come down from the cross* (*Matt.* 27, 40, 42).

But what could he do to him who was sitting in heaven? What harm coud his words do? What harm could his shouting do? What harm could crucifying do? What harm the lance? Nothing more could happen to him and yet he cried: *Why do you persecute me?* When he said *you persecute me,* he indicated that we are his members.

Turn to the Almighty

4. Let the love of Christ, then, which we love in you and which you love in us, in spite of temptations, toils, exhaustive enterprises, cares, miseries, and groanings, lead us where there is no toil, no miseries, no groanings, no exhaustion, no anguish, no trouble, no births and no deaths, no fear of the strong man's anger, in cleaving to the face of the Almighty.

THE LOVE OF PETER[1]

You have heard Peter's confession when questioned by the Lord as you have already heard his denial when terrified by the servant girl. When he was presumptuous the words *"You will deny me"* were uttered. When he was loving he heard the words: *Do you love me?* Therefore, what led to the apostle Peter's fall was his presumption about his own strength of soul. For already the psalmist said: *They trust in their own strength* (*Ps.* 49, 7). Peter then had acted like the man sung about in the psalms: *And I said in my prosperity, I shall never be moved* (*Ps.* 30, 7). In his prosperity he had said to Christ: *I shall be with you until death;* in his abundance he had said: *I shall never be moved.* The Lord, however, like a resourceful physician, had known better than a weak human being how he would act in his weakness. For physicians act in physical conditions as the Lord can in weaknesses of soul. For why does it seem astonishing to you, I ask you, that a sick man waits to be told by his physician what is wrong with him? He indeed can know what ails him; but whether his pains are dangerous or not, or what caused them, and whether they are curable or not, (to learn this) the doctor inspects his pulse, and gives the sick man a report on his trouble. When, then, the Lord said to blessed Peter *"You will thrice deny me,"* he touched the beat of his heart.

His repentance

Thus the prediction of the physician was realized and the confidence of the sick man was proved false. The Holy Spirit says in the same psalm: *I said in my prosperity; I shall never*

---

1. Latin text: PLS 2, 582-585: Sermon Morin Guelferbytanus 17.

be moved, thus presuming on his own strength. But he soon
adds: *Lord, in your good pleasure you added strength to my
beauty; but you turned away your face and I was troubled*
(*Ps.* 30, 8). What did he mean? What I had I had without you,
and I believed it was from myself. You then turned away your
face; you took back your favors and I was troubled. I discovered
my true self when you withdrew yourself.

So the Lord deserted Peter for a while to teach him a salutary
lesson in humility. And when he looked at him again, Peter wept.
That is what we read in the Gospel: after he denied him thrice
and the Lord's prediction was fulfilled, what do we read? *The
Lord looked at him and Peter remembered that Jesus had said
to him: Before the cock crows you shall deny me thrice. And
going out he wept bitterly* (*Luke* 22, 61, 62). There was need for
Peter to wash away his sin of denial in a baptism of tears. But
from where would he have got this if the Lord had not granted
it to him? And so the Apostle Paul advises the people how they
should deal with those in dissent, saying: *gently admonishing
those who resist in case God should give them repentance* (II *Tim.*
2, 25). Thus repentance is a gift of God. The heart of the haughty
is rough ground: it is not softened for repentance unless it is
moistened by the grace of God.

Peter, do you love me?

2. After his resurrection, then, the Lord interrogates Peter:
his confession is elicited and his death announced. His love is
revealed and he is confirmed in virtue. The Lord says to him
after his resurrection: *Peter, do you love me more than these?*
You who denied me, do you love me? You have had your fill;
you see him alive whom you saw dying when you were afraid to
die. Behold, I live; here I am. Why were you afraid to die?
When you denied me you did not lose me. Do you love me?
Because here I am! And Peter said: *Yes, Lord, you know that I
love you.* Why do you ask me what you know? You knew it
when you foretold my denial to me. What I myself did not know,
you knew. And do you not know what I know? For I see in my
heart that I love you, and you see it too: for it is impossible that
you, who saw my future fear, do not see my present love. And
again the Lord knows, and he asks; and again Peter makes the
same response to the same question. And the Lord asked him a

third time so that his triple denial might be obliterated by his triple confession. Let us congratulate the apostle: *for he was dead and has come to life again; he was lost and is found (Luke 15, 32).*

Feed my sheep

3. He arms him for greater and more difficult combats: *Feed my sheep;* what he had to endure in the flesh would contribute to his spiritual glory. For in feeding the sheep of Christ how great would his sufferings be for Christ's name. *Feed my sheep, feed my lambs (John 21, 15-17).* What would you give me if you loved me? The prince of pastors made Peter a pastor that he might feed the sheep of Christ, not his own. For some people who wanted to be disciples of the apostles were recalled to their senses by the apostles themselves. They were Christ's sheep but wished to belong to mere men: *I am of Paul, or I am of Apollos, or I am of Cephas (I Cor. 1, 12).* But there were some who recognized their master: *I am of Christ.* Paul, knowing that Christ had confided his sheep to his apostles, denied that he had any sheep of his own: he confessed that he was not the Lord so that he might remain faithful to the Lord: *Was Paul crucified for you? Or were you baptized in the name of Paul?* (*I Cor. 1, 13*). You are his sheep and you do not know whose sheep you are. Recognize the marks that have been branded on you. *Feed my sheep.* Why? Because you love me, because you are enamored of me, I commit my sheep to you. Feed them, but remember that they are mine. The authors of heresy wish to make Christ's sheep their own; but whether they like it or not, they are compelled to put the seal of Christ on them; to make them belong to Christ and to inscribe on the sheep the Master's name. But what does the Sacred Scripture say to such men in the Canticle of Canticles? The spouse, Christ, calls the Church his bride and says: *If you know not yourself, you fair one among women (Cant. 1, 8).*

What is *the fair one among women?* The Catholic Church among the heresies. Hear how she is threatened. If you do not know yourself, whose you are, what you believe, to whom you belong, how far and wide you are extended, by whose blood you have been redeemed, if you know not yourself, you fair one among women, if you do not know yourself, I reject you, *go forth* (*Cant.* 1, 8). What means, *"go forth"?* John tells us in his Epistle: *they have gone forth from us but they were not of us* (I *John* 2, 19). *Go forth in the footsteps of the flocks* (*Cant.* 1, 8); not in the footsteps of the shepherd, but in the footsteps of the flocks: by following the footsteps of men, and not of Christ. *And feed your kids,* not like Peter, *my sheep.* And where is this *feed your kids? By the shepherds' tents* (*Cant.* 1, 8). There is division in the shepherds' tents, not in the shepherd's tent. *And other sheep I have that are not of this fold. Them also I must bring, and they shall hear my voice, and there shall be one fold and one shepherd* (*John* 10, 16).

Return to Christ's flock

4. I announce to you, dear brethren, that my severity with you yesterday was not in vain. My harsh remonstrances have had full effect. One of those four has today abjured the Arian and Eunomian heresy along with Arius and Eunomius, and become Catholic. And so the one I put you on your guard against yesterday, deserves your affection today. And so I commend to you him whom you look upon now in joy and without suspicion. I also commend the others to your prayers.

THE DAY THAT THE LORD HAS MADE[1]
(On Psalm 117, 24: *"This is the day the Lord has made;*
Let us be glad and rejoice in it.")

1. The Lord has made every day, and not merely has made, but continues to make. For he makes the day when *he makes his sun rise on the evil and on the good and sends rain on the just and on the unjust* (*Matt.* 5, 45). This regular day, common to the good and the wicked, is not what is referred to in the text which says: *This is the day which the Lord has made.* For he is speaking of some more illustrious day and fastens our attention on some special day when he says: *This is the day which the Lord has made.* What a wonderful day it must be when it is said: *let us be glad and rejoice in it.* It must be good; it must be desirable, lovable, delectable, a day such as holy Jeremiah

---

1. Latin text: PLS 2, 556-558, Sermon Morin Guelferbytanus 8.

said: *Nor have I desired the day of man, you know* (*Jer.* 17, 16).
What kind, then, is this day which the Lord has made? Live
well and you will be that day. For the apostle was not simply
thinking of the day that lasts from sunrise to sunset when he says:
Let us conduct ourselves becomingly as in the day (*Rom.* 13, 13).
Nor when he says: *For they who are drunk, are drunk at night*
(*I Thess.* 5, 7). No one sees men drunk at lunchtime; drunkenness occurs at night, not in the day which the Lord has made.
Just as day exists in those who live a holy and religious life, in
temperance, justice, and sobriety, likewise, on the other hand,
there will certainly be night — the night of which Scripture
speaks of those who live luxuriously, in a spirit of haughtiness
and irreligion, for it is written: *the day of the Lord will come
like a thief in the night* (*I Thess.* 5, 2). When the apostle gave
this testimony, he meant it for those to whom he had elsewhere
said: *for once you were darkness, but now you are light in the
Lord* (*Eph.* 5, 8). And when the day that the Lord has made is
made, he turned to those to whom he had said: *You know,
brethren, that the day of the Lord will come like a thief in the
night.* He said to them: *But you are not in darkness for that day
to surprise you like a thief. For you are all sons of light and sons
of the day; we are not of the night or of darkness* (*I Thess.* 5, 4-5).

Our hymn, then, exalts the good life. When we all exclaim in
harmony, with joy of spirit and heartfelt accord *"This is the day
which the Lord has made";* let us be in harmony lest our lips
testify against our conduct. If you intend to get drunk on the
day and you say: *This is the day which the Lord has made,* are
you not afraid to hear the reply: "The Lord did not make this
day? And you dare to call that day good which debauchery
appropriates and wickedness corrupts." ·

A joy which never fails

2. See what joy, brethren, the joy in your assembly, the joy
in chanting psalms and hymns, the joy of evoking Christ's passion
and resurrection, the joy of hope in life everlasting. And if mere
hope causes such joy, how great will be the joy of realization?
These are the days when we hear "Alleluia" and our spirit is
somehow transformed. Do we not get a certain foretaste of that
city on high? If these days cause us such joy how great will the

joy of that day be when we hear: *Come ye blessed of my Father, take possession of the kingdom* (*Mt.* 25, 34). Then all the saints will be assembled together, seeing themselves as they had never been seen before, and knowing themselves as they had never known. Their union there will be so close that no friend will be lost or no enemy ever feared.

For behold we chant "Alleluia." It is good, it is joyful, it is full of joy, grace and tenderness. Nevertheless we would tire if we were to say it always. When it recurs but once a year, how we delight when it returns and miss it when it stops! Surely will we not have a sense of regret as well as of joy in heaven? No. Perhaps someone will say: How can there always be joy and never weariness? Yet I can show an instance in this life where there is no growing tired, you will believe that in the next life it will all be like that. We can get too much to eat, too much to drink, too much entertainment, too much of this or that, but we can never get too much good health. So then in this life with its mortal flesh, its frailty, its tedium, if there cannot be too much good health, then in heaven we can never have too much of love, or immortality, or eternity.

THE NEW CHANT[1]

1. We are admonished to sing a new chant to the Lord. The new man knows this new chant. The chant is the expression of joy, and on reflection it is also an expression of love. The one then who knows how to love the new life knows how to sing this new song. We must learn what the new life is to learn what the new song is. All things belong to the one realm: the new man, the new song, the New Testament. Therefore the new man will both know the new chant and belong to the New Testament.

We love him because he loves us

2. There is no one who does not love. But whom does one love? There is no question of us stopping loving, but only choosing the object of our love. Or do we choose if we are first chosen. We do not love him if we are not loved first by him. Hear what

---

1. Latin text: PL 38, 210-213. Sermon 34 on Ps. 149.

the apostle John says, he who leaned on his Master's breast and at Supper imbibed the secrets of heaven. This drink, this blessed intoxication inspired him with the word: *in the beginning was the word* (*John* 1, 1). Sublime simplicity! Spiritual intoxication! But this man, full of inspiration, this pent-up preacher among the other secrets learned at the heart of his master produces this one: *We love him who has first loved us* (I *John* 4, 10). It was to accord too much to say in speaking of God: *we love.* We, him? Men, God? Mortals, the eternal? Sinners, the Just one? Frail beings, the immutable? Creatures the Creator? We love the beloved! And how can we? Because he has first loved us. Seek for the reason why man can love God and the only one you will find is this: God has first loved us. He whom we love gives himself. He gives himself that we may love him. Why has he given himself for us to love him? The Apostle Paul will tell us clearly: *The love of God is poured forth in our hearts* (*Rom.* 5, 5). By whom? Is it by us? No. By whom, then? *By the Holy Spirit who has been given to us.*

God the creator

3. On such great authority let us love God through God. Since the Holy Spirit is God let us love God through God. What more can I say? Let us love God through God. *The love of God is poured forth in our hearts by the Holy Spirit who has been given to us.* And since the Holy Spirit is God and we can only love God through the Holy Spirit it is clear that we love God through God. The conclusion is inescapable. John puts it even more precisely for us: *God is love and he who abides in love abides in God and God in him* (*John* 4, 8), that is to say, love comes from God.

Now what one of us will hesitate to repeat this word: *God is love?* It has been uttered by one who knew what he possessed. Why does the imagination of man, why does his fickle spirit represent God to him, why do they fashion an idol for his heart? Why give him an imaginary God in place of the real God whom he deserves to find? Is that God there? No, but he is here. Why do they sketch details of him? Why do they outline his members? Why trace these gracious lines? Why indulge in fantasies about the beauty of his body? God is love. How do you fashion and delineate that? We see nothing of it and yet we love.

Love is invisible

4. I venture to say to your Charity:[2] seek below what we would discover above. Love that is itself humble and lowly, love that is squalid and disgraceful and only concerned with physical love — that love, I maintain, urges and elevates us to nobler and better sentiments. A sensual wastrel may love a woman of outstanding beauty. He is disturbed by her bodily grace but inwardly he seeks a response to his fondness. Suppose he realizes that this woman hates him? All his fever, all the transports occasioned by her admirable traits collapse. For this being who fascinated him he now feels loathing. He becomes estranged, filled as he is with anger, and the object of his affection now begins to fill him with hatred. Has her body changed? Have her charms vanished? No. But he ardently desired what he saw, and demanded from the heart a sentiment which he did not see. Suppose, on the other hand, that he experienced a reciprocity of love? How his ardor would redouble. She sees him, he sees her, but nobody sees love and yet it is love though invisible which is loved.

To love God is to possess him

5. Get rid of those treacherous desires and abide in the pure light of love. You do not see God. Love him and you will possess him. So many goods, objects of base desires, are loved without being possessed. They are eagerly coveted but they cannot be possessed immediately. Does love of gold give us possession of it? Many love it but do not possess it. Does loving large and wealthy estates guarantee possessing them? Many love them but do not possess them. Does loving honors mean that we attain to them? Many are without them and yearn to have them. They exert themselves but generally their efforts are not crowned with success. But God offers himself to us first. Love me, he exclaims, and you will possess me. You cannot love me without possessing me.

A chant of praise

6. O brothers. O sons. O Catholic offshoots. O holy, celestial plants, O you who are regenerated in Jesus Christ and born in

---

2. Your Charity, like Your Holiness, was often used by St. Augustine in addressing his hearers.

heaven, listen to me, or rather hear from me the words: *Sing to the Lord a new chant.* Good, you say. I am singing. Yes, you are singing. I hear you. But let not your life belie your words. Sing with the voice, sing with the heart, sing with the mouth, but sing with your whole life: *sing to the Lord a new song.* But how should you sing of that which you love? Doubtless it is what you love that you wish to sing of. You would like to know his glory to sing of it. You have heard the words: *Sing to the Lord a new song.* You want to know what is his glory? *His glory is the assembly of the saints.* The glory of him who is sung about is nothing other than the one who sings about it. Become yourself the glory that you sing of. You are his glory if you lead the good life. For his glory is not in the synagogue of the Jews; it is not in the follies of the pagans; it is not in the errors of the heretics; it is not in the plaudits of the theatre. Do you search for where it is? Cast your glances on yourselves. Be his glory yourselves. *His glory is in the assembly of the saints.* Do you know the origin of your joy when you sing? *Let Israel rejoice in him who made it,* and Israel has found no joy other than God.

The price of love

7. Examine yourselves well, brethren. Pull down your interior barns. Open your eyes. Take stock of your store of love and augment what you will discover there. Watch over your treasures so that you may enrich yourselves. Goods are called dear which cost a high price and not by accident. Carefully note the expression — this is dearer than that. What means "is dearer"? Doesn't it mean "costs more"? If everything that is costly is called "is dearer" how dear is love itself, brethren? What does it cost in your terms? And how do you pay for it? You pay for wheat with money, for land with silver, for a gem with gold. The price of your love is yourself. If you wanted to buy a field, a gem, a beast of burden, and pay for it, you look to your estate, you look outside yourself. But if you want to possess love, do not search beyond yourself, do not find anything but yourself. What do you fear in giving yourself? Losing yourself? On the contrary it is in giving yourself that you avoid losing yourself. Love itself expresses itself in Wisdom and calms your confusion when this word reaches you: *Give me yourself.* For if a man wished to sell you a field he would say to you: Give me your

gold; or for something else, give me your money, give me your silver. Hear what Love tells you by the mouth of Wisdom: *My son, give me your heart (Prov. 23, 26)*. What? *Your heart*. When it was in you, when it was yours, it was bad. You were preyed on by frustrations, impure and destructive passions. Away from there!

Give me your heart. Let it be mine and you will not lose it. Take note: do you wish to leave nothing in yourself to make you more dear to yourself? *You shall love the Lord your God with your whole heart, and your whole soul, and your whole mind (Matt. 22, 37)*. What remains to you of your heart with which you can love yourself? What remains of your soul? And of your mind? "With it all" it says. He demands everything of you — he who has made you. But do not feel sorry for yourself, as if all joy were dead in you. *Let Israel rejoice*, not in itself but *in him who made it*.

What means to love oneself?

8. But you will answer: if nothing remains of me for me to love seeing that I am bound to love my maker with all my heart, all my soul and all my mind, how can I obey the second commandment which commands me to love my neighbor as myself? That is all the more reason you should love your neighbor with all your heart, all your soul, and all your mind. How? *You shall love your neighbor as yourself*. God is to be loved with all myself; my neighbor as myself. How do I love myself? How do you love yourself? Do you wish to know how to love yourself? This is the way: by loving God with all yourself. Do you think you help God in loving him? To what is the love applied that you bring him? And if you do not love him what will he lose? It is you who gains by loving him. You will attain immortality. But, your objection continues, am I not to love myself? No, no. You did not love yourself when you did not love God who made you. You hated yourself. You only thought that you were loving yourself. *He who loves violence hates his soul (Ps. 11, 5)*.

9. Addressing ourselves to God our Lord and Father almighty let us give exceeding thanks with a pure and grateful heart to the best of our poor ability. Beseeching his incomparable goodness with all our heart that he may deign to hear our prayers

and to keep far from us by his power what is inimical to our thoughts and actions, to increase our faith, direct our soul, inspire us with spiritual thoughts and lead us to his joy. Through Jesus Christ his son our Lord who lives and reigns with him in the unity of the Holy Spirit, God, for ever and ever. Amen.

ALLELUIA[1]

1. Since it has pleased the Lord our God to allow me to be physically present here, let us join in your charity, let us join with you in singing Alleluia, which in Latin means "Praise the Lord." Brethren, let us praise the Lord, in our life and on our lips, in heart and on mouth, by word and deed. God wants our "Praise the Lord" to be said without any lack of harmony in the one who praises: let what is in our life and on our lips then be harmonized in ourselves first; let our inner conscience square with our outer protestations, let our deeds, I say, match our words, lest our fine words be belied by evil conduct.

O blessed "Alleluia" in heaven where the angels are the temple of God. There, agreement is perfect among those praising God, joy is assured among those who chant; they have not to contend with the conflict between the law of the mind and the other law in the members; they have no struggle of concupiscence, in which the victory of charity is at stake. Here and now let us chant "Alleluia" with concern so that there we may chant it with complete freedom from care.

Why do I say "with concern"? How can I not be concerned when I read: *Is not man's life on earth a drudgery?* (*Job* 7, 1) How can I not be concerned when I read: *Watch and pray that you may not enter into temptation?* (*Mark* 14, 38) How can I not be concerned when temptations are so numerous that they force us to pray in these terms: *Forgive us our trespasses as we forgive those who trespass against us* (*Mark* 6, 12). Every day we ask forgiveness, every day we contract debts.

How can I not be concerned when every day I ask pardon for my sins, rescue in danger? For past sins I say: *Forgive us our trespasses as we forgive those who trespass against us,* but I

---

1. Latin text: PL 38, 1190-1193. Sermon 256.

add also, in view of the dangers that lie ahead, *and lead us not into temptation.* Does the Christian people possess happiness since it cries with me, *deliver us from evil?*

Brethren, in the midst of this evil let us chant "Alleluia" to the good God, who delivers us from evil. Why do you look outside yourself for what he would deliver you from, when he delivers you from evil? Do not go so far, do not let your gaze wander afar, look into yourself, examine yourself. You are the evil yourself. God delivers you from evil when he delivers you from yourself. Listen to the Apostle, who tells you from what evil he has to deliver you: *For I am delighted with the law of God according to the inner man, but I see another law in my members warring against the law of my mind and making me prisoner to the law of sin which is —* Where is it — *making me prisoner to the law of sin which is in my members* (Rom. 7, 22-23). I believed you would see a prisoner of some unknown barbarians, of some strange peoples, of some human masters? *Who is in my members.* Cry then with him: *Unhappy man that I am. Who is going to deliver me?* Deliver me from what? From whom? One asks to be delivered from the executioner, another from prison, this one from the oppression of barbarians, that one from fever and from some malady. Tell us, Apostle, not where we cannot be sent or led, but that which we carry in ourselves. What we ourselves are: *a body of death* (Rom. 7, 24). Yes, *a body of death.*

Awaiting deliverance

2. Another objects: the body of this death does not belong to me; it is my temporary prison, it keeps me in confinement for a time. I am in this body of death, but I am not a body of death. You argue but you are not liberated. I am, you say, a spirit. I am not flesh, I am in flesh. After I am freed from the flesh, what further business will I have with it? Who, brethren, would you have answer your argument, the Apostle or myself? If I answer myself the unworthiness of the minister may minimize the worth of the response. I prefer to say nothing on my own. But listen to the words of the Apostle of the Gentiles. Hear the vessel of election, put an end to your controversial argument. Hear, but repeat first what you have been saying. Your words were: I am

not flesh, but spirit. I groan in my prison; I will depart in freedom
when these bonds, this captivity has been dissolved. Dust returns to dust, spirit to heaven. I go, and what is not me is left
behind. Aren't those your words? Yes, you say.

I will not answer you myself. But let you answer, Apostle.
Answer, I beg you. You preached to be heard. You wrote to be
read, and everything was done to help belief. Speak: *who will
deliver me from this body of death? The grace of God by our
Lord Jesus Christ.* Liberate you from where? *From the body
of this death.*

But, aren't you yourself "the body of this death"? He answers:
*I myself with my mind serve the law of God but with my flesh
the law of sin* (Rom. 7, 25). Me, he says. Would you be different
from him? With the mind, he says, because I love. By the flesh
because I desire. I overcome provided I do not consent, but I
must beat myself and the enemy besieging me.

Once delivered from this flesh, Apostle, will you be spirit?
Freed with death, this debt which is inescapable, the Apostle
replies, I do not dispose of the flesh for ever.

You will return then in this body of death? But why? Listen
further to him. How can you return in this body from which
you have so fervently demanded to be liberated? It is true, he
replies, that I will return in this body, but not in this body of
death. Listen, you ignorant fellow, you who block your ears to
what is read to you each day. Hear how you return in this body,
but not in this body of death. This will not be another body but
*this corruptible body must put on incorruption and this mortal
body must put on immortality* (I Cor. 15, 33). My brothers,
when the Apostle speaks of a corruptible body, of a mortal body
he means his own body. Not some other body.

I do not put off the earthly body to take a body made of air
or ethereal substance. I take the same body, but not *of death.
This body* — not another one — *when this mortal body puts on
immortality then shall come to pass the word that is written:
Death is swallowed up in victory* (I Cor. 15, 54).

Let us chant Alleluia. Then the word of Scripture will be
accomplished, the word not of combatants any more, but of
victors; *Death has been swallowed up in victory.*

Let us chant Alleluia. *O death, where is your sting?*

Let us chant Alleluia. *The sting of death is sin* (I Cor. 15, 56).
You will seek its place and will not find it. (Ps. 37, 10).

Alleluia on the journey

3. Let us chant "Alleluia" here in the midst of dangers and temptations, we and the others. *God is faithful,* says the Apostle, *he will not allow us to be tempted above our ability* (I *Cor.* 10, 13). Let us then chant "Alleluia." Man is blameworthy but God is faithful. He does not say "He will not permit you to be tempted" but "he will not permit you to be tempted above your ability." *With the temptation he will also give you a way out that you may be able to bear it.* You have entered into a temptation. God arranges a way out so that you may not succumb. Preaching molds you like the potter's vase; the temptation hardens you. In entering think of the way out for God is faithful: *the Lord guards your going in and your coming out* (*Ps.* 121, 8).

Once this body becomes immortal and incorruptible all temptation will cease. For *it is a body of death.* Why is it death? *Because of sin.* But *the spirit is life,* says the Apostle. Why? *Because of justice.* Are we going then to regain this body of death? No. Listen: *If the spirit of him who has raised Christ from the dead lives in you he who has raised Christ from the dead will give life to your mortal body* (*Rom.* 8, 10-11). Today, animal, tomorrow spiritual. *The first man was a physical being endowed with life, the second will be a living spirit. He will give life to our mortal bodies because of the Spirit who dwells in you* (I *Cor.* 15, 45).

O blessed Alleluia of heaven! No more anguish, no more adversity. No more enemy. No more love of destruction. Up above, praise to God, and here below, praise to God. Praise mingled with fear here, but without disturbance above. Here the one who chants must die, but there he will live for ever. Here he chants in hope, there, in possession; here it is Alleluia *en route,* there it is Alleluia on arriving home.

Today let us chant, brethren, no longer to entice repose, but to lighten our burden. Chant as a man on a journey, but keep time. Chant to sustain your effort, do not cultivate laziness. Chant and march. What do I mean, "March"? Progress, make progress in good. For there are those, as the Apostle tells us (cf. II *Tim.* 3, 13) who make progress in evil.

As for you, march to make progress to advance in goodness, to progress in integrity of faith, and in purity of life. Chant and march, without straying, without going back, without marking time.

MAXIMUS OF TURIN
(† 408-420)

Like all the sermons of the bishop of Turin the three texts which are published here take the form of short, concentrated meditations which reveal Maximus, in Altaner's phrase, as "a truly popular preacher."[1] Here theological reflection is in fact sacrificed. The preaching confines itself to a development of the ancient Christian symbolism which identified Christ with day and Satan with darkness.

But Maximus is a poet and mystic and his paschal vision is enriched by all the requirements of an ardent sensibility, of a rather uncommon sense of the universal.

.What is the resurrection of Christ? Not just the exceptional destiny of a man who was God but the wholesale entry of man into a new life: "The Lord is risen and gives resurrection to the whole world." The resurrection of God coincides with that of the resurrection of the universe. That is what underlies the whole paschal vision of the bishop of Turin. One can see from that in what sense Maximus uses the symbol of Christ as the Light of Day. Day in the thought of Maximus is the finest expression for Christ eternal and omnipresent. Nothing resists his rays. As a being more creative than man, a force of the life of the universe, the days of which Maximus speaks unfolds itself throughout creation, "embraces" every being, passes beyond the limits of the world which it has already brightened to conquer spaces which have not yet come within its domain. A day which is "everywhere" but which is also "without end," and which the darkness cannot terminate or reduce to darkness. Maximus discovers in it a new fulfillment, that of time. In that day displaces night for ever it creates a new dimension of time for mankind. Time was hitherto a matter of succession, alternating amid opposites of shadow and light, divided into past, present and future. This

---

1. **Patrology**, New York 1961, p. 545.

changed at the resurrection, becoming a continuous present, an eternal today. The world and mankind enter through it into God's own time which is unbroken and perfect. In sermon 36 we will read the wonderful meditation on the entry of this new time into human life — God's today.

This day, which is the risen Christ, once again only exists for and through the renewal of the world. What is this renewal of the world to which it is joined? A massive rising of the dead, but also the common momentum which lifts up all of creation and takes it along to the heaven of paschal joy. "Opened up, hell yields up its dead; renewed, earth causes the risen to blossom forth, and heaven once opened welcomes those who ascend to it." Nothing escapes from this day; nothing escapes from this elevation of all things to eternal blessedness. "In one and the same movement the Lord's passion takes the dead from the abyss, raises them from the earth, and confirms them in the heights of heaven. Christ's resurrection is life for the dead, pardon for sinners, and glory for the saints." A vision of a world in change which is reminiscent of the lyricism of an Agrippa of Aubigné.

But the Latin Maximus has not merely experienced the Pasch as a visionary: cosmic fusion and incandescence. To an epic and cosmic style is added a most intimately felt experience. This interior resurrection is described for us in sermon 58 as a passage from age to infancy. Infancy, the source of life, the bond of strength and virtues, is here the interior rendering of the renewal of the world to which the eternal light comes to give purity and vigor. The very intimate poetry to which birth inspires Maximus inevitably makes us reflect on the sermon[2] of Peter Chrysologus devoted to the same theme. There is the same feeling in the presence of the newly born's grace, the same emotion in presence of his innocence. It is there no doubt that the two Fathers are most closely joined and base their common originality. Let us not conclude from that to an identity of paschal vision in them. On the contrary, in this they differ profoundly. For the one the Pasch is a confrontation, a long and difficult quest. For the other it is an irresistible union of God and man, a joyous and total blossoming of man in the radiance of eternity.

---

2. **Sermon on the Epiphany**, PL 50, 30.

THE JOY OF CREATION
(Homily 57:[1] on Psalm 14)

The Psalm of David

1. Brethren, it is not by chance that we read today this Psalm in which the prophet bids us rejoice and be glad. For holy David invites all of creation to today's festivity. Today, by Christ's resurrection, the gates of hell are opened, the earth is renewed by the neophytes of the Church, heaven is reached by the Holy Spirit. Hell once opened yields up its dead, the renewed earth raises up the dead, heaven made blessed receives those ascending to it.

Then the thief ascends to paradise, the bodies of the saints enter the holy city, the dead return to life, and by progressing in the resurrection of Christ they raise themselves to all the higher elements. Hell yields up its inhabitants to the upper regions, earth sends its buried to heaven, heaven presents its new arrivals to the Lord, and by one and the same operation the passion of the Savior elevates from the abyss, raises from the earth and confirms in the highest heavens. For Christ's resurrection is life for the dead, pardon for sinners, and glory for the saints. Therefore, holy David invites the whole of creation to the celebration of Christ's resurrection, for he says that we should rejoice and be glad on that day which the Lord has made.

The whole universe ought to celebrate

2. But, you may say, if congratulations are in order on the day, the ones to congratulate are those whom the day itself embraces: but heaven and hell are constituted outside this world's "day." How then can those elements be called to the celebration of this day which are not' within its ambit? But "this day" which the Lord has made penetrates all things, contains all things, and embraces heaven, earth, and hell. For the light of Christ is not obstructed by walls, nor divided by elements, nor obscured by darkness. Christ's light, I say, is a day without night, a day without end; it is everywhere resplendent, everywhere radiant, everywhere unfailing.

---

1. Latin text: CC (Ser. Lat) 23, 214-216.

This day is Christ

That this day is Christ the Apostle says: *The night has passed; the day however has approached.* "Night," it says "has passed," not "follows," so that you may know that the diabolical darkness is put to flight by the intervention of Christ's light, and that the darkness of sins does not follow, that the mists of the past are dissipated by the yoke of splendor, and surreptitious crimes are prevented. For Scripture testifies that Christ this day shed his light on heaven, on earth, and on hell. John tells us that he shone on the earth: *He was the true light which illuminated every man coming into the world* (*John* 1, 9). The prophet tells us that he shone in hell: *Upon those who sat in the region of the shadow of death a light has shone* (*Isa.* 9, 1). And David tells us that this day endured in the heavens, saying: *His posterity shall continue for ever, and his throne shall be like heaven's day before me* (*Ps.* 88, 37). What is this heavenly day except Christ the Lord concerning whom it is said through the prophet: *Day pours out the word to day* (*Ps.* 19. 3). For this day is the Son to whom the Father poured out the secret day of his divinity. It is this day, I claim, who says through Solomon: *I made that in the heavens there should rise light that never fails* (*Ecclus.* 24, 6). Just then as night does not at all follow the day of heaven, so the darkness of sins does not at all follow the justice of Christ. For the day of heaven is always shining, is always resplendent, is always refulgent and cannot be hedged in by any darkness; likewise the light of Christ always gleams, always radiates, always shines, and cannot be darkened by any fog of sin, whence the evangelist John says: *And the light shines in the darkness and the darkness did not engulf it* (*John* 1, 5).

The sun's grief and joy

3. In the resurrection of Christ, then, all the elements get glory. For I think that the sun itself is brighter on this glorious day. It is necessary that the sun should rejoice at the resurrection of him at whose death it was saddened; and that it should welcome him alive with a brighter burst of light whose death it shrouded with a mourning veil of mist; and as a good servant it then was draped in mourning for the burial rites, so now it

should shine in observing the resurrection. For during the passion of Christ it enveloped itself in the mist of night, and bewailed the deed of the Jews as the world can testify. The sun indicated its grief at such a crime by refusing to shed its light, and it poured darkness on the Jews' eyes as a sort of vengeance, that darkness might seize the eyes of those whose minds were already blinded, and that the light of the world might not shine for them in whom the light of salvation was extinguished. A sort of damnation, then, descended on the Pharisees so that they might suffer in advance on earth the darkness at the day of judgment promised to sinners. And so darkness prevailed on the earth at the crucifixion of Christ. Small wonder that there was darkness in the world since the light had descended to the underworld.

A perfect joy

4. Therefore, brethren, let us all rejoice on this holy day. Let no one, in his consciousness of being a sinner, withdraw himself from the common rejoicing. Let no one be called back from the public prayers by the burden of his crimes. However much a sinner one is, he must not despair of forgiveness on this day; for there is no small precedent. If the thief entered paradise, why won't the Christian deserve forgiveness? And if the Lord showed mercy to the thief at his crucifixion, will he not be much more merciful at his resurrection, and if the lowliness of suffering bestowed so much on one who trusted, how much more will the glory of resurrection bestow on him who prays? For as you yourselves know, the joy of victory is more generous in largess than the confines of captivity.

THE BIRTH OF FAITH[1]
The Pasch is the rejuvenation of men

Brethren, God has granted us a great and marvelous gift of faith. On the Pasch, the day of salvation, he has risen and granted resurrection to all. Rising from the depths to the heights himself, he has raised us too on high. For all of us Christians, the Apostle says, are the body of Christ and his members. In

---

1. Latin text: CC 23, 218-219, sermon 54.

Christ's resurrection all of necessity have raised their vitals with him. In passing from hell to heaven he has caused us to pass from death to life. The Pasch in Hebrew means "passage" or "departure," doubtless because through this mystery there is a passage from evil to good. It is a good passage to pass from sin to justice, from vice to virtue, from infancy to old age, I refer to infancy of simplicity, not of years. For virtue too has its ages. By our previous falls we were established in the seniority of sin, but by Christ's resurrection we were renewed in the innocence of little children.

Faith in Jesus Christ is an infancy

For Christian simplicity also has its infancy; just as an infant does not know how to be angry, or cheat, or does not dare to strike back, so also among Christians infancy is not perturbed by those who do us injuries, or does not offer resistance to or does not fight against those who kill. In a word, as the Lord has ordered, it even prays for its enemy, lets go its shirt to those who would take its coat, offers the other cheek to one slapping it on the face, except that in this Christ's infancy is better than normal infancy: the latter does not know how to sin, the former rises above it, the latter is harmless through weakness, the former is innocent through virtue. And so he is more praiseworthy in being not so much incapable of committing sin as unwilling to commit it.

And so, as we have said, there are ages in merit. For the young can be found morally mature, and the old are sometimes as innocent as children. In fine, the prophet tells us that there is a certain ageing of honesty in the young, saying: *For the age that is honorable comes not with the passing of time, nor can it be measured in terms of years. Rather, understanding is the hoary crown for men* (Wisd. 4, 8). But the Lord said to the apostles already well on in years: *Unless you return and become like this little child you will not enter into the Kingdom of Heaven* (Matt. 18, 3). He recalls them then to the source of their beginning, so that of course, though old and fragile in body, they might be reborn in innocence of character, as the Savior says: *unless a man be born again of water and the spirit he cannot enter the Kingdom of God* (John 3, 5). Therefore, the apostles are told, *unless you return and become like this little child*. He does not say "like these little children" but "like this little child," he selects and proposes just one.

Jesus Himself is the Child

Let us see, then, who is so great as to be proposed for imitation to the disciples. I do not think this is an ordinary individual, a man in the street, one of the multitude, especially as he is proposed as an example of sanctity to the whole world through the apostles. As I say, I do not think he is from the street, but from heaven. For he is the boy from Heaven of whom Isaiah, the prophet, spoke: *For a child is born to us, a son is given us* (*Isa.* 9, 5). Assuredly he like an innocent boy did not curse back when he was cursed, did not strike back when he was struck, nay rather during his very passion he prayed for his enemies saying: *Father, forgive them, for they know not what they do* (*Luke* 23, 34). So, the simplicity, which is nature's gift to the young, was crowned with goodness by the Lord of mercy. Therefore, he is the boy who is to be imitated and followed, and proposed as such to youth, for he says: *Take up your cross and follow me* (*Matt.* 16, 24).

TODAY[1]

Man's today

Brethren, today as yesterday let us celebrate our joy. If the shadows of night have interrupted our celebrations, it is nonetheless the same day of celebration. The darkness of evening separates day and night, but the brightness which suffuses the joy of the Lord is eternal. Christ gave us illumination yesterday; today again we are in the warm glow of his presence. *Jesus Christ is the same yesterday and today* (*Heb.* 13, 8), says the blessed Apostle.

Yes, for us he has made this day. For us this day is born, as God his father announced by the voice of David: *You are my son, today I have begotten you* (*Ps.* 2, 7). That is to say, not

---

1. Latin text: PL 57, 605-607, sermon 36.

that he has begotten his son in the day, but that he has begotten the Son himself like day and light. And so today when Christ the only begotten is born, we discover in the coming of this Savior not so much a man being born as a brightness which shines on the world and illuminates all.

This is called "today" because like a living, unfailing splendor, it does not cease to inflame the world in perpetual light and because this unceasing flame seems to be one uninterrupted day. *A thousand years are in your sight as one day* (Ps. 89, 4), writes the prophet. Yes, Christ is clearly this one day, because the eternity of divinity in him is one.

It is our "today": the past, by reason of antiquity, does not escape him; and the future, which is unknown, has no secrets for him. But like a sovereign light, he contains all things, he knows all things, he is ever present and possesses all things. Before him the past cannot escape, and the future cannot hide. And when God said to his Son, *Today I have begotten you,* understand that this "today" is not the time in his humanity when he was born of Virgin Mary, nor in his divinity when he proceeded from the mouth of God, his Father, but the time when he rose from the dead. *He has raised up the Lord Jesus Christ,* says the Apostle Paul, *as also it is written in the second Psalm, you are my son, this day have I begotten you* (Acts 13, 33).

Truly, then, this is our "today" when he rises from the dense night of hell to illumine men like a bright light. That is rightly called day when the black deed of the Jews could not obscure. And nothing could be better than for today to accept the light; he has restored day and salvation to all the dead; by the presence of life today he has raised up men long dissolved in death.

The kiss of peace

Brethren, let us rejoice then and be glad on this day on which the Lord has brought us light, salvation and peace. For by rising, I say, Christ has brought us peace because when he was about to suffer he did not deny peace to the disciple who was a traitor; he gave the kiss of peace to faithful and renegade alike. For I would not have you think that the kiss to Judas Iscariot was inspired by any sentiment other than tenderness; the Savior already knew that he would betray him. He knew obviously that this kiss was a pledge of love, yet he did not deny it to him, for it is the mark of love not to refuse a final embrace to those who are about to die, but to give final solace to the ones we have loved. Likewise Jesus hoped to correct Judas by this show of affection, feeling that a friendly rebuke would prevent him from deserting one who loved him, from betraying one who kissed him. And so this kiss was given to Judas as a test: if he amended, it would be a bond of peace for the disciple; if he proved traitor, it would seal his traitorous guilt.

The Lord said to him: *Judas, do you betray the son of man with a kiss (Luke 22, 48)*? Where is the subtlety of the enemy plot? Where the secret trap? Everything secret and wicked is laid bare. The traitor is betrayed before the betrayal: *Do you betray*, he says, *the son of man with a kiss?* that is, with the seal of love do you inflict a wound? With the proof of tenderness do you cause bloodshed? With the kiss of peace do you bring death? Tell me, what kind of love is this? Do you kiss and threaten? This is not a kiss, but poison, when the servant betrays his Lord, the disciple, his Master, the chosen follower, his creator.

PETER CHRYSOLOGUS
(† 450)

Almost nothing is known of Peter Chrysologus, archbishop of Ravenna. His work although important (176 sermons) has long remained in obscurity. Nevertheless it has considerable charm, revealing its author as a regular moralist, an extremely competent analyst of the human heart.

Doubtless the chief care of Peter Chrysologus was his pastoral concern to indoctrinate his faithful in their faith. One of his sermons reproduced here gives an exposition of the faith which for its clarity bears comparison with the preaching of Leo the Great. The faithful of Ravenna were unsophisticated and unmoved by the theological subtleties which captivated the East. So their pastor confined himself to a portrayal of the faith that appealed to the senses. He emphasizes the human witnesses to the Resurrection.

Behind this apparently simple approach, however, is a method of exegesis of great value: psychological analysis. All the scriptural commentaries try to go beyond the literal to the spiritual

meaning. The driest quotations are charged by Peter with spiritual resonances. We will see his analysis of a simple text like: *they
were seated at table.* Everything had retired within itself witnessing the disorder of the world at the death of Christ. All is
full of love – a disturbed and divided love.

That was the way with the disciples: in the house where
they had taken refuge they lay prostrate and despondent. Then
their heaviness gave place to a violent conflict of opposing
forces.

While Augustine condemned the anguish of the apostles and
their lack of faith in the risen Christ, Chrysologus understands
them, takes their part, even praises them: does he not see – a
profound insight – that love's very progress is a state of anguish,
a straining of self toward a difficult acquisition? That is how
Chrysologus depicts even the most characteristic faults of the
disciples: flight, treason, denial. These are manifestations of a
fundamental anguish which he tries to explain. They stem from
a feeling of human anguish which the episode on the road to
Emmaus brings into sharp relief. Man's solitude is tragic in its
abandonment. Sin has consummated the break between God and
men abandoned to the confused forces of night, death, chaos,
and the threats of eternal punishments.

The profound compassion with which the archbishop of
Ravenna is inspired by man's misery and fundamental solitude
is what shapes his theology. It is constructed around the idea
of a God as mediator who restores peace and hope to man
through faith. It would take too long to cite his suggestive images
of man in his misery, in his childish helplessness, and of God
as his physician and Father. In any case his concern is to rescue
man from his misery, from the disorder by which he is rent and
to achieve salvation not in a faraway heaven but in man's
troubled heart itself.

THE SIN OF THE CHURCH[1]
(On John 21, 4-8)

After the Passion whose tumult was unprecedented on earth
and unheard of in the heavens, which was without parallel in

---

1. Latin text: PL 52, 420-422.

history and had desolated hell, the Lord came to the sea and found his disciples being buffeted by storm in the depths of the night. Once the sun had set what solace could they get from the moon or stars? Earth was one dark, misty confusion, blinding not just the sight of the eye but all mental perception, and making it impossible to head for the shore of faith, the port of salvation, or even to rescue those on the sea. *But when day was breaking,* the Gospel says, *Jesus stood on the beach yet the disciples did not know that it was Jesus* (*John* 21, 4). All creation had fled the outrage inflicted on its creator: the world had tried to flee the death of its Lord, knowing that the slaughter would be avenged on the whole household since the servants had criminally killed their master. Hence it is that the earth trembled as its foundations deserted it, the sun fled so as not to see, the day departed so as not to be a witness, the rocks, since they could not physically depart, were rent by a fresh wound, condemning this dreadful deed by their crash since they could not do so in word. Hell when it saw its Judge penetrating its bosom yielded up its dead in a gesture of defeat with piteous cry.

Return to peace

Then souls restored to their bodies announced to the living that the dead, whom the world had regarded as perished, would rise again. Therefore the entire world was rocked to its foundations by confusion and believed that the death of its creator had cast it back to primordial darkness and primitive chaos. But suddenly in the light of his resurrection the Lord restored day and gave back its regular appearance to the world. He came to unite with himself in his resurrection what he had seen to sympathize so much within his passion.

As the Gospel says, *but when day was break*ing, that is when the night of the Lord's passion had passed, *Jesus stood on the beach.* He came to restore all things to their former limits, to banish doubts, to calm the tempest, to restore order, and to reestablish the foundations of the earth which had been so badly disturbed. Thus the world would promptly return to its devotion to its creator after its temporary rebellion and injury.

Jesus comes to his disciples' rescue

When day was breaking Jesus stood on the beach. His first purpose was to restore his Church, in which his disciples were being buffeted by the waves of the sea, to the solid ground of the faith. Secondly, because he found them bereft of the virtue of faith and robbed of their manly strength, he treated them as children, saying: *Young men, have you anything to eat?* For Peter was there who denied him; Thomas was there who had doubted; John, who had fled. So he addresses them not as brave soldiers but as frightened children. And he invites those timid creatures to eat whom he found not yet ready for combat, saying: *Young men, have you anything to eat?* So his humanity recalled them to grace, the bread to renewed confidence, the meal to faith. For they would not believe that his body had risen if they had not seen him behaving in a completely human fashion and eating. That is why the all sufficient nourishment himself seeks the commonest piece of nourishment to eat. The Bread himself eats, because he is hungry not for their food but for their continued love. *Young men, have you anything to eat? They answered him, No.* And what had they, seeing that they had not Christ who was beside them, failing as yet to recognize their Lord although he was standing beside them? *For the disciples did not yet know that it was Jesus.*

The discovery of the Lord

He said to them, "Cast the net to the right of the boat and you will find them." He recalls them to the right for the turmoil of his passion had led them to the left. *They cast therefore, and now they were unable to draw it up for the great number of the fishes.* They had cast to the right, to the men's side, but being young boys they were not yet able to draw it up. They felt, however, from the very weight that the fish had come in response to the Master's bidding and that the catch was not due to human skill.

The disciple whom Jesus loved said therefore, "It is the Lord." The one who is loved is the first to see because the eye of the lover is always keener and more sensitive. *When Peter heard*: Why was Peter's mind so slow that he had to hear from

another of the Lord whom he had been in the habit of announcing to others? Where was that singular intuition of his which
made him exclaim: *You are the Christ the son of the living God*
(*Matt.* 16, 16). Peter had taken refuge in the house of Caiaphas,
the chief priest of the Jews. He was slower to recognize his
Lord although he had easily recognized the whisper of the
maid-servant.

Why did Peter gird his tunic?

*Hearing that it was the Lord he girt his tunic about him
for he was stripped* (*John* 21, 7). It is very strange, brethren;
when the Lord was uncovered John let go his tunic and Peter
is taken naked by surprise. As flight had clothed John so betrayal
had stripped Peter. It is strange, brethren, and passing strange
that he who was stripped in the boat had plunged clothed into
the sea (cf. *Matt.* 14, 29): it is because innocence never feels
naked, and guilt always seeks to hide itself. Like Adam Peter
after his fall wants to conceal his nakedness, yet the two before
they fell were naked and unashamed.

He girt his tunic about him and threw himself into the sea.
His hope was that the sea would wash away his filthy sin of
betrayal. *He threw himself into the sea.* He wanted to be the
first to return for he had received primacy of rank. *He girt his
tunic about him,* for he was going to be girt with the passion
of martyrdom, according to the Lord's words, *another will gird
you and lead you where you would not* (*John* 21, 18).

*The other disciples came in the boat for they were not far
from land but only about two hundred cubits dragging the net
of fishes* (*John* 21, 8). The others came with the boat, dragging
the net full of fishes: this is the Church, buffeted by the storms
of the world, which they were bringing to the light of day, raising the men caught in the Gospel net from the deep and bringing them to the Lord by faithful toil. It says: *They were not far
from land.* They were not far from the land of the living. Their
abandonment of the present brought them into proximity with
the next life. *About two hundred cubits off.* From Jews and
pagans it is double the number one hundred, which joins the
life and salvation of the two peoples.

The rest of the reading we will explain, please God, in our
next sermon.

THE DISQUIETUDE OF FAITH[1]
(On Luke 24, 36-41)

The gift of peace

When rebellious Judea proceeded to war on its creator and raised impious hands to slaughter the author of its being, it took away peace from the earth, broke the concord which reigned in the world, and so ruptured the alliance of the elements that the universe returned to primordial chaos. It put day to flight and plunged everything into night. It turned light into darkness and took the sky from the world. It caused the earth to tremble, mingling the dead with the living, confounding hell and heaven, turning everything into disorder, and not leaving the slightest trace of peace or love in its war with the creator.

So it is that Christ returning from hell to restore peace to the world exclaims: *Peace be to you. And while the disciples were speaking Jesus appeared in the midst of them and said to them, Peace be to you.* Fittingly "to you" is add, because the earth was already steadied, the day had returned, the sun had regained its course, and the world had rediscovered its order and harmony. But with the disciples the war was still going on. Faith and doubt remained in furious conflict. The trouble of the passion had not disturbed the earth as it did their hearts; the battlelines of faith and doubt were drawn and their hearts were devastated in a merciless war. Hordes of thoughts besieged their minds and in the conflict of despair and hope their hearts were broken despite their toughness. Between the countless miracles which Christ had performed as signs and the diverse humiliations of his passion, between the marks of his divinity and the weaknesses of his flesh, between the horrors of his death and the graces of his life the disciples were torn in heart and mind. At one moment their spirits were raised to the heavens, at another dashed to the earth. While such a storm raged in their inner souls they could find no port of refuge, no haven of peace.

When Christ saw this — he who searches hearts and commands the winds, he who directs the storms and by a mere nod of his head turns the tempests to calm — he soon confirmed them in his peace, saying: *Peace be to you. It is I. Fear not.* I am he who

---

1. PL 52, 427-430.

was crucified, died and was buried. *It is I.* God for myself; man for you. *It is I.* Not just a spirit in the figure of a body but truth itself incarnate. *It is I.* I am risen live from the dead, come up from hell. *It is I.* I whom death flees from, in whose presence the infernal regions tremble. Hell confesses that I am God when it quakes. *Fear not,* Peter, because of your denial. *Fear not,* John in spite of your flight. *Fear not,* though you all have deserted me, though you betrayed me with thoughts that completely lacked faith, though you failed to believe in me even after seeing me (cf. *Matt.* 26; *Mark* 14). *Fear not. It is I.* I who have called you by grace, chosen you in condescension, sustained you by piety, upheld you by charity, and now receive you back out of sheer goodness of heart. For the father has no eyes for evil when he receives back his son, or affection when he restores his own to his embrace.

The coming of Christ

But they were terrified and afraid, it goes on, *and they thought that they had seen a ghost.* Why? Because the Lord had entered through closed doors. Therefore the disciples in consternation and the delirium of grief were attributing to Christ not what divine power was capable of but mere natural capabilities. *They thought that they had seen a ghost (Luke* 24, 37). For the ghost of a man goes through the maternal womb, passes through walls and penetrates the barriers of solid objects. So when the soul reaches the end of its life, when it quits the sweet resting place of the body it is no longer held back by domestic or earthly obstacles. A heavenly substance cannot allow itself to be confined in an earthly prison; *for you know not whence the spirit comes or whither it goes (John* 3, 8).

So when the Lord after the resurrection entered through closed doors the disciples did not believe that he brought with him the bulk of his body: they thought that only his soul had come through with the appearance of a body, just as in sleep one sees images of bodies. *They thought that they saw a ghost.* Therefore, as we have said, the conflicting thoughts in the minds of the disciples were not resolved but were rather magnified and their mental anguish was increased by his appearances; the very proof of the resurrection gave rise instead to scruples about its fulfillment. That he had come was a fact. That he had entered through closed doors was an illusion, not a fact. But it was not an illusion; it was the result of his power. He was not like men, but he was a man. He was a real body manifesting the power of God, and not a fictitious being doing violence to the resurrection. Therefore to appease the mental conflicts which his appearance had given rise to, Christ said to them: *Why are you troubled? And wherefore do these questionings arise in your heart?* (*Luke* 24, 38) Note the questions *arise;* they do not descend. For human thought oppressed by the weight of the flesh tries to rise to the lofty mysteries of God but they fail in the attempt, fall to the ground and remain there unless help is provided by him who leads man to divine thoughts.

The testimony of the senses

Why are you troubled? And why do questionings arise in your heart? See my hands and feet (*Luke* 24, 38-39). *See,* that is to say, be observant. Why? Because it is not an apparition that you have seen. *See my hands and my feet,* for you have not yet the power to raise your heavy eyes to my head. See the wounds on my body, for you do not see the works of God; see the marks made by my enemies for you have not yet seen the marks of God. Touch me so that your hand will convince you, for your eye sees but fails to contemplate, so let your touch see for your eyes that fail to see. Let your fingers enter the place of the nails, let your hands reach to the depths of wounds; open the gaping wounds of my hands, furrow my side, renew my wounds for I cannot deny to my disciples in their search for faith what I did not deny to my enemies in their frenzy for punishment. Touch me, touch me, and in the ardor of your quest reach to my very bones so that at least the bones of my flesh will lend credence and the wounds that remain will testify to my identity.

The other miracles of Christ

Why, I ask you, do you not believe in my resurrection? Have not I raised countless people from the dead before your very eyes? Or can I help others by my power yet fail to help myself, as was said in insult to me as I hung on the cross, *he saved others; himself he cannot save. If he is the king of Israel let him now come down from the cross and we will believe in him*

(*Matt.* 27, 42). And which is greater, to pull out the nails and come down from the cross, or to trample on death and ascend from hell. For behold I have saved myself. I have broken the chains of hell and risen to the heavens and nevertheless I do not find among you any faith in my divinity.

Or does a three day death, perhaps, deny faith to the believer? Did not my voice call back before your eyes Lazarus from the dead after four days when he was already stinking? Did he not return to life at my bidding? And if the slave can be resurrected on the fourth day why cannot his Lord be resurrected on the third?

They still disbelieved for joy and wondered. Joys that are prayed for are with difficulty believed in even after they are granted. When what is longed for finally arrives it leaves us in a stupor. That is why the apostles *wondered* at the resurrection which came quicker than they had hoped. Their slowness to believe is due to love, not to lack of faith; their extensive investigation was not so much a denial of faith as a search for it. The deeper they probed the more they hoped for the truth of what they saw.

Brethren, it was not timid lack of faith that caused the disciples to hesitate and to wonder at such great things. It was the greatness of the mystery. It was not lack of faith but a unique miracle which prevents them from seeing what is obvious, from knowing what was evident, and from believing what was certain.

Brethren, nature is a mere infant in the presence of God's power. If God does not mature it it cannot grasp mature concepts or attain to perfect knowledge. May God therefore grant that we grasp and comprehend through his help what we cannot attain to of ourselves.

THE MOURNFUL FEAST[1]
(On Mark 16, 14-18)

An unusual joy

Today the blessed evangelist recounts that at the very time of the crucifixion the apostles were concerned with eating and engaged in conviviality forgetful of the Lord's passion. *As*

---

1. P.L., 52, 432-436. Sermon 83.

the eleven were at table, the Gospel says, *the Lord appeared to them* (*Mark* 16, 14). They were seated, where? At the sepulchre of the Lord, then at the table of the servant? Is this the loyalty of servants? Is this the love of disciples? Is this the ardor of Peter? Is this the love of John taken from the very breast of Christ? Is this all the love they acquired by such a death, such gifts, such virtues? At the very moment of the passion, when death was still fresh and the burial scarcely over, in the midst of exulting enemies and with all Judea overweening, were the disciples dining with lavish festivities and in complete relaxation?

Angels assisted at the death of Moses. God himself took care of the sepulchre. The Jewish camp came to a halt, interrupted its march, took a tiresome rest in the desert and went into mourning for thirty days. Lengthy lamentations were held in memory of the servant (cf. *Deut.* 34, 5-6). But Christ the one true Lord, creator of the universe, redeemer of all men, after his tragic passion, crucifixion and death, does he not deserve to be mourned for three days with the tears of his disciples?

The earth trembles, hell is disturbed, the rocks are rent, the monuments are set ajar, the sun hides its face, day is buried, all is black night, and do the disciples alone gather around a festive board in completely relaxed mood? Is that how the Master takes them by surprise, brethren, when he returns from hell? *Afterwards he was manifested to the eleven as they sat at table and he upbraided them with their unbelief and hardness of heart because they did not believe those that had seen him after he had risen.* What reply will we make to this, faithful Peter, devoted Peter?

The distress of the disciples

As they were at table: Surely they were not dining? Brethren, they were not sitting down, they were lying down. This was not a festive banquet; it was a gathering for mourning. There was no bread of joy there, only the bread of sorrow. There the cups were not filled with sweet wine but with the bitter vinegar of the cross. *The doors were shut,* the Gospel says (*John* 20, 19), *for fear of the Jews.* If they were afraid, if the doors were closed, then they were certainly not celebrating a banquet. And if they were not celebrating, then that was no house but a prison; that was no banquet but a funeral. All the sorrow of the Lord's death had passed on to the disciples. Not only their sides but also their hearts were transfixed with the lance of sorrow. Their hands and feet were riveted with the nails of sorrow. The cruelty of the Jews made them drink vinegar and gall. In them the sun had died, day had fled, and the depths of darkness had invaded their hearts and souls. Dreadful temptation had cast them on the reefs of doubt and broken their faith. Despair, the most cruel of evils, which crowns every sorrow, had put them to sleep on the tombs. Once again they were not men seated, nor at table, but men lying down, buried men. That is how they were when the Lord took them by surprise. He blamed their discouragement for despair had taken the place of hope in the resurrection which the Lord had predicted. His servants had announced it but it found in them no trace of faith or of life. Dead to the world, buried in the world, they regarded this house of theirs as their common tomb.

The gift of hope

Then the Lord seeing them retired from the world recalled them and sent them back into the world: *Go into the whole world proclaiming the good news to every creature.* Come into the world so that you who thought your heads were only covered by a mere roof may suddenly see the whole of creation extended at your feet. *Go into the whole world proclaiming the good news to every creature,* that is to say become the hope of every man, you who were yourselves a cause of despair. You will discover the magnitude of your incredulity when you see the world accepting your testimony — you who could not believe the testimony of your own eyes. You will realize how great has been the hardness of your hearts when you see throughout the world the most savage and barbarous peoples proclaiming my name without seeing me — you who denied me while I lived in your midst.

You will see men divided on earth, confined on islands, perched on rocks, lost in the desert, you will see pedantic soothsayers, prating Greeks, and eloquent Romans seeking faith by faith alone when you yourselves sought it with your hands and fingers in the depths of my wounds. But I send you as witnesses of my passion, death and resurrection; so I would like you to look a bit closer at these mysteries if you would fortify the faith of those who will believe on your word.

What our faith should be like?

He who believes and is baptized will be saved. Brethren, baptism is to faith as the soul is to the body. So he who is born of water is enlivened by faith. *The just man lives by faith (Rom. 1, 17).* He who has not faith dies.

He who believes: that there is one God and three persons; that in the Father, Son and Holy Spirit there is equal greatness, all the parts being equal the divinity is distinguished by the Trinity; that it is not a confused unity but is one in divinity and three in person; that God is the name of the Trinity; that Father and Son are not terms of precedence but of love; that the Holy Spirit must not be held as inferior, more or less, or exterior more or less; for the divinity has nothing exterior to itself; that Christ was made man without ceasing to be God and that he died in order to raise from the dead the dead of all time; that he did not rise for himself but for us; that by descending from heaven he has raised us to heaven; that he sits there not to rest from any weariness but to exercise sovereign sway; that he will come without any change in position since he is everywhere the cause of movement; that he will come, not to conquer the world which he already possesses but that the world may henceforth be worthy to contemplate its creator.

So man ought also believe in the forgiveness of sins, for the heavens however vast do not welcome sinners. A man's sins are great, perhaps? Let him not despair. God would not be almighty if he was not able to do all things. Man should believe too in eternal life where death cannot take place a second time. Let him believe that the demon, man's ancient enemy, is banished from man's body: that even one mouth can speak many languages. That, touched by Christ, the serpents lose their poison; that the poisoned cups, thanks to Christ, cannot harm those who drink them; that maladies quit the bodies which are touched by the messengers of Christ. Such, brethren, are the chief tenets of faith: *Faith will bring with it these miracles: believers will cast out devils in my name and speak in strange tongues; if they handle snakes or drink any deadly poison, they will come to no harm; and the sick on whom they lay their hands will recover.*

Man, make your faith your medicine in order that you may not have to trust in yourself, in your own resources, in extraneous medicines, and to pay dear for what you possess for nothing.

Pray, brethren, in order that we may experience the virtues of faith without ceasing, and that established in the expectation of Jesus Christ we can, at his coming, with tranquil consciences, enter into his glory.

LEO THE GREAT
(† 461)

Leo is one of the outstanding figures in the papacy. He sought to defend the Church against its enemies within and without. His name remains linked with christological quarrels so that there are repeated statements of the double nature of Christ in his writings and especially in his sermons.

Leo is the first pope to leave us a number of sermons preached on the chief liturgical feasts of the year. The resurrection inspired two of these sermons, one of which is published here. These texts witness to the twofold concern — theological and pastoral — which characterizes all his work.

Leo tries to give as rigorous a definition as possible to the divine person. All his vision of the resurrection is overshadowed by this didactic necessity: the Pasch is the clearest manifestation of the duality of natures in Jesus Christ: in raising himself from the dead the Lord demonstrates the indivisibility of his two substances, human and divine.

Moral exhortation is joined to the dogmatic affirmation. The Christian ought to achieve his own resurrection in imitating Christ, that is to say by exalting in himself the spiritual part at the expense of the flesh. Man possesses in himself too a twofold nature: an art of life is suggested to him in order that he may know how to direct it and to render to the soul the dignity which God has conferred on it.

FAITH IN THE RISEN ONE[1]

Fast and Resurrection

1. In my last sermon, dearly beloved, I called on you, not unreasonably if I may say so, to participate in the cross of Christ in such a way that the Paschal mystery might pass into the life

---

1.PL 54, 385-390.

of the faithful and what is honored in the feast might be celebrated in your daily lives. You yourselves have proved how
useful this is and your devotion has taught you the benefit to
soul and body of extended fasts, more frequent prayers, and
more generous almsgiving. Practically everybody has benefited
from this exercise and stored within his own conscience some
genuine cause for rejoicing.

These gains, however, must be jealously guarded. Any relaxation of our efforts may afford the devil in his envy a chance
to deprive us of the gift of God's grace. Since, then, our objective in the observance of Lent was to experience something of
the cross as Christ experienced it in the week of his passion, we
should strive to be found sharers too in Christ's resurrection,
passing from death to life even in our mortal state. For each
individual who by some conversion is changed from one state
to another aims not to be what he was and his object is to be
what he was not. But it makes a difference to know whether one
is alive or dead: because it is death which is the cause of life
and life which is the cause of death.

Nowhere else except in this ephemeral world are both
objectives pursued and the differences of eternal retributions
depend on the quality of our passing actions. We must die, then,
to the devil and live to God; we must become devoid of iniquity
to rise to justice. Let the old man subside so that the new man
may rise in his place. And since, as Truth says, *no man can
serve two masters* (*Matt.* 6, 24; *Luke* 16, 13), let us take for
our master not the one who drives those who stand to destruction
but he who raises the downcast to glory.

God's death was a sleep

2. St. Paul says: *The first man was of the earth, earthly; the
second man from heaven, heavenly. Such as is the earthly so
also are the earthly; and such as is the heavenly so also are the
heavenly. Therefore as we have borne the image of the earthly
let us bear also the image of the heavenly* (I *Cor.* 15, 47-49).
This change should inspire a profound joy in us. We are raised
from our earthly ignominy to the dignity of heaven by the ineffable mercy of Christ who descended to our state to raise us
to his own. He assumed not just the substance but even the
condition of sinful nature and allowed those sufferings to be

inflicted on his divine impassibility which human mortality suffers in its great misery. Whence he shortened the announced three-day delay with such speed that the last part of the first day and the first part of the third day are joined with the whole second day and in this way he prevents the disciples from being perturbed by a long delay. In this way the number of days is kept at three but the period is telescoped into a briefer span.

The Savior's resurrection, then, neither detained his soul in hell for long nor his body in the tomb; so speedy was the coming to life of his incorruptible flesh that it was more like sleep than death, for the divinity had not left the twofold nature of his assumed manhood; the natures were both divided and reunited by his power.

Two indivisible substances

3. There followed many signs that established the authority of the faith to be preached throughout the world. The stone rolled back, the empty tomb, the linen bands, and the account of the angels gave abundant proof of the truth of the Lord's resurrection. Nevertheless he appeared to the women and frequently manifested himself to the apostles not only speaking to them but even staying and eating with them, and permitting them to touch him to their complete satisfaction in order to eliminate their doubts. And so, though the doors were closed he went in to the disciples (cf. *John* 20, 19), and gave them the Holy Spirit by breathing on them and by enlightening their minds he opened to them the secrets of the Sacred Scriptures (cf. *Luke* 24, 27); again, he showed them the wound in his side, the marks of the nails, and all the signs of his recent passion, to convince them that what was proper to both his divine and human natures remained intact and that we might know that the Word was not the same as the flesh so that we might confess that both the Word and the flesh were the one Son of God.

The exaltation of the Cross

4. Dearly beloved, Paul, the Apostle of the Gentiles, does not contradict this belief when he says: *though we once regarded Christ according to the flesh we regard him thus no longer* (II *Cor.* 5, 16). The Lord's resurrection did not put an end to

his flesh: it transformed it but it was not substantially changed by its increase in virtue. It changed qualitatively but it experienced no deficiency in its nature. From being able to be crucified it became an impassible body; from being liable to death it became immortal; from being vulnerable it became incorruptible. St. Paul rightly says that the flesh of Christ is not known in the state in which it was previously known, for nothing remained passible in it, nothing infirm, so that it remains the same in essence, but it is now a glorified body. Why be astonished at St. Paul elsewhere attributing to the body of Christ what he says of all spiritual Christians: *So from now on we know nobody according to the flesh* (II *Cor.* 5, 16). From now on, he means, a beginning of resurrection in Christ is made by us from the fact that in him who died for all has proceeded the form of our whole hope. Let us not hesitate by diffidence, nor be in suspense through uncertain expectation, but accepting the beginning of the promise we already see the future with the eyes of faith and rejoicing in the progress of nature let us now hold on to what we believe.

To live outside the flesh

5. Let us not be distracted by the appearance of ephemeral things nor turn our gaze from heavenly things to earthly. Let earthly things be regarded as past and gone for by and large they no longer exist. Let our mind be fixed and our yearning directed to what is destined to last, since what it offers is eternal. For although we are saved by hope and are still decked out in a corruptible and mortal flesh nevertheless we are rightly said to be outside the flesh if we are not dominated by carnal affections. No, we no longer deserve to be called by the name of this flesh if we have suppressed its appeals. So when the Apostle says: *Make no provision for the flesh to gratify its desires* (*Rom.* 13, 14), we do not interpret it as prohibiting those things which help salvation and are necessary for our weak human nature. What is meant is that we must not be the slave of every desire or gratify every prompting of the flesh. What it teaches us is to observe the due measure of temperance neither according anything superfluous to the flesh which is created subject to the spirit's judgment, nor denying it anything that is absolutely necessary. Hence the Apostle says elsewhere: *For no man ever*

hates his own flesh, but nourishes and cherishes it (*Eph.* 5, 29). It should be nourished and cherished, of course, not with a view to vice and luxury but to fulfill its role of service, so that nature after its renewal might maintain its proper role; the inferior parts should not perversely and disgracefully prevail over the higher faculties, nor should the higher yield to the lower. For if vice prevails in the soul what should be the master is turned into a mere slave.

Imitate the resurrection

6. Let the people of God recognize, therefore, that they constitute a new creation in Christ. Let them take care to understand by whom they have been adopted and whom they have adopted. Let what has become new not return to the instability of its own state. Let the man not forget his proper task once he has put his hand to the plough, but let him attend to what he sows and not look back at what he has left behind. Let no one relapse into the state from which he has risen. And if perchance he lapses into some of his maladies (for the flesh is weak), let him immediately want to be healed and lifted up. For this is the way of salvation and the imitation of the resurrection begun in Christ. But since mishaps and falls are not lacking on the slippery road of this life, let our footsteps be transferred from slippery to solid ground since it is written: *The steps of a man are directed by the Lord and he establishes his way; though the just man fall he shall not be cast headlong, for the Lord is the stay of his hand* (*Ps.* 37, 23-24).

Dearly beloved, these considerations should be reflected upon, not just on this feast day of Easter but for the sanctification of our entire lives. This present exercise should aim at translating into practice what is observed to be beneficial to the life of the faithful from this brief experience. This passing experience should become an abiding one, and any lapse in behavior should be quickly remedied by repentance.

And since the correction of inveterate faults is difficult and slow the more recent the wound the quicker should we apply remedies, so that always rising afresh from all our lapses we may deserve to come to that incorruptible resurrection of the glorified flesh in Christ Jesus our Lord who lives and reigns with the Father and the Holy Spirit for ever and ever. Amen.

GREGORY THE GREAT
(† 604)

Gregory was born at the end of Christian antiquity, at a time when the foundations of the medieval papacy were taking root. The son of a patrician family, a Roman by birth, he first embarked on a political career, becoming prefect of the city of Rome, then becoming a monk under the rule of St. Benedict. His austerities definitely affected his health of which he frequently complains in his sermons.

In 590 he was made Pope. He declined the title "universal pope," taking in its place "servant of the servants of God." He preached homilies on the Gospel to the Roman people. Here we publish one given during the Easter festivities. His word is simple, direct, and without affectation. His thought is not venturesome but touches us by its simplicity of tone and penetration of psychological analysis. He cannot speak of Mary Magdalene without communicating his emotion. Mary Magdalene, Mary the sister of Martha and the sinful woman in Luke are one and the same person for Gregory.

THE GRACE OF GOD[1]
(On John 20, 11-18)

I. WHAT WAS MARY SEEKING?

The Sorrow of Mary

1. Mary Magdalene was a public sinner. But in loving the truth, she obliterated with tears her criminal failings, and the word of the truth is fulfilled which says: *many sins are forgiven her because she has loved much* (*Luke* 7, 47). She who previously had remained frigid in sinning later glowed strongly in her love. For after she came to the tomb and failed to find the body of the Lord there, she believed in his resurrection and announced it to the disciples. They came and saw, and believed in what the woman had told them. And about them it is written, *the disciples, therefore, went again to their home,* with the additional remark, *but Mary was standing outside, weeping at the tomb* (*John* 20, 10). In this matter we must reckon how

---

1. PL 76, 1188-1196.

great was the fire of love which enflamed the mind of this woman who did not retire from the tomb of the Lord when the disciples departed. She sought whom she did not find, she wept in her search, and enflamed with the fire of her love, she ardently desired him whom taken away she believed in.

So it comes about that she who remained to seek was the only one to see him, because of course perseverance is a quality of a work well done and it is said by the word of truth: *he who has persevered to the end will be saved* (*Matt.* 10, 22). It is prescribed in the law that the tail of the victim be offered (*Lev.* 3, 9). For in the tail is the end of the body, and he sacrifices well who extends the sacrifice of a good work to its due end.

So, Joseph is described as having a tunic reaching his ankles among the rest of his brethren (*Gen.* 37, 3). The ankle-length tunic is a good work brought to a perfect conclusion.

An ardent quest

2. Mary, when she wept, bowed her head and looked into the tomb. Certainly she had already seen that the tomb was empty and had announced that the Lord had disappeared; why does she stoop again and want to look once more? To a lover one look is not enough because the power of love increases the ardor of the seeker. She looked once and did not find; she perseveres in her search and the result is that she finds. It happens that her desires intensify and increase and, increasing, receive what they have sought. Hence it is that the Church in the *Canticle of Canticles* says of the same spouse: *On my bed at night I sought him whom my heart loves. I sought him but did not find him. I will rise then and go about the city, in the streets and crossings. I will seek him whom my heart loves* (*Cant.* 3, 1-2). Twice she experienced failure to find, saying, *I sought him but I did not find him.* But success finally crowns her effort. *The watchmen came upon me as they made their rounds of the city: Have you seen him whom my heart loves? I had hardly left them when I found him whom my heart loves* (*Cant.* 3, 4). For we seek the beloved in bed, when in the brief repose of the present life we sigh with yearning for our Redeemer. We search through the night because even though the mind is vigilant in it, nevertheless the eye is still clouded. But he who does not find his beloved, has to rise and go around the city, that is he runs through the holy Church of the elect mentally in his search;

through streets and crossings he seeks her, that is he looks in the narrow places and the wide streets to see if he can find her footsteps in them, because there are some, even in secular life, who have something imitable in the realm of virtue. We who seek find those vigilant who guard the city, because the holy fathers, who guard the state of the Church, run to our good desires, to teach us by their spoken or written word. When we have gone through a little of these we find him whom we love, because our Redeemer even if by humility he is a man among men, nevertheless was superior to mankind by his divinity. When, then, the search is ended, the beloved is found because we see that the prophets and apostles are beneath him, he who by nature is God we consider to be above men. At first then the one who cannot be found is sought so that after he is found he be held on to all the more closely. Holy desires, as we have said, increase by being extended. If they shrink in the process they were not desires to begin with. Whoever can reach the truth is consumed in the fire of this love. This is why David says: *Athirst is my soul for the living God. When shall I go and behold the face of God* (Ps. 41, 3)? In this he advises us, saying: *Go and behold the face of God* (Ps. 104, 4). And the prophet is inspired to say: *My soul has desired you in the night and my spirit within me seeks for you* (Isa. 26, 9). And the Church says in the Canticle of Canticles: *You have ravished my heart* (Cant. 4, 9). Therefore, it is just that from the vision of the physician salvation should be reached, who through the heat of her desire carries in her breast a wound of love. Again it is said. *my soul is delighted at what my beloved has spoken* (Cant. 5, 8). For the mind of man which does not seek the face of his creator is very hard, because it remains frigid within itself. But if it begins to glow in a desire to follow the one it loves, liquified by the fire of love it runs. It becomes anxious in its desire, and all earthly things which were pleasing decrease in value; there is nothing outside the creator that is pleasing, and the things which formerly pleased the soul now oppress it exceedingly. Nothing consoles its gloom, so long as the object of its yearning is not beheld. The mind is dejected, its light is darkness, and the rust of sin is roasted with such fire in the mind and the soul so enkindled, as in the process of smelting gold, that it loses its appearance in the process and glows in the fire.

II. THE FINDING OF JESUS CHRIST

The two angels of knowledge

3. She then who so loved, who inclined herself a second time to the monument to what she had seen, let us see with what fruit the power of love redoubled in her the work of searching. It continues: *She saw two angels in white sitting, one at the head, the other at the feet where the body of the Lord had been placed.*

Why is it that in place of the Lord's body two angels are seen, one at the head, and the other sitting at the feet, except that in Latin angel means announcer and he had to be announced from his passion who is God before the ages, and man to the end of the ages. The angel sat at the head as it were when it is proclaimed through the apostle, John that *in the beginning was the word and word was with God and the word was God* (*John* 1,1). And an angel sat at the feet as it were when it says: *the word was made flesh and dwelt among us* (*John* 1, 14). We can also recognize the two testaments in the two angels, the Old and the New. Like the one sitting at the head and the other at the feet such are the testaments which announce in the same voice the birth, death and resurrection of our Lord. Whence also *the two cherubim who stand guard on the mercy seat are facing each other, turned toward the mercy seat* (*Exod.* 25, 20). The cherubim symbolize perfect knowledge; and the two cherubim symbolize the two Testaments. And what is the meaning of the mercy seat except the incarnate Lord? Concerning whom John says: *He is himself the remedy for the defilement of our sins* (I *John* 2, 2). And while the Old Testament announces that this has yet to take place the New Testament proclaims that it has already been accomplished by the Lord. So both cherubim look at each other while their countenances turned toward the mercy seat. They see between them the incarnate Lord. They turn the same gaze on him and in the same voice they proclaim the mystery of his coming.

A lucid error

4. The angels ask Mary, *Woman, why do you weep?* And she replied: *Because they have taken away my Lord and I do not know where they have laid him.* Those very sacred words

which stir us to tears of love also help to wipe away those very tears when they promise us the appearance of our Redeemer. But it must be noted in the narrative that the woman did not say, "They have taken away the body of my Lord" but *they have taken away my Lord.* Now in Sacred Scripture the part is often used for the whole, or the whole for the part. For instance the whole is signified by the part in the account of the sons of Jacob: *Jacob went down to Egypt with seventy souls (Gen. 46, 27).* Now incorporeal souls did not go down to Egypt, but here "soul" means the whole man — the whole expressed by the part. And only the Lord's body had lain in the tomb and Mary complains not that the Lord's body but that the Lord had been taken away — the part expressed by the whole.

When she had said this she turned around and saw Jesus standing and she did not know that it was Jesus. It should be noted that Mary who had previously doubted the Lord's resurrection turned back again to see Jesus; doubt had turned her back, so to speak, on the face of the Lord whom she did not believe had risen. Torn between love and doubt she saw him but failed to recognize him. Love revealed him to her and dissipated her doubts. Her failure to comprehend him is indicated in the words: *And she did not know that it was Jesus. He said to her, woman, why do you weep? Whom do you seek?* The cause of her sorrow is sought to increase her sense of loss. In the act of naming the one whom she sought the ardor of her love for him would be increased. *She thinking that it was the gardener says to him, Sir, if you have taken him away tell me where you have laid him and I will take him.* Perhaps the woman was not too far wrong in thinking that Jesus was the gardener. For was he not a spiritual gardener to her in that he planted in her heart the plants of virtue by the seeds of his love?

Jesus reveals himself

5. But why is it that when she mistakes him for the gardener and before telling him for whom she is seeking she says: *Sir, if you have taken him away?* It is as if she had already told him the cause of her flowing tears. She speaks of "him" without using his name. That is a trait of love: it thinks that everybody must know the permanent object of its own love. So this woman too does not name the one she is seeking but simply says: *If you*

have taken him away because she thinks he has to be known to everybody, the one whom she weeps for continuously and misses so much. *Jesus said to her, Mary.* After he had called her by the common title of her sex "woman" and was not recognized, he calls her now by name. As if he were to say openly, Recognize him by whom you yourself have been recognized. God said the same thing to a perfect man, *I know you by name* (*Exod.* 33, 12). "Man" is a name common to all but "Moses" is a proper name and the Lord said to him very properly that he knew him by name; as if he were to say: I do not just know you in a general way like the others but in a more special fashion. Mary then, because she is called by name, recognizes the one that calls her and straightway calls him "Rabboni," that is Master, because it was he who was sought without and he it was who taught her to seek for him within. Now the evangelist does not describe what Mary did but it is suggested by the words. Jesus said to her: *Do not touch me for I have not yet ascended to my Father.* In these words it is shown that Mary wished to embrace the feet of him whom she had just recognized. But the Master says to her, *Do not touch me.* Not that the Lord rejected the touch of women after his resurrection. For we are told of the two women who came to his tomb that *they approached and held his feet in their embrace* (*Matt.* 28, 9).

What means to ascend to the Father?

6. But the reason for not touching him is added in the words, *for I have not yet ascended to my Father.* Jesus ascends to the Father when he is regarded as equal to the Father. For whoever does not believe that he is equal to the Father the Lord has not yet ascended to the Father in his heart. Therefore he truly touches Jesus who believes that the Son is coeternal with the Father. Now in Paul's heart Jesus had already ascended to the Father when Paul used the words: *who although he was in the form of God did not think it was theft to make himself equal to God* (*Phil.* 2, 6). Likewise John also touched our redeemer with the finger of faith when he said, *in the beginning was the word and the word was with God and the word was God. This was in the beginning with God. All things were made by him* (*John* 1, 1-2). Therefore a man touches the Lord who believes that he is equal to the Father in eternity of substance.

Now somebody perhaps will venture to object with a question

that may be troubling you and say: how can the Son be equal to the Father? The human spirit is astonished at this and cannot grasp it. But you have only to think of another surprising thing and this one will not seem to you any more impossible. It is in fact easy to find something just as extraordinary. For as you know it was he himself who created the mother whose virginal womb gave himself birth among men. Is it surprising that he who existed before his own mother should be equal to his Father? Hear again the testimony of St. Paul: *Christ is the power of God and the wisdom of God* (I *Cor.* 1, 24). To claim that the Son is inferior to him is nothing else than to make little of the Father in denying him the wisdom of the Son. What a come-down for him to be told: You are mighty but somewhat deficient in wisdom! But the Lord also says: *The Father and I are one* (*John* 10, 30), and *The Father is greater than I* (*John* 14, 28). It is also written about him: *He was subject to* his parents (cf. *Luke* 2, 51). Will you be astonished then if he is thought to be inferior to his Father in the heavens when on earth and in human terms he was even obedient to his own parents?

It is because he is man that he says to Mary: *Go, find my brothers and tell them that I ascend to my Father and your Father, to my God and your God.* Instead of saying "my" and "your" why did he not say "our" father? The distinction made here indicates that God the Father is not the same for him and for us. *I go to my Father* which he is, obviously, by nature; *and to your Father* which he is by grace. *To my Father,* because I am descended from him. *To your Father* because you will ascend to him. He is God to me because I am also man; he is God to you because you have been delivered from error. But God the Father is not the same for you and for me: he engendered me as God before time began; he has created you as man with me at the end of time.

Mary Magdalene went then to announce to the disciples: I have seen the Lord and listen to what he has told me. The sin of man here leaves the heart from which it issued. For it was a woman in paradise who gave man the fruit of death. It is a woman at the tomb who now announces life to man and reports the words of him who gives life after having reported the words of the dread serpent. As if the Lord said to men, not in so many words but in deeds, the hand which extended to you the drink of death presents you this day with the cup of life!

III. THE PROFUNDITY OF GRACE

God's blessings

7. We have run through the Gospel reading, explaining it as succinctly as possible. Now with the help of the Lord of whom we speak let us consider the glory of his resurrection and the profundity of his love. He wished to rise so promptly from the dead lest our soul might remain too long in the death of unbelief. The saying of the psalmist is apt: *From the torrent on the way he will drink; therefore he will raise up his head* (Ps. 109, 7).

From the very beginning a torrent of death had flowed. But the Lord drank on the way from this torrent in that he had tasted death on the way. And so he raised his head that what by death he had laid in the tomb he might place above the angels by rising, and so he overthrew the ancient enemy for ever, committing him to that place from which for a time he had permitted the bands of his pursuers to rage against him. This the Lord openly indicated to Job saying: *Will you never catch Leviathan with the hook?* (Job. 40, 5).

Leviathan is pierced by the Lord's hook

8. By "Leviathan" of course, an additional enemy, is meant the monster that devours the human race. He took away immortality while promising to add divinity to man. He had thrown the first man into alliance with the devil. He forced his descendants to the same crime without let-up and increased their penalties. On a fish hook only the bait is exposed but the actual hook is hidden. The almighty Father then caught him on a hook because he sent his incarnate only begotten son to his death. In him the passible flesh was exposed but the impassible divinity lay hidden. When, then, that serpent, by the hands of the persecutors, bit into the bait of his flesh he was hooked by the divinity. Previously he had recognized him as God in his miracles but had lapsed from knowledge to doubt when he saw that he was capable of suffering. The hook then held the jaws of the devourer while the bait of the flesh was exposed on it which the devourer sought. And the divinity was hidden at the time of the passion when he was put to death. On the hook of his incarnation

the devourer was caught; he sought the bait of the flesh, but was hooked by the divinity. Humanity was there to lure the devourer on; divinity was also there to pierce him. Infirmity was there to provoke him; virtue was concealed to pierce the jaws of the devourer. He was caught on the hook and perished from what he had bitten. And he lost those whom he rightly regarded as subject to mortality because he dared to visit death on him in whom death had no sway.

Jesus saves us from death

9. So it is that Mary of whom we speak is living because he who owed nothing to death is nevertheless reposing in death in order to save mankind. So it is that we are regenerated every day to life in spite of sin because the creator, exempt from sin, humbles himself to accept our chastisement. Henceforth the ancient enemy lost the spoils which he had stolen from man and his crafty victory was reduced to naught. Each day sinners return to life; each day the Savior's hand plucks them from the jaws of the monster. So the Lord's voice says again to blessed Job: *With a hook shall you pierce his jaw?* (*Job* 40, 26). The hook encloses its prey and fastens itself on it. What is the meaning of the hook only the entry of our Lord who loves us? He pierces the jaws of Leviathan and in spite of our infidelity shows us the road to repentance. The Lord transfixes with a hook the jaws of Leviathan when with the invincible power of his compassion he strikes so forcibly the craftiness of his ancient enemy that the latter loses all his victims for all time. They had fallen into the jaws of Leviathan yet in spite of their faults they recovered their innocence. What prey can escape its jaws once it has been swallowed if a hand had not pierced it through? Was Peter not enclosed in its jaws at the moment of his denial? Was David not enclosed in its jaws when he wallowed in the depths of pleasure? And yet when they both returned to life by repentance Leviathan somehow allowed them to escape through a gap in his jaws. They took flight through a gaping wound and were restored to life by repentance after a great number of faults.

Now who among men would be able to flee the jaws of Leviathan without encountering the least evil? We know at present how we are indebted to our Redeemer who does not limit himself to putting us on our guard against the jaws of

Leviathan but even brings us back. In place of casting the sinner into despair he has transfixed the jaws of the monster and has made an opening in it to allow a way of escape to those who allowed themselves to swallow the bait.

Everywhere the Lord lavishes his heavenly assistance on us. He has given men laws to forestall sin; but he has also given his help to the one who falls into sin to rescue him from despair. Therefore take the greatest precautions not to be snapped up in the jaws of Leviathan, but if unfortunately we should fall into them let us not despair. With sincere repentance we can discover a new opening in his jaws through which we can escape.

Mary, proof of divine compassion

10. Mary is a standing proof of divine mercy. This Mary of whom we speak, of whom the Pharisee, in his wish to destroy the outburst of her tenderness, said: *This man if he were a prophet would surely know who and what kind of woman touches him that she is a sinner* (*Luke* 7, 39). But with her tears she washed away the stains of her soul and body, and threw herself at the feet of him whose ways she had abandoned in her sin. She sat at the feet of Jesus and heard the words from his mouth. She clung to him in life and found him in death. She found him alive whom she had sought dead. And she found such grace with him that she was his messenger to his own apostles, God's own messengers. Brethren, what should we see in this but the immense mercy of our creator who as a sign for us and an example of penance places before us those whom he had restored to life by penance after falling? I look at Peter, I consider the thief, I see Zacchaeus, I look at Mary, and I see nothing in them but examples of repentance and hope placed before our eyes.

Perhaps somebody has lapsed from the faith? Let him look at Peter who wept bitterly for his timid denial (*Matt.* 26, 75). Perhaps another has blazed forth in anger against his neighbor? Let him look at the thief who at the instant of death came by repentance to the rewards of life (*Luke* 23, 43). A third, seething with avarice, may have despoiled his neighbor's goods? Let him look to Zacchaeus who if he took anything from his neighbor restored it fourfold (*Luke* 19, 8). Yet another may be on fire with lust leading to a loss of purity. Let him look to Mary who purified in herself the lust of the flesh by the fire of divine love. Behold the omnipotent God everywhere places within our view examples which we should imitate, and everywhere proposes precedents of his mercy.

Let our sins, then, be displeasing, even the ones long since committed. The omnipotent God gladly overlooks the fact that we are wrongdoers. He is ready to accept our penance as innocence itself. If we have been defiled after the waters of salvation let us be reborn in our tears. And so, in the words of our first shepherd, *like the new-born infants you are, you must crave for milk* (I Pet. 2, 2). Return, little babes to the bosom of your eternally wise mother, be breast-fed by God's teeming mercy. Bewail your past sins, avoid menacing dangers in the future. Our Redeemer will console our ephemeral tears with an eternity of joy, he who lives and reigns with God our Father in the unity of the Holy Spirit God for ever and ever. Amen.

BIBLIOGRAPHY

TEXTS

PS.-Ambrose, **Sermons** 34 and 35; PL 17, 671-675,
Anastasius of Antioch, **Discourse on the Resurrection,** PG 89, 1355-1362.
Aphraates, **Demonstration** 12; PS 1, 105.
Apostolic Constitutions 5, 17-19; PG 1, 888-896.
Asterius the Sophist, PG 40, 389-477; cf. PG 55, 35-39, 539-544, 549-558.
Augustine of Hippo, **Sermons** 219-260; PL 38, 1087-1202.
Sermon 376, PL 39, 1669-1671.
Sermones Mai 86, 87, 89, 92, 94, 95; PLS 2, 475-494.
Sermones Guelferbytani 4-19; PLS 2, 548-588.
Sermones Wilmart 4-9; PLS 2, 717-725, 739-743.
Sermones Denis, PL 46, 821-841.
Ps.-Augustine, **Sermones** 157-172; PLS 2, 1255-1272.
Sermones Caillau-Saint-Yves, PLS 2, 946-991, 1019-1020, 1073-1081.
Sermones Mai 36-38, 40, 42; PLS 2, 1135-1143.
Basil of Seleucia, **Homily on the Pasch,** PG 28, 1073-1081.
Bede the Venerable, **Homilies,** PL 94, 133-154.
Caesarius of Arles, **Sermones** 203-205, ed. Morin, CC 2, 817-824.
Chromatius of Aquileia, **Homélies,** ed. J. LeMarié, **Revue Benedictine,** 72 (1962), 273-277, 73 (1963), 181-243, 75 (1965), 136-142, 76 (1966), 7-40.
Cyril of Alexandris, **Paschal Letters** 1-29; PG 77, 401-968.
Didascalia of the Twelve Apostles, XXII, trad. NAU (Paris 1912), 163-178.
Ps.-Epiphanius, **Homilies,** PG 43 465-477, 505-508.
Ps.-Eusebius of Alexandria, PG 61, 733-738, 775-778; cf. 86, 423.
Eusebius of Caesarea, **On the Feast of the Pasch,** PG 24, 693-706.
Eusebius of Gallican, **Sermones** 17-22; PLS 3, 589-605; cf. **ibid.,** 547.
Eutychius, **Sermon on the Pasch and Eucharist,** PG 86, 2391-2402.
Ps.-Fulgentius of Ruspe, **Sermones** 35-44; PL 65, 897-910; cf. PLS 1363.
Gaudentius of Brescia, **Sermons** 1-7; PL 20, 843-886.
Gregory of Antioch, **In Mulieres Unguentiferas,** PG 88, 1847-1866.
Gregory of Nazianzus, **Homilies** 44, 45; PG 36, 607-664.
Hymn 38; PG 37, 1326-1330.
Gregory of Nyssa, **Five Sermons,** PG 46, 599-690. The second belong to Severus of Antioch, the fifth is doubtful.
Gregory the Great, **Homilies on the Gospels** 21-26; PL 76, 1160-1204.

Hippolytus of Rome, **On the Holy Pasch** (lost), cf. PG 59, 735-746; SC 27, 117-191.

John Chrysostom, **Sermons for Easter,** PG 50, 433-442 821-824 are authentic. PG 52, 765-772 is doubtful. Cf. De Aldama, Repertorium Pseudo-Chrysostomicum, 144; PG 59, 721-756 are spurius. Cf. **Homélie Pascales** 1, 11, 111, ed. Nautin, SC 27, 36, 48.

John Damascene, **In Sabbatum Sanctum,** PG 96, 601-644. Chant for Easter Sunday, PG 96, 839-844.

John Mediocre, **2 sermons for Easter,** ed. A. Mai, Nova Patrum Bibl. Serm., 35, 41, pp. 75-76, 83-85.

Jerome, **Letters** 28, 29, De Exodo in Vig. Paschae; PL 30, 224-226, **In die dominicae Paschae** (1 and 2), PL 30, 211; 39, 2059; PL 40, 1201-1204. In Ps. 41 **ad neophytos,** PL 40, 1203-1206.

Ps.Jerome, **Letter** 24=Eusebius the Gallican, Homily 12; PL 30, 215.

Leo the Great, **Sermons** 71-72; PL 54, 385-394; 56, 1134-1138. **Sermons** 8-10 (PL 54, 495-499) are not authentic.

Maximus the Arian, **In Sancta Pascha,** PLS 1, 737-739.

Maximus of Braga, probable author of ps.-Athanasius, **De ratione paschae,** PG 28, 1605-1610.

Maximus of Turin, **Homilies** 55-59; PL 57, 355-368 (55 belongs to Eusebius the Gallican=sermon 13). **Sermons** 29-43 spurius; cf. PLS 111, 354-359.

Nilus, 2 sermons, PG 79, 1489-1497.

Optatus of Milevis, **Sermo paschalis,** PLS 1, 295-296 doubtful.

Origen, **Two homilies on the Pasch** (text mutilated), ed. O. Guéraud, RHR 131 (1946), 92-94.

Peter Chrysologus, **Sermons** 73-84; PL 52, 406-440.

Proclus of Constantinople, **Sermons** 12-15; PG 65, 788-805.

Quodvultdeus, **De cantico novo,** PL 40, 677-686.

Rupert of Deutz, **De div. off.,** PL 170, 193-197.

Sedulius, **Carmen Paschale,** PL 19, 533-752; **Opus Paschale, ibid.**

Severus of Antioch, PG 46, 627-652=ps.-Gregory of Nyssa.

Synesius of Cyrus, **Homily** 2; PG 66, 1563-1564.

Theophanes, **Homilies** 28-37; PG 132, 605-719.

STUDIES

Baumstark, A., **Nocturna Laus,** Münster 1957.

Becker, C., **La Nuit Paschale,** Bruges-Paris 1954.

Botte, B., **La Question paschale,** La Maison-Dieu 41 (1955), 84-95; Pascha, **Or. Syr.** 8 (1963), 213-226.

Bouyer, L., **Le Mystère pascal,** Paris 1945.

Callewaert, C., **Sacris erudiri.** Fragmenta liturgica collecta, Steenbrugghe 1940, 449-671.

Casel, O., La fête de Paques dans l'Eglise des Pères, Lex orandi 37, Paris 1964.

Chavasse, A., Le Sacramentaire gélasien, Paris 1958; "Le Cycle Paschal," L'Eglise en prière, Paris 1961, 693-713.

Collins, T. P. ed., The Risen Christ in the Fathers of the Church, Westminster, Md. 1968.

Fisher, B. Wagner J., Paschatis Sollemnia, Freiburg 1961.

Flicoteaux, E., Le Triomphe de Pàques, La cinquantaine pascale, Paris 1957.

Jerermia, J., "Pascha" in Theologisches Wörterbuch zum Neuen Testament, 5, 900-903.

Kunze, G., Leiturgia 1, Kassel 1954, 443-460.

Leclercq, H., "Pâques" in Dict. d'arch. et de liturg., 13, 1521.

Le Déaut, R., Le Nuit Pascale, Rome 1963; along with J. Lécuyer, art. "Éxode," in Dict., de Spiritualité, 4, 1973-1995.

Llopart, E., Liturgia 1, 1956, 387-522.

Lohse, B., Das Passafest der Quartadecimaner, Gutersloh 1953.

"La liturgie du mystère pascal," La Maison-Dieu 67 (1967).

Merendino, P., Paschale Sacramentum, Münster 1965.

Mohrmann, Ch., "Pascha, Passio, Transitus," Ephemer. liturg. 66 (1952), 37-52.

Nesmy, J. C., La Spiritualité pascale, Paris 1957.

Pinell, J. M., Liturgia 11, Montserrat.

Rahner, H., Greek myth and Christian mystery.

Richard, M., La Question pascale au IIe sìecle, L'Orient Syrien 6 (1961), 179-212.

Righetti, M., Manuale di storia liturgica 11, Milan 1955, 183-227.

Schmidt, H. A. P., Hebdomada sancta, 2 vols., Rome 1956-57.

Schurmann, H., in Theologische Quartalschrift 131 (1951), 414-425.

Watts, A. W., Easter, Its Story and Meaning, London 1959.

Weller, P. T., The Easter Sermons of St. Augustine, Washington D.C. 1955.

—————, Selected Easter Sermons of St. Augustine, St. Louis 1959.

INDEX

Abraham 36, 40-41, 70, 77, 90, 158.
Adam 63, 71, 84, 100, 103, 117, 121, 154, 160, 201.
Alms 125.
Angel 46, 51, 101, 105, 116-117, 127, 136, 217.
Apostles 59, 87, 105, 141.
Azymes 37, 60, 76, 118.

Baptism 104, 111, 123, 140, 176, 208.
Birth 61-62, 160.
Blood see Body.
Body 63, 84, 93, 157, 186, 218.
Bread 58, 170, 199.

Church 30, 60, 71-72, 108, 132, 141, 142, 148, 149, 173, 177, 201, 215, 216.
Circumcision 60.
Contemplation 48, 131.
Creation 31, 84, 86, 87, 151, 152-154, 178.
Cross 37, 44, 64-66, 97, 100-101, 149, 209.

Dawn 50, 61.
Death 28, 32, 60, 67, 69, 84, 96, 98, 101, 107, 136, 150, 162, 165.
Devil 100-101, 123, 124, 221.
Drunkenness 81, 179.

Egypt 27-29, 33, 54-55, 76, 110.
Eucharist 103, 131.
Eve 100, 120.

Faith 45, 56, 122, 127, 165, 167-169, 171, 202, 205, 207, 208, 212, 223.
Fasting 59, 107, 210.
Fear 38, 66, 202.
Figures 26, 29, 51, 69, 118.

Greeks 79, 207.

Hell 109, 115, 116, 120, 136, 191.
Heresies 72, 77, 177-178, 183.
Heritage 30, 31, 36, 84, 108, 112.

Idolatry 55.
Incredulity 67, 79, 84, 87, 207, 221.
Israel 29, 35, 36, 55, 58, 66.

Jerusalem 30, 35, 37.
Jews 69, 79, 105, 111, 115, 118, 137, 139, 142, 149, 159, 183, 202.
John the Baptist 73, 108.
Jordan 105.
Joseph 33-34, 36, 110-112, 215.
Judas 37, 81, 111
Judgment 56, 82, 92, 95, 123, 172.

Lamb 50, 58, 69, 73.
Lazarus 35, 67, 87, 92, 204.
Life, Christian 76-77, 103.
Love, Human 42, 155, 172-173, 180-182, 184, 214, 215, 216.

Man 31, 73, 90-91, 92, 163, 165.
Manna 36, 58, 118.
Martyr 46, 165.
Mary 34, 100, 115, 129, 131, 182.
Moses 27, 33-34, 45, 54, 59, 69, 75, 115, 138, 157, 206, 219.

Noah 36, 70, 142.

Pagan 55, 81, 137, 155, 159, 183.
Pardon 20, 107, 193, 203, 208.
Paradise 31, 96, 143.
Peace 48, 203.
Peter 55, 172, 174-176, 203, 220-223.
Pharaoh 27, 34, 55, 76, 82, 117-118, 176.

Poor 46, 79, 81, 84, 92, 102, 107.
Prayer 137, 148, 209.
Priest 44-45, 72.

Rahab 71.
Red Sea 36-37, 118.
Regeneration 69, 89, 114, 212.
Repentance 82, 175, 212.
Riches 76, 124, 182, 183.

Scripture 36, 141, 152, 169, 211, 217.
Sick 63, 81, 84, 175, 212.
Sin 32, 67, 123, 222.
Sleep 92, 98, 135, 150, 210.

Temple of God 77, 130, 185.
Temptation 123-124, 185, 206.
Thieves 54, 65-66, 111, 143, 193, 223.
Thomas 121, 199.

Unity 71, 174, 179.

Woman 48, 65, 67, 86, 120, 151, 161, 182, 221.
World 47, 142, 149, 160, 207, 218.

Years 58, 69, 73.